MATH

BIG 8 REVIEW

Intermediate Level
Test Preparation

Authors
Norman Levy & Joan Levy

Editors
Wayne Garnsey & Paul Stich
Judith Shuback – Associate Editor

Artwork
Eugene B. Fairbanks & Howard VanAckooy

N&N Publishing Company, Inc.
18 Montgomery Street   Middletown, New York 10940-5116

For Ordering & Information
1-800-NN 4 TEXT
Internet: www.nn4text.com   email: nn4text@warwick.net

ACKNOWLEDGEMENTS

The authors would like to acknowledge Joshua Levy for his word processing expertise; Dawn Levy for being in the right grade at the right time; Rabbi Schonbrun for his continued support; Wayne Garnsey of N&N Publishing for his support, and to our family for putting up with us during this project.

DEDICATION

During the writing of this book, "the Attack on America" (9-11-2001) occurred. The hijacking of United States airplanes, the attack on the Pentagon, the destruction of property, the World Trade Center collapse and the killing of innocent people weighs heavily on us all. This book is dedicated to those who died or were injured as a result of the attack.

———————————

Special thanks to these educators for their editorial assistance in the preparation of this manuscript.

Chris Armstrong,
Nancy Biamonte,
Toni Forsythe,
Fran Harrison,
John Lewis, and
Joanne Prunty

———————————

Front Cover: Photo courtesy of NASA. STS108-S-008 (5 December 2001) Smoke billows from Launch Pad 39B as the Space Shuttle Endeavour lifts off into an afternoon sky to begin the STS-108 mission to the International Space Station (ISS).

NORMAN LEVY

Executive Director: NJL College Preparation
Mathematics Coordinator: Hebrew Academy of Nassau County

JOAN LEVY

Executive Director: National Learning Systems
Director: NJL College Preparation

© Copyright 2003

N&N Publishing Company, Inc.

Internet: www.nn4text.com   phone: 1-800-NN 4 TEXT   email: nn4text@warwick.net

SAN # - 216-4221   ISBN # - 0935487-77-8

2 3 4 5 6 7 8 9 10 11 12 13 14 15 BookMart Press 2008 2007 2006 2005 2004 2003

TABLE OF CONTENTS

TO THE STUDENT

Hello Eighth Grader!

This workbook is designed to help you achieve success on the New York State 8th Grade Math Assessment Test.

Each chapter contains:

- **FAST FACTS**
  These are a quick chart and picture reviews of the topic. We do not give long, wordy details – just the necessary facts.

- **OUR TURN**
  We ask the questions and *we* work out the solutions.

- **YOUR TURN**
  You get plenty of practice problems in each subject area.

In addition there are special features:

- **PIZZA π PIZZERIA**
  A fun scenario to practice what you have learned.

- **2 COMPLETE TESTS**
  All questions are on the level of the Assessment Test and are just what you need to know in order to do well.

⑧ "BIG 8" SPECIAL NOTES

- **SYMBOLS AND REFERENCES**
  A comprehensive guide to many of the standard signs and symbols used in math operations

Good luck!

CHAPTER ONE

STRATEGIES

STRATEGIES: "HOW DO I APPROACH A PROBLEM?"

For example:

1 Scott's mom wins a $1,200 lottery. She gives half to her sister who shared the ticket purchase. She gives $\frac{1}{4}$ of the balance to her husband and $\frac{1}{5}$ of the remainder of that to each of her two sons. She then spends $\frac{1}{9}$ of the remainder on herself. How much does she have left?

2 There are nine camp bunks being assigned in order to the campers. The first camper goes to Bunk 1; the second camper to Bunk 2; the ninth camper to Bunk 9 and the tenth camper goes to Bunk 1, etc. To which bunk is the 243rd camper going to be assigned?

Knowing *how to approach* a problem is the key to a solution. That's what this chapter is all about.

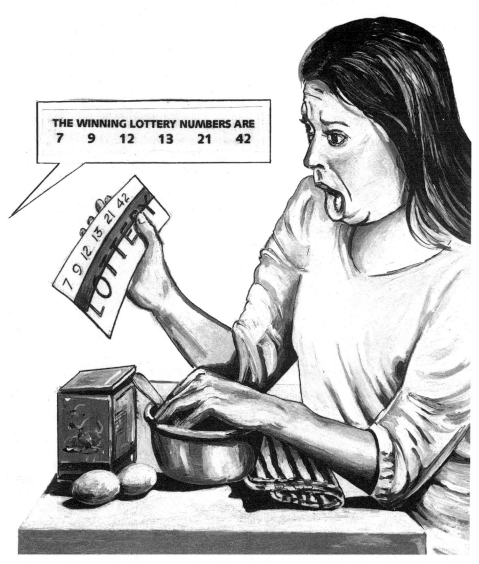

THE WINNING LOTTERY NUMBERS ARE
7   9   12   13   21   42

1.1 TYPES OF STRATEGIES

Some helpful problem solving strategies are introduced with this section.

SUMMARY OF STRATEGIES

1. Estimate
2. Pictures and Diagrams
3. Trial and Error (Guess and Verify)
4. Simpler but Related Problem
5. Proportional Reasoning
6. Equations (Math Sentences)

7. Patterns
8. Separate Relevant from Irrelevant
9. Work Backwards
10. Multiple Representation
11. Try the Answer Choices

1.2 ESTIMATE

Make a rough calculation to identify a reasonable answer.
Check the answer choices to see if all but one are unreasonable.

OUR TURN

Q: Find the product of 652 and 18 and divide by 15.

- **A** 7.824
- **B** 78.24
- **C** 782.4
- **D** 7824
- **E** 78240

A: C

SOLUTION BY ESTIMATING

Estimate by broad rounding to get a "feel" for the answer:

$$652 \Rightarrow 700$$
$$15 \Rightarrow 20$$
$$18 \Rightarrow 20$$

$$\frac{652 \times (18)}{15} \approx \frac{700 \times (20)}{20} = 700$$

Only answer **C** is possible.

YOUR TURN

1 What is the product of 1.25 and 10^5 ?

- **A** 12,500,000
- **B** 1,250,000
- **C** 125,000
- **D** 12,500

2 In a 40 hour work week, Sam earns $340. What is his wage per hour?

- **F** $17,600
- **G** $85
- **H** $10.25
- **J** $8.50

3 What is the correct solution to the question
$3x - 10 = 1268$?

A 426

B 42.6

C 4260

D 622

4 ABC toy company pays $16,000 a month rent for
a store whose area is 500 square feet. How many
dollars is ABC paying per square foot?

F $320

G $32

H $3,200

J $32,000

5 The circus is in town for seven days. The Chart
below shows the attendance for each day. Which
of the following is the total attendance for the
seven days?

A 82,926

B 104,726

C 117,926

D 134,026

DAY	Attendance
Sunday	22,751
Monday	16,582
Tuesday	13,212
Wednesday	15,921
Thursday	17,852
Friday	23,702
Saturday	24,006

6 What is the value of $(199)^3$?

F 7880599

G 3780599

H 99359

J 780599

7 7839 × 568 = ?

A 4452552

B 4454553

C 4452554

D 44525558

8 At the Troy Widget Factory, 6.3% of the widgets
are purple. If 386,269 widgets are made,
estimate how many would be purple.

F 1,800

G 2,400

H 24,000

J 240,000

1.3 PICTURES AND DIAGRAMS

Draw a diagram to assist in the visualization of the problem.

OUR TURN

Q: Sally has 12 marbles. She gives 2 to George and 3 to Ed. Ed
gives 2 each to George and Sally, and George gives 1 to Sally
and 2 to Ed. How many marbles does Sally now have?

A: 10

SOLUTION USING A PICTURE OR DIAGRAM

Using the diagram, Sally gave
away 5 and received 3. She
therefore lost 2. She now
has 10 (12 – 2)

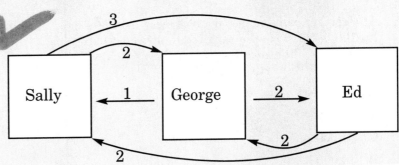

NO PERMISSION HAS BEEN GRANTED BY N&N PUBLISHING COMPANY, INC TO REPRODUCE ANY PART OF THIS BOOK BY ANY MECHANICAL, PHOTOGRAPHIC, OR ELECTRONIC PROCESS.

YOUR TURN

1 A, B, C, D are points on a line segment AD in that order. $\overline{AD}$ is 20 cm long. C is the midpoint of $\overline{AD}$. If $\overline{AB}$ is 7 cm long, how long is $\overline{BC}$?

A 17 cm

B 3 cm

C 10 cm

D 13 cm

2 On Monday, John has $20. Bill has twice as much as John and Ken has half as much as John. On Tuesday John gives Bill $10. Bill then gives half of his money to Ken. How much money does Ken now have?

F $35

G $30

H $40

J $50

3 There are two roads from Jericho to Albertson and seven roads from Albertson to Great Neck. If Carol drives from Jericho to Great Neck, passing through Albertson, how many different routes are possible?

A 14

B 10

C 9

D 5

4 Jane decides to enlarge a picture. The original photo is 3 cm by 5 cm. If it is enlarged so that the new smaller dimension is 15 cm, what is the perimeter of the enlarged photo?

F 25 cm

G 16 cm

H 70 cm

J 80 cm

5 At a certain bank, money doubles every 10 years. If $100 is placed in the bank today, and no other deposits or withdrawals are made, how much will the account be worth in 40 years?

A $400

B $1,200

C $1,600

D $4,000

6 Which set of polygons has all members similar?

F triangles

G octagons

H squares

J parallelograms

7 Points A, B, C, and D are on the same line. Given the following information, in what order do the letters occur, going from left to right?

- C is 7 units to the right of D
- B is 2 units to the left of A
- D is 4 units to the right of A

A A, B, C, D

B B, A, C, D

C B, A, D, C

D A, B, D, C

8 P is the center of a circle. $\overline{AB}$ is a diameter of the circle and M is a point on the circumference of the circle. Radius $\overline{PM}$ is drawn. If angle MPA measures 43°, what is the measure of $\angle MPB$?

F 47°

G 43°

H 147°

J 137°

9 A is taller than B and C. C is taller than D but shorter than E. E is taller than F. Which one of the following people cannot be the shortest?

A B

B F

C D

D E

1.4 TRIAL AND ERROR (GUESS AND VERIFY)

Estimate a guess at the answer and see if it works. If not, adjust your guess appropriately and now see if it works.

OUR TURN

Q: If $a \cdot a$ is less than a, what is a possible value of a?

A:

SOLUTION BY TRIAL AND ERROR

Guess	Verification	
$a = 1$	$1 \cdot 1 < 1$	No
$a = 5$	$5 \cdot 5 < 5$	No
$a = -2$	$(-2) \cdot (-2) < -2$	No
$a = 0$	$0 \cdot 0 < 0$	No
$a = \frac{1}{2}$	$\frac{1}{2} \cdot \frac{1}{2} < \frac{1}{2}$	Yes

A possible value of $a = \frac{1}{2}$

YOUR TURN

1 Which value of n satisfies the following inequality?
$$12 < 3n - 6 < 54$$

   A 4

   B 6

   C 20

   D 8

2 If shirts costs $12.50 each, what is the maximum number of shirts that could be purchased for $100.

   F 9

   G 8

   H 7

   J 87

3 Paul needs $350 to buy a TV set. He already has saved $70. If he wants to buy the TV set in 10 weeks, what is the average amount he must save each week?

   A $280

   B $2.80

   C $28

   D $35

4 A circle has a circumference of 50 cm. A chord in the circle could be which of the following lengths?

   F 15 cm

   G 16 cm

   H 17 cm

   J 20 cm

5 A state has a 4% sales tax. If an item costs $124.80 with the sales tax, what is the price of the item not including the sales tax?

   A $119.81

   B $120.80

   C $120

   D $129.79

6 In ten years Mary will be 5 years less than twice as old as she is now. What is Mary's age now?

   F 8

   G 10

   H 15

   J 20

7 What is the maximum integer value of n that satisfies the following inequality?

$$2^n < 10{,}000$$

A 10

B 12

C 13

D 14

8 Which of the following is in the solution set of the inequality?

$$x^3 < x^2 < x$$

F -1

G $-\frac{1}{2}$

H $\frac{1}{2}$

J 2

9 Bob has test scores of 75, 80, and 85. What score must Bob get on his next test so that his average is 85?

A 85

B 90

C 95

D 100

10 What is one solution to the following equation?

$$x^2 - 5x + 6 = 0$$

F -2

G 2

H 0

J -3

1.5 SIMPLER BUT RELATED PROBLEM

Break the problem into smaller pieces or a simpler problem that is easier to solve.

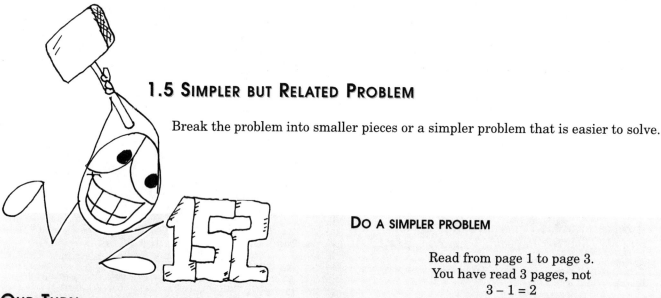

OUR TURN

Q: In a book, you read from the top of page 7 to the bottom of page 241. How many pages have you read?

A: 235

DO A SIMPLER PROBLEM

Read from page 1 to page 3.
You have read 3 pages, not
$$3 - 1 = 2$$

Read from page 7 to page 10.
You have read 4 pages, not
$$10 - 7 = 3$$

Note: Subtracting the page numbers gives a result one less than the correct answer

Therefore: page 7 to page 241

$$\begin{array}{r} 241 \\ -\ 7 \\ \hline 234 \end{array} \quad \text{is off by 1}$$

The correct answer is 235.

YOUR TURN

1 If $A \Delta B$ is defined as $A^2 - B$, evaluate $(5 \Delta 20) \Delta 20$.

   A 405

   B 5

   C 620

   D 952

2 How many numbers from 1 to 100 are multiples of both 4 and 3?

   F 58

   G 25

   H 8

   J 14

3 A large block of ice is in the shape of a cube and its edge is 10 in. A machine cuts it into cubes that are 2 in. on edge. How many smaller ice cubes are obtained?

   A 50

   B 125

   C 250

   D 500

4 The fraction $\frac{1}{7} = .\overline{142857}142857$. Which of the following is the 82nd decimal digit?

   F 8

   G 7

   H 5

   J 4

5 The accompanying figure represents a semicircle inside a square. To the nearest integer, find the shaded area (use $\pi = 3.14$)

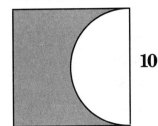

10

   A 11

   B 21

   C 61

   D 84

6 Karen visits her grandmother once every two weeks, goes to the movies once every three weeks, and goes bowling once every five weeks. How often will all three events occur in the same week?

   F every 10 weeks

   G every 20 weeks

   H every 30 weeks

   J every 40 weeks

7 Find the value of $\dfrac{(100!) \times (2!)}{99!}$.

   A 200

   B 400

   C 600

   D 2000

1.6 PROPORTIONAL REASONING

Calculate appropriate ratio, proportions, and unit costs.

OUR TURN

Q: In the country of Neval, 4 VIMS = 3 dollars. How many VIMS can you get for 12 dollars?

A: 16

SOLUTION BY RATIO

Ratio of VIMS to dollars is $\dfrac{\text{VIMS}}{\text{Dollars}}$

$$\frac{\text{VIMS}}{\text{Dollars}} : \frac{4}{3} = \frac{x}{12}$$

$$3x = 48 \quad \text{cross multiply}$$
$$x = 16 \quad \text{divide by 3}$$

SOLUTION BY UNIT PRICE

Find a unit price. Four VIMS for 3 dollars.
Divide 4 VIMS by 3 dollars $\Rightarrow \frac{4}{3}$ VIMS per dollar

$$\$12 \times \left(\frac{4}{3}\right) = 16 \text{ VIMS}$$

YOUR TURN

1 If 3 cans of peas cost 55 cents, how much will 12 cans cost?

   A $6.60

   B $2.20

   C $4.95

   D $2.00

2 In a recipe for a cake for 4 people, you need 3 eggs and 4 cups of sugar. How many eggs should you use if you are making a cake to serve 8 people?

   F 6 eggs

   G 8 eggs

   H 7 eggs

   J 12 eggs

3 A class consists of 12 boys and 15 girls. How many boys should there be in a class of 36 students if the ratio of boys to girls is the same as in the 1st class?

   A 15 boys

   B 20 boys

   C 16 boys

   D 17 boys

4 If the U.S. dollar is worth 1.8 Canadian dollars, how many U.S. dollars will 9 Canadian dollars be worth?

   F 16.2

   G 10.8

   H 5

   J 2

5 A 20 ft. tree casts a shadow 4 ft. long. At the same time and place, how long will the shadow be of a 6 ft. man?

   A 30 ft.

   B 1.2 ft.

   C 22 ft.

   D 2 ft.

6 A set of marbles has 2 green, 3 black, and 5 blue marbles. What percent of the marbles are green?

   F $\frac{2}{10}$

   G 2

   H 20

   J 200

7 A triangle has sides of 4 cm, 5 cm, 6 cm. If the longest side of a similar triangle has length 120 cm, how long is the shortest side of the similar triangle?

   A 100 cm

   B 180 cm

   C 118 cm

   D 80 cm

8 If 7 widgets = 9 gidgets, how many widgets are equal to 11 gidgets? Which equation can be used to solve the question?

   F $7 + 9 = 11 + n$

   G $\frac{7}{9} = \frac{11}{n}$

   H $\frac{9}{7} = \frac{11}{n}$

   J $9 - 7 = 11 - n$

9 A car uses 4 gallons of gasoline on a trip of 92 miles. At the same rate, how far could the car go on a full tank if the capacity of the tank is 17 gallons?

   A 107 miles

   B 391 miles

   C 368 miles

   D 408 miles

1.7 Mathematical Sentences (Equations)

Express the problem algebraically and solve.

Our Turn

Q:
Tam has 4 more marbles than Juan. Together they have 20. How many does Juan have?

A: 8

Solution by Equation

Let x = number of marbles Juan has
Let $x + 4$ = number of marbles Tam has

$$x + (x + 4) = 20$$
$$2x + 4 = 20$$
$$2x = 16$$
$$x = 8$$

Juan has 8 marbles.

Your Turn

1 Jeff is 3 years more than twice Bob's age. If Bob's age is represented by n, which expression correctly represents Jeff's age?

  A $n + 3$

  B $2n + 3$

  C $2n - 3$

  D $2 \times (n + 3)$

2 If the angles of a triangle are represented by 3 consecutive integers, which equation can be used to find the measures of the angles?

  F $n + 2n + 3n = 360$

  G $n + (n + 1) + (n + 2) = 180$

  H $n + (n + 2) + (n + 4) = 180$

  J $n + 10n + 20n = 180$

3 Norm has twice as many dimes as quarters. Norm has $9.00. If x equals the number of quarters, which of the following equations could be used to find the number of quarters?

  A $25(x) + 10(2x) = 9$

  B $25(x) + 10(2x) = 900$

  C $25x + 10x = 90$

  D $x + 2x = 9$

4 The length of a rectangle is 3 more than the width. Let x equal the width of the rectangle. If the perimeter of the rectangle is 42, which equation can be used to solve for x?

  F $x + (x + 3) = 42$

  G $x + x + (x + 3) = 42$

  H $x + x + (x + 3) + (x + 3) = 42$

  J $x + x + x + (x + 3) + (x + 3) = 42$

5 A cardboard box has a length of $x - 2$, width of $x + 1$, and height of $2x$. Which of the following expressions represents the volume of the box?

  A $x (x - 2) (x + 1)$

  B $x + (x - 2) + (x + 1)$

  C $\pi (x + 1)^2$

  D $2(x) (x - 2) (x + 1)$

6 A florist charges $6 for delivery and $1.25 per rose. If x represents the quantity of roses, which of the following equations can be used to find the number of roses that can be delivered for $26?

  F $1.25x - 6 = 26$

  G $1.25x + 26 = 6$

  H $1.25x = 26 + 6$

  J $6 + 1.25x = 26$

7 Twice a number is 8 less than three times the number. If x represents the number, which of the following equations be used to solve for x?

A $2(x - 8) = 3x$

B $3(x - 8) = 2x$

C $3x = 2x - 8$

D $2x = 3x - 8$

1.8 PATTERNS

Develop a pattern that can be extended to find a solution.

OUR TURN

Q: What is the next number in the pattern: 3, 4, 6, 9, 13, 18, 24, _____ ?

A: 31

SOLUTION BY DEVELOPING A PATTERN

3 → 4	Increases by 1
4 → 6	Increases by 2
6 → 9	Increases by 3
9 → 13	Increases by 4
13 → 18	Increases by 5
18 → 24	Increases by 6

We expect 31 to be the next number.
Twenty-four increased by 7.

YOUR TURN

1 What is the next number in the sequence: 64, 32, 16, 8, 4, 2, ____

A 4

B 2

C 0

D 1

2 Which number should be the 8ᵗʰ number in the pattern: 3, 7, 13, 21, 31, ____ , ____ , ____

F 61

G 73

H 7

J 66

3 Find the missing number in the following sequence: 37, 41, 43, ____ , 53, 59, 61

A 45

B 51

C 46

D 47

4 Find the next number in the pattern: 5, 3, 10, 6, 15, 9, 20, 12, 25, ____

F 15

G 16

H 30

J 18

5 Use the information below to help answer this question.

$$(11)^2 = 121$$
$$(111)^2 = 12321$$
$$(1111)^2 = 1234321$$

How many digits will be in $(111111)^2$?

A 9

B 10

C 11

D 12

E 13

6 Use the information below to help answer this question.

$$1 = 1^2$$
$$1 + 3 = 2^2$$
$$1 + 3 + 5 = 3^2$$
$$1 + 3 + 5 + 7 = 4^2$$

Which of the following represents the sum of the first fifteen consecutive odd whole numbers?

F 100

G 121

H 144

J 225

8 A palindrome number reads the same forward or backward. For example, 797 is a palindrome number. How many of the following numbers are palindrome numbers?

777
12221
12345
54945

F none

G one

H two

J three

7

1ˢᵗ	2ⁿᵈ	3ʳᵈ	4ᵗʰ	5ᵗʰ	6ᵗʰ	7ᵗʰ

If the pattern above continues, how many dots will be in the 7ᵗʰ figure?

A 21

B 28

C 36

D 45

1.9 SEPARATE RELEVANT FROM IRRELEVANT

Separate out the irrelevant information to clarify the problem.

OUR TURN

Q: Traveling directly from A to B, a distance of 480 miles, Aldo travels at an average speed of 60 mph. Traveling directly from B to C, Aldo travels at an average speed of 50 mph and covers a distance of 200 miles in 4 hours. What was the total distance Aldo traveled from A to C, through B.

A: 680

SOLUTION BY ELIMINATING IRRELEVANT DATA

To find the total distance traveled:

$$\begin{array}{ll} \text{Distance } A \to B = & 480 \\ \text{Distance } B \to C = & 200 \\ \hline \text{Total} \quad = & 680 \end{array}$$

The rest of the data was not necessary.

YOUR TURN

1 A class of 40 students has 23 boys and 17 girls. The class size increased in October by 20%. How many students were added to the class?

  A 48

  B 20

  C 8

  D 17

2 A recipe that serves 4 people uses 2 cups of sugar, 1 egg, and 3 cups of milk. If we want to serve 6 people, how many cups of sugar would we need?

  F 3

  G 4

  H 5

  J $4\frac{1}{2}$

3 In parallelogram $ABCD$, $\overline{AB}$ measures 10 cm and $\overline{BC}$ measures 8 cm. If the height to side $\overline{BC}$ is 9 cm, find the perimeter of the parallelogram.

  A 18 cm

  B 72 cm

  C 45 cm

  D 36 cm

4 Alice usually has an 80% shooting percentage in basketball. On Monday, she scored 16 baskets in 22 attempts. If she scores her usual percentage on Tuesday by scoring 20 baskets, how many shots did she attempt?

  F 24

  G 25

  H 28

  J 30

5 Frank weighed 20 lbs. as a 1-year-old and 30 lbs. as a 2-year-old. Each year since he was 2, he has gained 12 lbs. How much does Frank weigh on his 10th birthday?

  A 110

  B 152

  C 126

  D 114

6 Joe is 6 ft. tall and owns a boat that is 65 ft. long. His brother Frank has a boat that is 64 ft. 8 in. long. If Frank is 5 in. shorter than Joe, how tall is Frank?

  F 5' 7"

  G 5' 8"

  H 6' 5"

  J 6' 7"

7 If $A - B = 5$, $B + C = 12$, and $A - B + C = 14$, how much is C?

   A 8

   B 9

   C 5

   D cannot be determined

8 A bag contains 5 red, 4 white, and 6 blue marbles. Another bag with 9 blue marbles has the same ratio of blue to white marbles as the first bag. How many white marbles are there in the second bag?

   F 7

   G 8

   H 6

   J 5

1.10 WORK BACKWARDS

Use a piece of given information and try to work the problem backwards to arrive at the solution.

OUR TURN

Q: A has twice the number of coins that B has. C has 2 less coins than D and 4 more than E. D has 4 more coins than B. If E has 12 coins, how many coins does A have?

A: 28

SOLUTION BY WORKING BACKWARDS

Begin with the given $\Rightarrow E$ has 12

Work backwards:

C has 4 more than $E \Rightarrow C$ has 16

C has 2 less than $D \Rightarrow D$ has 18

D has 4 more coins than $B \Rightarrow B$ has 14

A has twice $B \Rightarrow A$ has 28

YOUR TURN

1 Postage is 34 cents for the first ounce and 21 cents for each additional ounce. If the cost of mailing a package is $2.23, how much does the package weigh?

   A 12 ounces

   B 11 ounces

   C 10 ounces

   D 9 ounces

2 During Halloween, Lisa went trick or treating and collected candy. She ate half her candy the 1st week, half the remainder the 2nd week, and the 3rd week she ate half her remaining candy. If she still had 5 pieces of candy after the 3rd week, how many pieces did she collect on Halloween?

   F 40

   G 20

   H 10

   J 80

3   Fred goes to the gym every week. Every week he lifts 8 lbs. more than the previous week. During the ninth week he lifts 250 lbs. How much was he lifting during his 1st week?

   A   178 lbs.

   B   170 lbs.

   C   242 lbs.

   D   186 lbs.

4   After improving his batting average by .015 each month during June, July, and August, Marty is now hitting .300. What was his average at the beginning of June?

   F   .255

   G   .345

   H   .240

   J   .270

5   If $a + b = 6$, $b + c = 11$, and $c + d = 4$, find the value of a if $d = 1$.

   A   – 4

   B   – 2

   C   2

   D   4

6   To be ready to watch a TV concert special at 8 PM, Dawn wants to finish her 2 hours of homework, allow 35 minutes for dinner, and 30 minutes to practice her bassoon. What is the latest time she can begin these activities and still be finished by 8 PM?

   F   4:25

   G   4:35

   H   4:45

   J   4:55

7   Which of the following is a correct solution to the inequality:

$$3y - 7 > 50$$

   A   5

   B   10

   C   15

   D   20

8   At a store in Port Washington, a new MP3 player came on the market during July. In August, the price increased by $5. In September, the price increased by $12. In October, the price decreased by $13. At this point, the price had become $120. What was the price of the MP3 player back in July?

1.11 MULTIPLE REPRESENTATIONS

Display the problem using an equivalent but different representation to better define the solution path and possibly find an easier solution.

OUR TURN

Q: On a particular day, the school cafeteria offered 3 types of juice, 2 types of cereal, and 3 types of bread during breakfast. How many different meals can be formed of one juice, 1 cereal, and 1 type of bread?

A: 18

SOLUTION BY MULTIPLE REPRESENTATION

Method 1: Tree Diagram

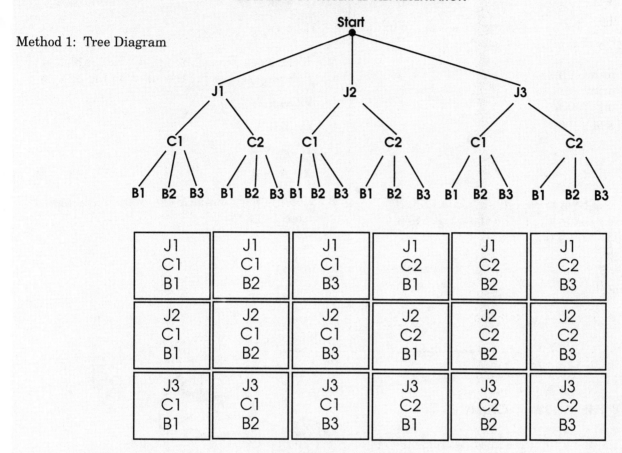

18 different combinations

Method 2: Counting Principle

$$3 \quad \times \quad 2 \quad \times \quad 3 \quad = \quad 18$$

Juices   Cereals   Breads

YOUR TURN

1 There are 5 teams in a basketball tournament. If each teams plays every other team once, how many games are played?

   A 20

   B 25

   C 120

   D 10

2 A six-sided die is rolled and a two-sided coin is tossed at the same time. How many outcomes are there?

   F 12

   G 8

   H 6

   J 2

3 Marsha is on a line. She is the 8th person from the front but the 11th person from the back. How many people are on line?

   A 19

   B 18

   C 3

   D 20

4 Three dimes are tossed at the same time. What is the probability that all three land on heads?

   F $\frac{1}{2}$

   G $\frac{3}{2}$

   H $\frac{1}{8}$

   J $\frac{1}{6}$

5 The ratio of boys to girls in a class is 4 : 5. If there are 27 students in the class, there how many girls are in the class?

   A 6

   B 9

   C 12

   D 15

6 The sum of the ages of the three Smith brothers is 63. If their ages can be represented as consecutive integers, what is the age of the middle brother?

7 If the sides of a square are doubled, which of the following represents the effect on the area "A"?

   F $A + 2$

   G $A + 4$

   H $A \times 2$

   J $A \times 4$

8 What is the average of the consecutive integers from 1 to 29?

   A 14

   B $14\frac{1}{2}$

   C 15

   D $15\frac{1}{2}$

1.12 TRY THE ANSWER CHOICES

Substitute the answer choices into the problem and see which one works.

OUR TURN

Q: Solve $|2x - 3| = 5$ for a possible value of x.

   A -2

   B -1

   C 0

   D 1

   E 2

A: B

SOLUTION USING "TEST THE ANSWER CHOICES"

If $x = -2$ $|2 \times (-2) - 3| = |-4 - 3| = |-7| = 7$ this $\neq 5$

If $x = -1$ $|2 \times (-1) - 3| = |-2 - 3| = |-5| = 5$ this $= 5$

Answer is choice B

1 What value(s) of x make the following statement true?

$$x = x^2$$

I   1
II -1
III   0

A   I, only

B   II, only

C   III, only

D   I and III

2 Which value solves the following equation?

$$x^3 - x^2 = 48$$

F   5

G   6

H   4

J   3

3 Which value satisfies the following inequality?

$$5(x + 4) - 3x^2 > 9$$

A   2

B   4

C   5

D   10

4 When is $x^2 > x^3$?

I x is negative
II x is positive integer
III x is a fraction

F   I, only

G   II, only

H   I and II

J   I and III

5 Which set of angles could be the angles of a triangle?

A   {25, 45, 70}

B   {51, 70, 59}

C   {40, 50, 100}

D   {110, 120, 130}

6 A triangle is isosceles. Which set of numbers could be the sides of the triangle?

F   {2, 8, 8}

G   {3, 4, 5}

H   {5, 12, 13}

J   {30, 30, 120}

7 Which value of n will make the equation true?

$$5^n = 3125$$

A   3

B   4

C   5

D   6

8 Which set consists solely of prime numbers?

F   {3, 7, 19, 51}

G   {1, 11, 19, 23}

H   {17, 29, 39, 49}

J   {2, 31, 37, 41}

1.13 Long Answers for Chapter 1

1 To begin, Ricardo has 4 more marbles than Juanita. Juanita has 2 more than Alfredo, and Ricardo started with 20 marbles. If Alfredo gives Ricardo 6 and Juanita 2, Juanita gives Ricardo 3, and Ricardo gives Juanita and Alfredo each one, how many marbles does Alfredo have after all the above transactions?

Answer _____ marbles

Explain how you arrived at your answer. Show all necessary work.

2 The time in San Francisco is 3 hours earlier than the time in New York. If a 6-hour flight leaves San Francisco at 5:00 P.M. Monday, at what New York time does it arrive in New York?

Answer _____

Explain how you arrived at your answer.

_____

_____

_____

_____

_____

_____

3 Ling sold 45 bottles of water and 85 cans of soda at the beach last weekend. She collected a total of $183.75.

Part A

If the bottles of water sold for $1.25 each, write an equation to find the cost C of each can of soda.

Equation : _____

Part B

Using the equation in Part A, what is the cost of a can of soda?
Show your work.

Answer _____

Part C

The cost of a can of soda is what percent greater than the cost of a bottle of water?
Show your work.

Answer: _____%

4   Between 1990 and 1995, the tuition of a private school doubled. It stayed the same in 1996 and 1997. In 1998, the tuition went up another $340 per year. It stayed the same in 1999 and 2000. In the year 2001, the tuition was $4320, which was a rise of $80. What was the tuition per year in 1990, before these increases?

Show your work or explain your method of arriving at the solution.

Answer _____dollars

5   For the school Halloween party, Brad and Eric had a total of 20 yards of material from which to make costumes. Brad used three times more material to make his costume than Eric used and 2 yards of material were left over.

Part A

If x represents the amount of material Eric used, write an equation which can be used to solve for x.

Equation : _____

Part B

Solve the equation and determine the amount of material each person used. Show all of your work

Brad used _____ yards.

Eric used _____ yards.

6 If $(11)^2 = 121$
   $(111)^2 = 12321$
   $(1111)^2 = 1234321$

What is the value of $(1111111)^2$

Use the space below to show your work and/or explain how you arrived at your answer.

Answer: _____

7 Four Syosset Middle School students (Mark, David, Marshall, and Jonathan) competed in three events. The results were partially erased and only those standings shown in the table below remained. There were no ties and the points awarded for each standing are indicated in the chart.

Event	1st Place (5 points)	2nd Place (3 points)	3rd Place (1 points)	4th Place (0 points)
1	Mark			David
2		Mark	David	
3			Mark	Marshall

PART A

What is the highest combined point total Jonathan could have received for all three events? Explain how you arrived at your answer.

	1st	2nd	3rd	4th
1	Mark			David
2		Mark	David	
3			Mark	Marshall

Answer: _____ points

PART B

What is the minimum combined point total Jonathan could have received for all three events? Explain how you arrived at your answer.

	1st	2nd	3rd	4th
1	Mark			David
2		Mark	David	
3			Mark	Marshall

Answer: _____ points

PART C

Could Marshall have finished with the highest combined point total? Explain your answer.

	1st	2nd	3rd	4th
1	Mark			David
2		Mark	David	
3			Mark	Marshall

Answer: _____ (yes or no)

CHAPTER TWO
TYPES OF NUMBERS

Numbers are used for expression of size and for comparison. They come in many forms, e.g., 6, 181, 8.2×10^5, $\sqrt{17}$, $\frac{1}{3}$, 18%, 18.3, 4 : 3, 5^7. Each form has its use. We can use numbers to express very great distances, as with stars, or very small distances, as with atoms. We use them to compare things such as: which garden has the most space to plant flowers, what portion of a group is a particular category or activity, or to express the ratio between items.

Numbers help us understand questions such as:

Dawn read that the Alpha Centuri star is 2.5×10^{13} miles from our Sun. How many miles is that?

One recipe calls for $\frac{1}{3}$ teaspoon of vanilla. Cara measures out the vanilla that she has and it measures $\frac{5}{16}$ teaspoon. Does she have enough vanilla for the recipe?

Numbers are the key.

2.1 CLASSIFICATION OF NUMBERS

CLASSIFICATION OF NUMBERS (PICTORIAL)

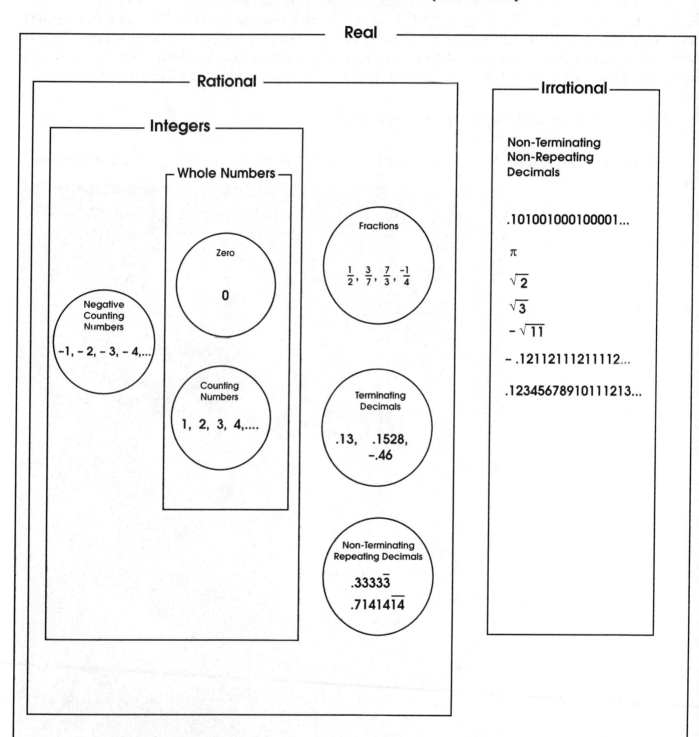

Real

Rational

Integers

Whole Numbers

Negative Counting Numbers
$-1, -2, -3, -4,...$

Zero
0

Counting Numbers
$1, 2, 3, 4,....$

Fractions
$\frac{1}{2}, \frac{3}{7}, \frac{7}{3}, \frac{-1}{4}$

Terminating Decimals
$.13, \quad .1528, \quad -.46$

Non-Terminating Repeating Decimals
$.3333\overline{3}$
$.71414\overline{14}$

Irrational

Non-Terminating Non-Repeating Decimals

$.101001000100001...$

π

$\sqrt{2}$

$\sqrt{3}$

$-\sqrt{11}$

$-.12112111211112...$

$.12345678910111213...$

CLASSIFICATION OF NUMBERS (TABULAR)

Family				Description	Example
Real	Rational	Integers	Whole	Counting: like counting sheep "One, two, 3, 4,.."	1, 2, 3, 4, ...
				Zero: the number 0, as in no sheep	0
				Negative counting numbers: the counting numbers with a minus sign in front	–1, – 2, – 3, – 4,...
				Fractions: an integer divided by a non-zero integer	$\frac{1}{5}$, $\frac{7}{4}$
				Terminating decimals: Decimal numbers that end	.46208
				Non-terminating, repeating decimals: decimal numbers that go on forever, but they repeat uniformly	.147147147...
	Irrational			Non-terminating, Non-repeating decimals: decimal numbers that extend forever, but do not repeat	$\sqrt{3}$, $\sqrt{5}$ .61661666166661... π

OUR TURN

Q: Let W = family of whole numbers, I = family of Integers
R = family of rational numbers, H = family of Irrational numbers

To which family or families do each of the following numbers belong?

1 $\sqrt{16}$

2 $-\frac{1}{2}$

3 .1010010010001...

4 .101010101...

A:

1 $\sqrt{16}$ = 4   belongs to W, I, and R families

2 $-\frac{1}{2}$ belongs to the R family

3 .101010010001... is a never ending non-repeating decimal. It belongs to the H family.

4 .1010101...   is never ending and repeats. It belongs to the R family.

YOUR TURN

Using the letters W, I, R, and H as defined in the 'Our Turn' the on previous page, identify the family or families to which each of the following numbers belong.

____ **1** $\sqrt{5}$

____ **2** π

____ **3** 8.14

____ **4** 6.301010101...

____ **5** $\frac{1}{4}$

____ **6** $-\sqrt{4}$

____ **7** 62.62627

____ **8** $\sqrt{25}$

____ **9** 3^2

____ **10** 0

11 Which of the following is rational?

   A $\sqrt{13}$

   B π

   C $\sqrt{3}$

   D $\sqrt{.16}$

12 Which of the following is a whole number?

   F -7

   G 0

   H $\frac{3}{4}$

   J $2\frac{1}{2}$

2.2 NUMBER LINE AND ABSOLUTE VALUE

NUMBER LINE

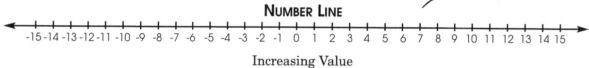

Increasing Value ⟶

ABSOLUTE VALUE/OPPOSITES

Symbol	Terminology	Description	Example
$\lvert-4\rvert$ $\lvert 5 \rvert$	Absolute Value	the distance a number is from zero on the number line	$\lvert-4\rvert = 4$ because -4 is four units from zero $\lvert 5 \rvert = 5$ because 5 is five units from zero
$6, -6$ $5, -5$ $\frac{1}{4}, -\frac{1}{4}$	Opposites	two numbers that are the same distance from zero but in opposite directions	3 and -3 are opposite, each is 3 units from the origin, but in opposite directions

❽ Absolute Value – The two vertical bars, one on each side of the number, indicate absolute value:

$$\lvert 6 \rvert, \lvert-2\rvert, \lvert-\tfrac{3}{4}\rvert$$

❽ Absolute Value – The absolute value of a number is never negative.

❽ Opposites – An integer and its opposite add to zero.

OUR TURN

Q: Write the opposite of each of the following:

1 $-\frac{1}{2}$

2 $\sqrt{5}$

3 .402

Find the value (evaluate) of each of the following:

4 $|-3|$

5 $|-2| + |-1|$

6 $|2| + |-2|$

A:

1 $\frac{1}{2}$

2 $-\sqrt{5}$

3 $-.402$

The opposite of a number is basically the same number with the sign changed

4 3

$|-3| = 3$

$|-2| = 2, |-1 = 1|$

5 3

$|-2| + |-1| = 2 + 1 = 3$

$|2| = 2, |-2| = 2$

6 4

$|2| + |-2| = 2 + 2 = 4$

YOUR TURN

Write the opposite of each of following:

1 3.7

2 -4

3 $\frac{2}{3}$

4 π

Evaluate (find the value):

5 $|-11|$

6 $|-1| - |-1| + |1|$

7 $3 + |-3|$

8 $|-\frac{1}{2}| + |\frac{1}{2}|$

9 Which one of the following is the opposite of -2?

A $-\frac{2}{1}$

B $-\frac{1}{2}$

C $\frac{1}{2}$

D $\sqrt{4}$

10 If $|n| + |n| = 4$, which of the following could be the value of n?

F -1

G -2

H -3

J -4

2.3 INVERSES

ADDITIVE AND MULTIPLICATIVE INVERSES

Types of Inverses	Other name (terminology)	Description	Example
Additive Inverse	Opposite	that which adds to a given number to get zero ⎯⎯⎯⎯ the given number with sign changed	$-2, 2$ $\frac{1}{2}, -\frac{1}{2}$ $\sqrt{2}, -\sqrt{2}$ are pairs of opposites
Multiplicative Inverse	Reciprocal	that which multiplies with a given number to get one ⎯⎯⎯⎯ the "up-side-down" of the given number	$\frac{1}{2}, 2$ $-3, -\frac{1}{3}$ $1, 1$ are pairs of reciprocals

OUR TURN

Q: Write the additive and multiplicative inverses of each of the following:

1 6

2 – 6

3 $\frac{2}{3}$

4 .5

A:

1 AI = – 6, MI = $\frac{1}{6}$

2 AI = 6, MI = $-\frac{1}{6}$

3 AI = $-\frac{2}{3}$, MI = $\frac{3}{2}$

4 AI = – .5, MI = $\frac{1}{.5}$ = 2

YOUR TURN

For each of the following numbers write the reciprocal, the opposite, and identify if it is a whole number.

1 $-\frac{7}{3}$

2 $\frac{1}{4}$

3 7

4 $2\frac{1}{2}$

5 .02

6 $-\sqrt{16}$

7 –1

8 The product of two non-zero opposites is always

    A even

    B odd

    C positive

    D negative

9 Which of the following shows the numbers in decreasing order?

F – 3, |– 3|, reciprocal of – 3

G |– 3|, – 3, reciprocal of – 3

H reciprocal of – 3, |– 3|, – 3

J |– 3|, reciprocal of – 3, – 3

10 What is the additive inverse of the reciprocal of |– 5|?

A – 5

B $-\frac{1}{5}$

C $\frac{1}{5}$

D 5

2.4 DIVISIBILITY

DEFINITION

A whole number is divisible by a second whole number if you can divide the first by the second and get a whole number answer (meaning: **No remainder**).

DIVISIBILITY RULES

A number is divisible by:	If
2	the last digit is divisible by 2 (last digit is even)
3	the sum of its digits is divisible by 3
4	the last two digits, read as a two digit number, is divisible by 4
5	it ends in 0 or 5
6	It is divisible by 2 and by 3
8	the last three digits, read as a three digit number, is divisible by 8
9	the sum of its digits is divisible by 9
10	it ends in 0
12	it is divisible by 3 and by 4

EVEN/ODD INTEGERS

Examples	Terminology	Description
... – 10, – 8, – 6, – 4, – 2, 0, 2, 4, 6, 8, 10, 12,...	Even Integers	Each is divisible by 2.
... – 11, – 9, – 7, – 5, – 3, – 1, 1, 3, 5, 7, 9, 11,...	Odd Integers	Cannot be divided by 2 without a remander.

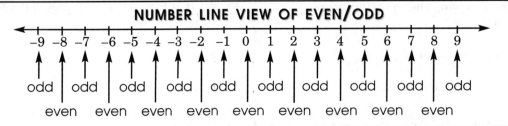

NUMBER LINE VIEW OF EVEN/ODD

- Between any two consecutive even integers is an odd integer
- Between any two consecutive odd integers is an even integer

❽ Zero - zero is an even integer

OUR TURN

Q: Is 3142278 divisible by 2, 3, 4, 5, 6, 8, 9, 10, or 12?

A:

It is divisible by 2 . . . . because the last digit is even

It is divisible by 3 . . . . because the sum of the digits $(3 + 1 + 4 + 2 + 2 + 7 + 8 = 27)$ is divisible by 3

It is **not** divisible by 4 . . . . because 78, the two digit number based on the last two digits, is **not** divisible by 4

It is **not** divisible by 5 . . . . because it does not end in 0 or 5

It is divisible by 6 . . . . because it is divisible by 2 and 3

It is **not** divisible by 8 . . . . because 278, the 3 digit number based on the last three digits, is **not** divisible by 8

It is divisible by 9 . . . . because the sum of the digits $3 + 1 + 4 + 2 + 2 + 7 + 8 = 27$, which is divisible by 9

It is **not** divisible by 10 . . . . because it does **not** end in 0

It is **not** divisible by 12...because it is **not** divisible 4. To be divisible by 12, the number must be divisible by 3 and 4

YOUR TURN

1 Which one of the following numbers is divisible by 3?

A 1,111

B 11,111

C 111,111

D 1,111,111

2 Which one of the following is divisible by 6?

F 2,222

G 2,322

H 2,323

J 3,332

3 Let n represent the 3rd digit of the five digit number, 17, n21. For what value of n will 17, n21 be divisible by 9?

A 3

B 5

C 7

D 9

4 The sum of two even integers is always:

F even

G odd

H positive

J negative

5 Which of the following is divisible by 9?

    A 9,993

    B 9,393

    C 3,939

    D 3,339

6 Which one of the following is divisible by 5 and 2?

    F 22,225

    G 55,552

    H 86,720

    J 95,355

7 Let n represent the tens digit of the four digit number 7, 6n4. For what value(s) of n is 7, 6n4 divisible by 3?

    A 1 and 4, only

    B 1 and 7, only

    C 4 and 7, only

    D 1, 4, and 7

8 If a number is divisible by 9 it must also be divisible by:

    F 3

    G 6

    H 3 and 6

    J 18

9 The number 641,247 is divisible by which of the following?

    A 2

    B 3

    C 6

    D 9

10 The product of two odd integers is always:

    F positive

    G negative

    H even

    J odd

2.5 PRIME NUMBERS

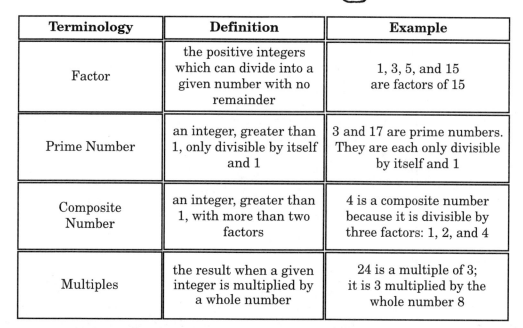

DEFINITION OF TERMS

Terminology	Definition	Example
Factor	the positive integers which can divide into a given number with no remainder	1, 3, 5, and 15 are factors of 15
Prime Number	an integer, greater than 1, only divisible by itself and 1	3 and 17 are prime numbers. They are each only divisible by itself and 1
Composite Number	an integer, greater than 1, with more than two factors	4 is a composite number because it is divisible by three factors: 1, 2, and 4
Multiples	the result when a given integer is multiplied by a whole number	24 is a multiple of 3; it is 3 multiplied by the whole number 8

* Prime Numbers - The number two is the only even prime number.

FACTOR VS. MULTIPLE

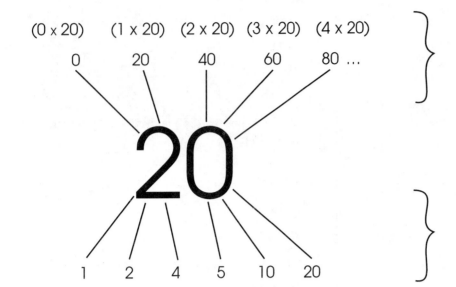

(0 x 20)   (1 x 20)   (2 x 20)   (3 x 20)   (4 x 20)

0   20   40   60   80 ...

20

1   2   4   5   10   20

Multiples of 20
_____
the product of 20 and a
whole number

Factors of 20
_____
integers that divide into 20
with no remainder

PRIME FACTORIZATION AND THE FACTOR TREE

Terminology	Description/Procedure/Example
Prime Factorization	writing a positive integer as a product of its prime factors
Factor Tree	a method of finding the prime factorization of a number
	Step 1: Split the number into two factors each greater than 1 (split 24 into 8 · 3). **Step 2:** Split each of the factors in Step 1 into two factors each greater then 1, if possible. **Step 3:** Repeatedly continue Step 2 until no numbers remain that can be separated into factors. **Step 4:** Write the prime factorization. 24 = 2 · 2 · 2 · 3. Example using 24 24 → 8, 3 → 4, 2 → 2, 2

❽ Prime Factorization - If you had split 24 into 6 and 4, the same final prime factorization would have resulted.

OUR TURN

Q: Find the prime factorization of 42.

A:
Construct the factorization tree.

$$42 = 2 \cdot 3 \cdot 7$$

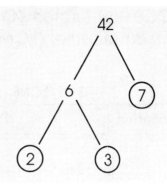

YOUR TURN

What is the prime factorization of each of the following composite numbers?

1 50

2 32

3 28

4 100

5 3000

6 Which of the following represents the prime factorization of 420?

   A $2 \cdot 2 \cdot 3 \cdot 3 \cdot 5 \cdot 7$

   B $2 \cdot 2 \cdot 3 \cdot 5 \cdot 7$

   C $2 \cdot 3 \cdot 5 \cdot 7 \cdot 10$

   D $2 \cdot 3 \cdot 5 \cdot 14$

7 Which of the following is a multiple of 12?

   F 2

   G 8

   H 16

   J 24

8 Which of the following is a prime number?

   A 1

   B 37

   C 51

   D 57

9 Which of the following has a prime factorization containing all the same number?

   F 12

   G 24

   H 36

   J 64

10 What is the value of n to correctly complete the following factor tree?

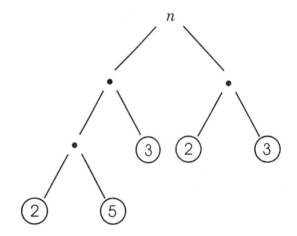

   A 180

   B 160

   C 140

   D 120

2.6 GREATEST COMMON FACTOR (GCF)
LEAST COMMON MULTIPLE (LCM)

GCF/LCM

Terminology	Description	Procedure/Example
Greatest Common Factor (GCF)	the largest factor a given group of numbers has in common	**Step 1:** List the factors of each number in the given group. **Step 2:** Search for the greatest common factor. For example: Factors of 30: 1, ②, 3, 5, 6, 10, 15, 30 Factors of 16: 1, ②, 4, 8, 16 Two is the greatest common factor.
Least Common Multiple (LCM)	the smallest positive integer a given group of numbers can each divide into without a remainder	**Step 1:** List several multiples of each number in the given group. **Step 2:** Search for the first non-zero multiple they have in common. For example: Multiples of 6: 6, 12, 18, ㉔, 36, 42, 48 Multiples of 8: 8, 16, ㉔ Twenty-four is the least common multiple.

❸ GCF - If two numbers do not have GCF greater than 1 the pair is called relatively prime.

OUR TURN

Q:

1 What is the greatest common factor (GCF) of 24 and 30?

2 What is the least common multiple (LCM) of 24 and 30?

A:

1 List the factors of 24 and 30

Factors of 24: 1, 2, 3, 4, ⑥, 8, 12, 24
Factors of 30: 1, 2, 3, 5, ⑥, 10, 15, 30
The GCF is 6

2 List several multiples of 24 and 30

Multiples of 24: 0, 24, 48, 72, 96, ⑫⓪, 144
Multiples of 30: 0, 30, 60, 90, ⑫⓪, 150
The LCM is 120

❸ Remember: The LCM is a positive integer, therefore 0 is not the LCM.

YOUR TURN

Find the GCF of each of the following pairs of numbers.

1 12 and 30

2 18 and 50

3 24 and 40

4 13 and 52

5 100 and 250

Find the LCM of each of the following pairs of numbers.

6 12 and 30

7 9 and 10

8 8 and 24

9 3 and 7

10 4 and 6

11 What is the greatest common factor (GCF) of the numbers 26 and 39?

    A 1

    B 3

    C 13

    D 23

12 If the factors of every positive integer were listed respectively, what number would be on every list?

    F 0

    G 1

    H 2

    J 10

13 If a list was made of all the factors of 24 and another list of all the multiples of 24, what number would be on both lists?

    A 0

    B 1

    C 3

    D 24

14 What is the least common multiple (LCM) of 2, 6, 12, and 24?

    F 2

    G 18

    H 24

    J 36

15 If the multiples of all the positive integers were listed respectively, what number is a multiple of every integer?

    A 0

    B 1

    C 10

    D 100

2.7 EXPONENTS

SYMBOL DEFINITIONS AND MEANING

Symbol	Description	Examples
x^a	$\underbrace{x \cdot x \cdot x \cdot x \,....\, x}_{a \text{ times}}$ the value x, multiplied by itself "a" times	$7^3 = 7 \cdot 7 \cdot 7$ $3^7 = 3 \cdot 3 \cdot 3 \cdot 3 \cdot 3 \cdot 3 \cdot 3$
x^0	1 any non zero number to the zero power equals 1	$8^0 = 1 \qquad 6^0 = 1$ $(\tfrac{1}{2})^0 = 1 \qquad (.137)^0 = 1$
x^{-a}	$\dfrac{1}{x^a}$ the reciprocal of x^a	$7^{-2} = \dfrac{1}{7^2} = \dfrac{1}{7 \cdot 7} = \dfrac{1}{49}$ $3^{-1} = \dfrac{1}{3^1} = \dfrac{1}{3}$

OUR TURN

Q:

1 Evaluate $2^0 + 3^0 + 4^0$.

2 Which is larger, 3^4 or 4^3?

3 Express $3 \cdot 3 \cdot 3 \cdot 5 \cdot 5 \cdot 5 \cdot 5$ using exponents.

A:

1 3 Any number to the zero power is 1.

$2^0 = 1 \qquad 3^0 = 1 \qquad 4^0 = 1$
$\Rightarrow 2^0 + 3^0 + 4^0 = 1 + 1 + 1 = 3$

2 3^4 $3^4 = 3 \cdot 3 \cdot 3 \cdot 3 = 81$

$4^3 = 4 \cdot 4 \cdot 4 = 64$

3 $3^3 \cdot 5^4$ $3 \cdot 3 \cdot 3 = 3^3$
$5 \cdot 5 \cdot 5 \cdot 5 = 5^4$
$\underline{3 \cdot 3 \cdot 3} \bullet \underline{5 \cdot 5 \cdot 5 \cdot 5} = 3^3 \cdot 5^4$

YOUR TURN

Evaluate:

1 2^4

2 3^2

3 2^3

4 7^2

Expand the following:

5 4^3

6 3^4

7 5^2

8 9^6

9 Which of the following expressions has a value of 64?

A 2^{32}

B 3^4

C 4^3

D 32^2

10 Evaluate 3^{-2}:

F -9

G -6

H $\frac{1}{9}$

J $\frac{1}{6}$

11 Evaluate 1^{12}:

A 0

B 1

C 2

D 12

12 Which is equivalent to $2^3 + 2^3$?

F 2^4

G 2^5

H 2^6

J 2^9

13 Which choice shows the numbers in increasing order of value?

A $4^{-2}, 3^{-2}, 2^{-2}$

B $3^{-2}, 4^{-2}, 2^{-2}$

C $2^{-2}, 3^{-2}, 4^{-2}$

D $4^{-2}, 2^{-2}, 3^{-2}$

14 Which choice shows the numbers in decreasing order of value?

F $4^0, 4^2, 4^{-3}$

G $4^2, 4^0, 4^{-3}$

H $4^{-3}, 4^0, 4^2$

J $4^{-3}, 4^2, 4^0$

15 Which of the following represents the prime factorization of 72?

A $2^3 \cdot 3^2$

B $2^3 \cdot 3^3$

C $2^2 \cdot 3^3$

D $2^2 \cdot 3^2$

16 Evaluate $7^{-2} \cdot 7^2$:

   F   0

   G   1

   H   49

   J 7^{-4}

17 Find the value of n for which $n^3 = 27$.

   A   3

   B   6

   C   9

   D   12

18 If $2^n = 8$ and $3^m = 9$ what is the value of $n + m$?

   F   2

   G   3

   H   4

   J   5

2.8 SCIENTIFIC NOTATION

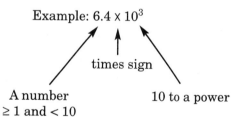

DEFINITION

A method of expressing very big or very small numbers

Standard Scientific Notation has 3 parts:

Example: 6.4×10^3

times sign

A number
≥ 1 and < 10

10 to a power

READING A NUMBER WITH A TIMES TEN TO A POWER

$a \times 10^n$	
Multiplying a number by 10 to a power moves the decimal point of the number a quantity of decimal places equal to the absolute value of the power.	
If the exponent on the 10 is:	Decimal point moves:
+	Right (→)
–	Left (←)

	Steps	Example 1	Example 2
Step 1	Move the decimal point of the given number to create a new number from 1 to 10. This yields the beginning portion of Scientific Notations.	Express 7839 in Scientific Notation: 7839 ⇓ 7.839	Express .04391 in Scientific Notation: .04391 ⇓ 4.391
Step 2	Count the number of decimal places moved.	Decimal point moved ③ places 7.839.	Decimal point moved ② places .04.391
Step 3	If the original number is greater than 10, use the answer in Step 2 as a positive power of 10. If the original number is less than 1, use the answer in Step 2 as a negative power of 10.	7839 is greater than 10 Use + 3	.04391 is less than 1 Use – 2
Step 4	Combine Steps 1 and 3 in the proper format.	7.839×10^3	4.391×10^{-2}

OUR TURN

Q: Evaluate.

1 3.14×10^{-2}

2 37×10^4

Express in Scientific Notation.

3 74200

4 .000342

A:

1 .3014   The – 2 power on the 10 means move the decimal point 2 places to the left. .03.14

2 370000   The 4 power on the 10 means move the decimal point 4 places to the right. 37.0000. ⇒ 370000

3 7.42×10^4

Step 1: Moving the decimal point to create a number ≥ 1 and < 10. 74200 ⇒ 7.42

Step 2: The decimal point was moved 4 places.

Step 3: The original number 74200 is greater than ten, therefore the power of the 10 will be +4.

Step 4: 7.42×10^4

4 3.42×10^{-4}

Step 1: .000342 ⇒ 3.42

Step 2: Decimal point moved 4 places.

Step 3: The original number is less than one, therefore use – 4 as the power of the 10.

Step 4: 3.42×10^{-4}

YOUR TURN

Evaluate:

1 7.32×10^4

2 6.42×10^{-2}

3 $.042 \times 10^3$

4 4200×10^2

5 $.006 \times 10^1$

Change to Scientific Notation:

6 4300

7 430

8 43

9 4.3

10 .43

11 .043

12 .0043

13 Which of the following is equal to 34.2×10^3?

A $.342 \times 10^4$

B 3.42×10^5

C 342×10^2

D 3420×10^2

14 The diameter of the Sun is about 333,000 kilometers. Express 333,000 in Scientific Notation.

F $.333 \times 10^4$

G 3.33×10^4

H 3.33×10^5

J 33.3×10^4

15 The half-life of Potassium 40 is 1.3×10^9 years. This is the same as:

A 130,000,000 years

B 1,300,000,000 years

C 13,000,000,000 years

D 130,000,000,000 years

2.9 PERFECT SQUARES AND SQUARE ROOTS

DEFINITIONS

A perfect square is the square of an integer.

The square root of a number (the symbol $\sqrt{}$) answers the question "what number squared is equal to my inside number?"

PRINCIPAL AND NEGATIVE SQUARE ROOTS

$3^2 = 9$ and $(-3)^2 = 9$ both 3 and -3 are square roots of 9		
Symbol	Description	Example
$\sqrt{}$	The principal square root or The positive square root	$\sqrt{36} = 6$
$-\sqrt{}$	The negative square root	$-\sqrt{36} = -6$

❽ Square: 13^2 is read as 13 squared or the square of 13.

❽ Square Root: $\sqrt{11}$ is read as the square root of 11.

❽ Squares/Square Roots: If $x^2 = y$, then y is the square of x and x is the square root of y.

OUR TURN

Q:

1 Evaluate $\sqrt{25}$

2 Evaluate $\sqrt{121}$

3 The $\sqrt{28}$ is between what two consecutive integers

4 What value(s) of n make the equation $n^2 + 1 = 17$ true?

A:

1   5 $\sqrt{25}$ represents the principal square root of 25, which is 5.

2   11 $\sqrt{121}$ represents the principal square root of 121, which is 11

3   5 and 6 $\sqrt{28}$ is between the $\sqrt{25}$ and $\sqrt{36}$ the $\sqrt{25} = 5$, $\sqrt{36} = 6$.

           We chose $\sqrt{25}$ and $\sqrt{36}$ because they are the closest square roots which gives an integer value, one above and one below the $\sqrt{28}$

4   4 and – 4   Use trial and error, or

           Solve by algebra: $n^2 + 1 = 17$

$$n^2 = 16$$

$$n = \pm\sqrt{16}$$

$$n = \pm 4$$

YOUR TURN

Evaluate:

1   $\sqrt{100}$

2   $\sqrt{40,000}$

3   $\sqrt{81}$

4   $\sqrt{625}$

5   $\sqrt{\frac{1}{4}}$

Between what two consecutive integers are the following square roots?

6   $\sqrt{38}$

7   $\sqrt{1000}$

8   $\sqrt{8}$

9   $\sqrt{106}$

10 Which value of n makes the following equation true?

$$\sqrt{n} = 4$$

A   2

B   4

C   8

D   16

11 The square root of 87 is between which two consecutive integers?

F   6 and 7

G   7 and 8

H   8 and 9

J   9 and 10

12 $\sqrt{16} + \sqrt{9} = ?$

A $\sqrt{25}$

B $\sqrt{36}$

C $\sqrt{49}$

D $\sqrt{64}$

13 Evaluate $\sqrt{4} + \sqrt{9} + \sqrt{16}$:

   F $\sqrt{20}$

   G $\sqrt{29}$

   H $\sqrt{42}$

   J $\sqrt{81}$

14 Which of the following is between 6 and 8?

   A $\sqrt{15}$

   B $\sqrt{36}$

   C $\sqrt{56}$

   D $\sqrt{65}$

15 Which square root is between 7 and 8?

   F $\sqrt{48}$

   G $\sqrt{58}$

   H $\sqrt{68}$

   J $\sqrt{78}$

2.10 FRACTIONS, DECIMALS, PERCENTS

CONVERSIONS

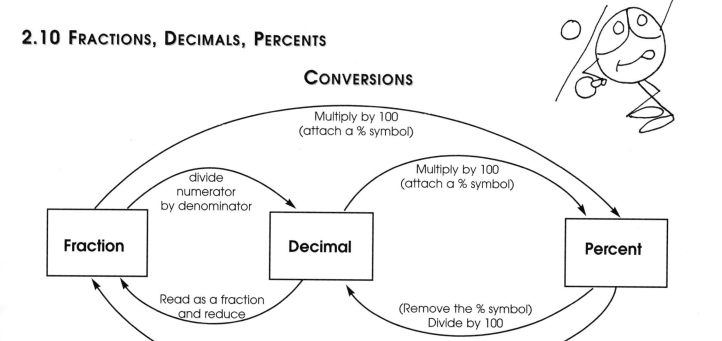

From	To	Procedure
Fraction Fraction	Decimal Percent	Divide (long division). Multiply by 100 (attach a "%" symbol).
Decimal Decimal	Fraction Percent	Read as a fraction and reduce. Multiply by 100 (attach a "%" symbol).
Percent Percent	Fraction Decimal	Remove "%" symbol. Divide by 100 in fraction form. Remove "%" symbol. Divide by 100 (shift decimal point two places to the left).

OUR TURN

Q:

1 Change $\frac{3}{5}$ into a decimal and a percent

2 Change .7 into a fraction and a percent.

3 Change 30% into a fraction and a decimal.

A:

1 .6, 60%

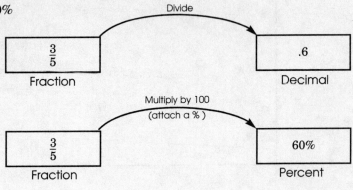

$\frac{3}{5} \Rightarrow 3 \div 5 \Rightarrow 5\overline{)3.0}^{.6} \Rightarrow .6$

$\frac{3}{5} \times 100 = \frac{300}{5} = 60 \Rightarrow 60\%$

2 $\frac{7}{10}$, .7

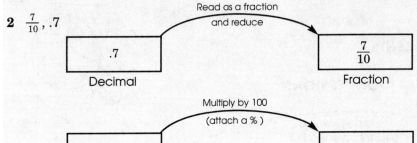

.7 is $\frac{7}{10}$

.7 x 100 = 70 $\Rightarrow$ 70%

3 $\frac{3}{10}$, .3

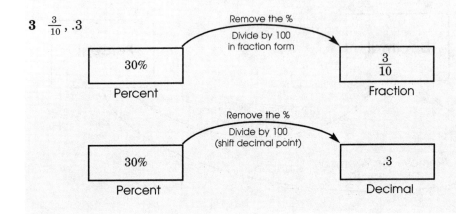

30% $\Rightarrow$ 30 $\Rightarrow \frac{30}{100} \Rightarrow \frac{3}{10}$

30% $\Rightarrow$ 30. $\Rightarrow$ .30. $\Rightarrow$ .3

YOUR TURN

Convert to a percent:

1 $\frac{3}{4}$

2 $\frac{5}{8}$

3 $1\frac{1}{2}$

4 .78

5 .042

6 $\frac{1}{1000}$

7 20

Convert to a fraction:

8 6%

9 .42

10 .402

11 74%

12 300%

13 100%

14 40%

Convert to a decimal:

15 35%

16 $\frac{4}{5}$

17 $\frac{7}{8}$

18 83%

19 4.2%

20 $\frac{1}{4}$

21 $\frac{4}{9}$

22 Five percent is equivalent to which of the following?

A $\frac{1}{20}$

B $\frac{1}{5}$

C .2

D .5

23 Which choice shows the values in decreasing order?

F 3, 200%, $\frac{100}{25}$

G 200%, $\frac{100}{25}$, 3

H 3, $\frac{100}{25}$, 200%

J $\frac{100}{25}$, 3, 200%

yes

2.11 REPEATING DECIMALS

HOW TO WRITE A NEVER-ENDING REPEATED DECIMAL

A never-ending decimal with a repeated pattern is expressed by placing a bar over the repeated pattern.

❽ Terminating - Terminating means ending, the opposite of never-ending.

A "PURE" REPEATING DECIMAL

A "pure" never-ending, repeated decimal has no digits other than those that repeat.

Our Turn

Q:

1 Write .333... using bar notation

2 Write .712434343... using bar notation

3 Write .427427427... using bar notation

4 Is .333... a "pure" repeating decimal?

5 Is .$\overline{21}$ a "pure" repeating decimal?

6 Is .2373737... a "pure" repeating decimal?

A:

1 .333... ⇒ .33$\overline{3}$ or .3$\overline{3}$ or .$\overline{3}$

2 .712434343 ⇒ .712$\overline{43}$

3 .427427427... ⇒ .427$\overline{427}$ or .$\overline{427}$

4 Yes
.333 ⇒ .$\overline{3}$
It is "pure" because it consists only of the repeated digit "3"

5 Yes

.$\overline{21}$
It is "pure" because it consists only of the repeated digits "21"

6 No
.2373737 ⇒ .2$\overline{37}$
It is **not** "pure" because the "2" is not part of the repeated pattern

---

Your Turn

Write each of the following as a never-ending repeating decimal using the bar notation.

1 .7777...

2 .7434343...

3 .606060...

4 .144144...

5 .12345555...

Display a representation of each decimal without the use of the bar.

6 .$\overline{6}$

7 .71$\overline{3}$

8 .7$\overline{13}$

9 .$\overline{713}$

10 .6$\overline{6}$

Indicate if the repeating decimal is "pure" or not.

11 .46$\overline{28}$

12 .4$\overline{628}$

13 .$\overline{4628}$

14 .1111$\overline{1}$

15 .$\overline{3}$

Identify the decimal as terminating or repeating.

16 .348

17 .4271354260

18 .$\overline{7}$

19 .70

20 .101010101010...

2.12 CONVERTING A "PURE" NEVER-ENDING DECIMAL INTO A FRACTION

PROCEDURE TO CONVERT A "PURE" NEVER-ENDING DECIMAL INTO A FRACTION

Step	Description	Examples	
		$.12\overline{12}$	$.437\overline{437}$
1	Write the repeated pattern once.	12	437
2	Count the digits in the pattern.	2 digits	3 digits
3	Step 2 digit count: Use: 1 → 9 2 → 99 3 → 999 4 → 9999 5 → 99999	Use 99	Use 999
4	Divide Step 1 by the 9 or 99 or 999 or 9999 from Step 3. Write the division as a fraction and simplify.	$\dfrac{12}{99} = \dfrac{4}{33}$	$\dfrac{437}{999}$

OUR TURN

Q: What fraction is equivalent to $.77\overline{7}$?

A: $\frac{7}{9}$

$.77\overline{7} \Rightarrow .\overline{7}$ ....This a "pure" never-ending decimal.

Step 1: 7 ....The repeated pattern is just the number 7.

Step 2: 1 digit ....The pattern consists of one repeated digit.

Step 3: 1 digit $\Rightarrow$ 9 ....The chart in Step 3 indicates that a 1 digit repeat uses a 9.

Step 4: $\frac{7}{9}$ ....The 7 from Step 1, divided in fraction formed by the 9 from step 3.

YOUR TURN

What never ending repeated decimal is each of these fractions (they may or may not necessarily be "pure")?

1 $\frac{1}{6}$

2 $\frac{4}{9}$

3 $\frac{7}{18}$

4 $\frac{1}{7}$

5 $\frac{5}{6}$

What fraction is each of these "pure" never ending repeated decimals?

6 $.88\overline{8}$

7 $.8282\overline{82}$

8 $.\overline{72}$

9 $.1111111...$

10 $.\overline{463}$

2.13 COMPARE TWO FRACTIONS...QUICKLY

HOW TO COMPARE TWO FRACTIONS QUICKLY

$$\frac{a \times d}{\frac{a}{b}} \qquad \frac{b \times c}{\frac{c}{d}}$$

Given two fractions $\frac{a}{b}$ and $\frac{c}{d}$

- Cross multiply the 1ˢᵗ and 4ᵗʰ number as shown and write the product above the first fraction.
- Cross multiply the 2ⁿᵈ and 3ʳᵈ number as shown and write the product above the second fraction.
- Whichever product is larger is above the greater fraction.

OUR TURN

Q: Which is greater $\frac{2}{5}$ or $\frac{3}{8}$?

A: $\frac{2}{5}$

$\frac{2}{5}$ or $\frac{3}{8}$

Cross multiply the 2 and the 8 and place the product (which is 16) above the first fraction and circle it.

Cross multiply the 5 and the 3 and place the product (which is 15) above the second fraction and circle it.

16 is greater than 15 therefore $\frac{2}{5}$ is greater than $\frac{3}{8}$

Your Turn

For each pair of fractions, indicate which is greater.

1   $\frac{2}{5}$, $\frac{4}{7}$

2   $\frac{5}{7}$, $\frac{2}{3}$

3   $\frac{3}{10}$, $\frac{1}{4}$

4   $\frac{5}{6}$, $\frac{3}{4}$

5   $\frac{2}{7}$, $\frac{4}{14}$

6   $\frac{1}{2}$, $\frac{4}{7}$

7   $\frac{2}{9}$, $\frac{3}{5}$

For each pair of fractions, indicate which is smaller.

8   $\frac{2}{5}$, $\frac{4}{9}$

9   $\frac{5}{11}$, $\frac{2}{3}$

10   $\frac{2}{13}$, $\frac{1}{6}$

11   $\frac{2}{5}$, $\frac{2}{7}$

12   $\frac{3}{8}$, $\frac{2}{5}$

13   $\frac{3}{8}$, $\frac{5}{13}$

14   $\frac{7}{3}$, $\frac{3}{1}$

15   Which choice shows the three fractions in ascending order?

A $\frac{2}{3}$, $\frac{1}{5}$, $\frac{3}{8}$

B $\frac{1}{5}$, $\frac{3}{8}$, $\frac{2}{3}$

C $\frac{1}{5}$, $\frac{2}{3}$, $\frac{3}{8}$

D $\frac{3}{8}$, $\frac{1}{5}$, $\frac{2}{3}$

16   Which of the following fractions is the greatest?

F $\frac{3}{5}$

G $\frac{2}{9}$

H $\frac{5}{8}$

J $\frac{2}{3}$

2.14 LONG ANSWER QUESTIONS FOR CHAPTER 2

1 The variables a, b and c each represent positive integers.
Use the following data to help answer the questions.

$$a + a + a = b$$
$$b + b + b = c$$

PART A

If c is a positive odd integer, is "a" always odd, always even, or sometimes even and sometimes odd?

Answer _____

Explain how you arrived at your answer.

_____

_____

_____

_____

_____

_____

PART B

If c is an even positive integer, is "a" always odd, always even, or sometimes odd and sometimes even?

Answer _____

Explain how you arrived at your answer.

_____

_____

_____

_____

_____

_____

2 Given the following six numbers

$$6, \quad \sqrt{100}, \quad 1\tfrac{3}{4}, \quad \sqrt{8}, \quad 14.67\overline{67}, \quad 1.5329$$

PART A

Which of the above numbers are integers? List all that apply.

Answer _____

Explain how you arrived at your answer.

_____

_____

_____

_____

_____

_____

PART B

Which of the above numbers are irrational? (List all that apply.)

Answer _____

3 Given: $5a = a^2$

Dawn argues a must equal 5.

Josh disagrees; he claims there is more than one value of a.

PART A

Who is right, Dawn or Josh?

Answer _____

Explain how you arrived at your decision as to who was right.

_____

_____

_____

_____

_____

_____

4 Let $\triangle{x}$ be defined as the greatest prime factor of x.

For example, $\triangle{6}$ = 3 because the factors of 6 are 1, 2, 3 and 6 and 3 is the largest prime factor of 6.

PART A

What is the value of $\triangle{64}$?

Show all your work.

Answer _____

PART B

Which is greater : $\triangle{7}$ or $\triangle{27}$?

Answer _____

Explain how you arrived at your answer and/or show supporting calculations.

_____

_____

_____

_____

CHAPTER THREE

OPERATIONS

3

This chapter discusses the basic rules of operations and the laws of exponents.

Sports are all played using rules. Can you imagine playing baseball, where some teams use the rule: 3 Strikes and you're Out; others use: 2 Strikes and you're Out; and still others use 4 Strikes? How could you play the game? Well, math also works on universal rules.

Operations are the manipulation of numbers according to defined rules. If you write a calculation, everyone should understand what that calculation means. Therefore, everyone will get the same answer. For example:

Order to use when calculating:

(Step 1) Work with any numbers within **parentheses** first.

(Step 2) If present, calculate any **exponents***
(Step 3) Then, **multiply** (ex. 1) or **divide** (ex. 2)
(Step 4) Finally, **add** (ex. 1) or **subtract** (ex. 2)

	Example 1	Example 2
Step 1	$6^2 + 2 \times (6 - 1)$	$(4 + 2)^2 \div 4 - 1$
Step 2	$6^2 + 2 \times 5$	$6^2 \div 4 - 1$
Step 3	$36 + 2 \times 5$	$36 \div 4 - 1$
Step 4	$36 + 10$	$9 - 1$
	answer = 46	answer = 8

*Exponents are the repeated multiplication of a number by itself.
It is a useful shorthand. Numbers like 6^2 can be used to express this.

3.1 BASICS

ORDER OF OPERATIONS

Abbreviation	Terminology	Notes
P	Parenthesis	work within the grouping symbols first
E	Exponents	sometimes called powers
M D	Multiplication Division	in order from left to right
A S	Addition Subtraction	in order from left to right

NAMES OF CALCULATION RESULTS

Calculation Type	Name of Result
Addition	Sum
Subtraction	Difference
Multiplication	Product
Division	Quotient

❽ PEMDAS – The mnemonic "<u>P</u>lease <u>E</u>xcuse <u>M</u>y <u>D</u>ear <u>A</u>unt <u>S</u>ally" helps to remember the order of operations

OUR TURN

Q:

1 What is the positive difference between 8 and 2?

2 In the calculation $3 + 2 \times 4 \div 2 - 1$, which operation should be done first?

3 What is the value of $2 + 3 \times 4 + 1$?

4 Evaluate $3a + b^2$ when $a = 4$ and $b = 5$

A:

1 6
Difference means subtraction.
$8 - 2 = 6$

2 x (multiplication)
Multiplication and Division come before Addition or Subtraction. Multiplication and Division are done left to right.

3 15

$2 + \underline{3 \times 4} + 1$

$2 + 12 + 1 = 15$

4 37

$3a + b^2 \Rightarrow 3(4) + (5)^2 =$
$12 + 25 = 37$

YOUR TURN

In each of the following sets, which calculation would be done first?

1 $4 \div 2 + 1$

2 $3 \div (4 + 1)$

3 $3^2 + 4$

4 $6 + 4 \div 2 \times 1 - 3$

5 $3 + 4 + 7 - 1$

Find the value of each of the following.

6 $6 \div 3 \times 4 - 1$

7 $4 + 3 \times 7$

8 $(3 + 5) \times 2 + 3$

9 $(1 + 4) \times (6 + 2)$

10 $(2 + 5) - (6 \times 1)$

11 $4 \div (3 - 1) + (2 \times 3)$

12 $(3 + 1)^2 - 4 \times 2$

13 $3^2 + 4^2$

14 $(3 + 4)^2$

15 $(7 - 3)^2 \div (1 + 3)$

Evaluate each of the following.

16 $2a + b$ when $a = 3$ and $b = 4$

17 $2a^2 - b$ when $a = 3$ and $b = 2$

18 $3a^2 + 4b$ when $a = 2$ and $b = 3$

19 $2a^2 - 3b^2$ when $a = 5$ and $b = 2$

20 $(a - b)^2 + a$ when $a = 4$ and $b = 1$

21 $6 + (2 \times 3) - 4 = ?$

   A 7

   B 8

   C 12

   D 20

22 $8^2 - (4 + 1)^2 = ?$

   F 6

   G 17

   H 37

   J 39

23 $(1 + 2)^2 - (5 - 4)^2 = ?$

   A 4

   B 8

   C 24

   D 36

24 $2 \times 3^2 + 1 = ?$

   F 19

   G 32

   H 37

   J 49

25 $(1 + 2 + 3)^2 + 4 = ?$

   A 16

   B 18

   C 40

   D 100

26 Which one of the following is equal to 10?

   F $(4 + 3) - (1 \times 2)$

   G $4 + (3 - 1) \times 2$

   H $(4 \times 3) - (1 \times 2)$

   J $(4 + 3 - 1) \times 2$

27 Which one of the following is equal to 14?

   A $(1 + 2 + 3)^2$

   B $(1 + 2)^2 + 3$

   C $1^2 + (2 + 3)^2$

   D $1^2 + 2^2 + 3^2$

28 Which one of the following is equal to 50?

   F $1 + (3 + 4)^2$

   G $1^2 + 3^2 + 4^2$

   H $(1 + 3)^2 + 4$

   J $(1 + 3 + 4)^2$

3.2 IMPLIED PARENTHESES (GROUPING SYMBOLS)

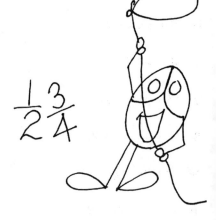

GROUPING SYMBOLS WITH INVISIBLE (IMPLIED) PARENTHESES

Symbol Name	Example	Implied Parentheses	Description
Fraction	$\dfrac{6+2}{7+1}$	$\dfrac{(6+2)}{(7+1)}$	Numerator - one group Denominator - second group
Square Root	$\sqrt{7+1}$	$\sqrt{(7+1)}$	Everything under the $\sqrt{\ }$ is one group
Absolute Value	$\|6+3\|$	$\|(6+3)\|$	Everything inside the absolute value symbol is grouped

OUR TURN

Q:

1 What is the value of $\dfrac{4+8}{1+2}$?

2 In this example, which operation do you perform first ?

$$\dfrac{5+3}{2 \times 2}$$

A:

1 4

$$\dfrac{4+8}{1+2} \Rightarrow \dfrac{(4+8)}{(1+2)} = \dfrac{12}{3} = 4$$

2 Adding

$$\dfrac{5+3}{2 \times 2} = \dfrac{(5+3)}{(2 \times 2)} = \dfrac{8}{4} = 2$$

YOUR TURN

Evaluate:

1 $\dfrac{6+2}{8 \div 2}$

2 $\dfrac{3+5}{3+1}$

3 $\dfrac{7-2}{2+3}$

4 $\dfrac{6+3 \times 2}{2+1}$

5 $\dfrac{3-(1+1)}{5-2}$

6 $\dfrac{2+2 \times 2}{2 \times 2 + 2}$

7 $\dfrac{12 \div 3 + 1}{(12 \div 3) + 1}$

8 $\dfrac{12 \div 3 + 1}{12 \div (3+1)}$

9 $\dfrac{8-1}{6+1}$

10 $\dfrac{3^2 - 1}{2^2}$

11 $\dfrac{6 + 3 \times (3^2 - 1)}{1^2 + 2^2} = ?$

A 6

B 7

C 8

D 9

12 $\dfrac{2 + 1}{4 - 1} + \dfrac{3 + 2}{6 - 1} = ?$

F 2

G 4

H 6

J 8

13 $\dfrac{6 + 4 + 2}{3 + 2 + 1} = ?$

A 1

B 2

C 6

D 10

14 $\dfrac{(1 + 2)^2 + 3}{1^2 + 2^2 + 3} = ?$

F $\frac{1}{2}$

G 1

H $\frac{3}{2}$

J 2

15 $\dfrac{6 \div (2^2 - 1)}{5 + 1} = ?$

A $\frac{1}{12}$

B $\frac{1}{6}$

C $\frac{1}{3}$

D 2

16 Which of the following is equal to 18?

F $|10 - 3 \times 2| + 4$

G $|10 - 3| \times 2 + 4$

H $|10 - 3| \times (2 + 4)$

J $|10 - 3 \times 2 + 4|$

17 $6 \times \sqrt{6 - 2} = ?$

A 4

B 12

C 24

D 34

18 $\sqrt{\dfrac{20}{5}} + 3 = ?$

F 5

G 7

H 9

J 13

19 Which of the following is equal to 2?

A $\dfrac{4 + 2 \times 3}{3^2 - 2^2}$

B $\dfrac{(4 + 2) \times 3}{3^2 - 2^2}$

C $\dfrac{4 + 2 \times 3}{(3 - 2)^2}$

D $\dfrac{4 + (2 \times 3)}{(3 - 2)^2}$

20 Which of the following is equal to 2?

F $\dfrac{1^2 + 2^2 + 3^2}{1 \times 2 + 3}$

G $\dfrac{(1 + 2^2) + 3^2}{1 \times 2 \times 3}$

H $\dfrac{1 + (2 \times 3)^2}{1 + 2 + 3}$

J $\dfrac{(1 + 2)^2 + 3}{1 + 2 + 3}$

21 Which of the following is equal to 10?

A $\dfrac{(6 + 8) \div (2 \times 2)}{5 - 2 - 1}$

B $\dfrac{6 + (8 \div 2) \times 2}{5 - (2 - 1)}$

C $\dfrac{(6 + 8 \div 2) \times 2}{(5 - 2) - 1}$

D $\dfrac{6 + (8 \div 2 \times 2)}{(5 - 2) - 1}$

22 $\dfrac{\sqrt{12 + 4} - 2}{\sqrt{12 + 4} - 7} = ?$

F $\frac{1}{4}$

G $\frac{1}{3}$

H $-\frac{2}{3}$

J $\frac{3}{4}$

23 $|5 - 1| \times 3 = ?$

A 2

B 9

C 12

D 15

Evaluate:

24 $\dfrac{2a - b^2}{a - b}$ when $a = 9$ and $b = 2$

25 $\dfrac{a + (b^2 - a)}{2 \times (a^2 - b)}$ when $a = 4$ and $b = 3$

3.3 PROPERTIES/LAWS

TABLE OF PROPERTIES/LAWS

Property	Sample	Explanation
Additive Identity	$a + 0 = a$ $2 + 0 = 2$	Adding a zero to a number maintains its value.
Multiplicative Identity	$a \cdot 1 = a$ $2 \cdot 1 = 2$	Multiplying by one maintains its value.
Associative Property of Addition	$(a + b) + c = a + (b + c)$ $(2 + 3) + 4 = 2 + (3 + 4)$	Regrouped addition maintains its sum.
Associative Property of Multiplication	$(a \cdot b) \cdot c = a \cdot (b \cdot c)$ $(2 \cdot 3) \cdot 4 = 2 \cdot (3 \cdot 4)$	Regrouped multiplication maintains its product.
Commutative Property of Addition	$a + b = b + a$ $2 + 3 = 3 + 2$	Adding can be done in any order.
Commutative Property of Multiplication	$a \cdot b = b \cdot a$ $2 \cdot 3 = 3 \cdot 2$	Multiplying can be done in any order.
Zero Product	$a \cdot 0 = 0$ $2 \cdot 0 = 0$	Multiplying by zero yields a zero product.
Distributive Property of Multiplication over Addition	$a(b + c) = a \cdot b + a \cdot c$ $2(3 + 4) = 2 \cdot 3 + 2 \cdot 4$	Multiplication can be distributed (given out) to each part of the addition.

Our Turn

Q:

1 The following is an example of which property?

$6 \cdot (4 + 3) = 6 \cdot 4 + 6 \cdot 3$

A:

1 Distributive Property of Multiplication over Addition

$6 \cdot (4 + 3) = 6 \cdot (4) + 6 \cdot (3)$

Your Turn

Identify the illustrated property.

1 $7 \cdot 1 = 7$

2 $7 + 0 = 7$

3 $7 \cdot 0 = 0$

4 $7 \cdot (3 + 4) = 7 \cdot (3) + 7 \cdot (4)$

5 $8 + (4 \cdot 3) = 8 + (3 \cdot 4)$

6 $(6 + 2) \cdot (8) = 8 \cdot (6 + 2)$

7 $(6 + 3) + 5 = (3 + 6) + 5$

8 $7 \cdot (2) + 7 \cdot (6) = 7 \cdot (2 + 6)$

9 $6 (2) + 5 (3) = 5 (3) + 6 (2)$

10 $6 (2) + 5 (3) = 6 (2) + 3 (5)$

11 $15 (17)$ is equivalent to which of the following?

A $5 (17) + 10 (17)$

B $5 (14) + 10 (3)$

C $3 (17) \cdot 5 (17)$

D $3 (10) + 12 (7)$

12 Which one of the following illustrates an associative rule?

F $8 + 0 = 8$

G $8 + (6 + 4) = (8 + 6) + 4$

H $8 \cdot (6 + 1) = 8 \cdot (6) + 8 \cdot (1)$

J $8 \cdot (4 \cdot 3) = 8 \cdot (3 \cdot 4)$

13 Which correctly illustrates the Commutative Property of Multiplication?

A $2 + 3 = 3 + 2$

B $2 \cdot (4 + 7) = 2 \cdot 4 + 2 \cdot 7$

C $2 \cdot (3 + 5) = (3 + 5) \cdot (2)$

D $2 (3) + 7 (3) = (2 + 7) (3)$

Rules of Exponents

Pictorial (rules)	Explanation	Example
$x^0 = 1$	Any number to the zero power is 1.	$7^0 = 1$
$x^1 = x$	Any number to the one power is itself.	$7^1 = 7$
$x^a \cdot x^b = x^{a+b}$	To multiply: If the bases are the same, keep the base and add the exponents.	$7^3 \cdot 7^9 = 7^{3+9} = 7^{12}$
$\dfrac{x^a}{x^b} = x^{a-b}$	To divide: If the bases are the same, keep the base and subtract the exponents.	$\dfrac{7^{12}}{7^6} = 7^{12-6} = 7^6$
$(x^a)^b = x^{ab}$	To power a power: Keep the bases and multiply the exponents.	$(7^2)^5 = 7^{2 \cdot 5} = 7^{10}$
$(x \cdot y)^a = x^a \cdot y^a$	A product to a power: Distribute the power.	$(7 \cdot 3)^4 = 7^4 \cdot 3^4$
$x^{-a} = \dfrac{1}{x^a}$	A base to a negative power: It is the reciprocal of the base to the positive exponent.	$7^{-2} = \dfrac{1}{7^2} = \dfrac{1}{49}$

❽ + or − : $x^a + x^b$ and $x^a - x^b$ do not have exponential rules. Just work them out.

❽ The letter x: As a rule, using the same letter means that they must have the same value.

Our Turn

Q: Perform the indicated operation and express the result in exponential form if possible.

1 $3^7 \cdot 3^2$

2 $\dfrac{4^8}{4^2}$

3 $3^{-2} \cdot 3^3$

4 $6^2 \cdot 7^1$

A:

1 3^9
$$x^a \cdot x^b = x^{a+b}$$
$$3^7 \cdot 3^2 = 3^{7+2} = 3^9$$

2 4^6
$$\dfrac{x^a}{x^b} = x^{a-b}$$

$$\dfrac{4^8}{4^2} = 4^{8-2} = 4^6$$

3 3^1 or 3
$$3^{-2} \cdot 3^3 = 3^{-2+3} = 3^1 = 3$$

4 No exponential solution.
However, the product is 252.

$x^a \cdot x^b$ requires the x values to be the same

$6^2 \cdot 7^1$: the base 6 and the base 7 are not the same; therefore, the exponential rule does not apply.

Without exponents $6^2 = 36, \; 7^1 = 7$
$\qquad\qquad\qquad\; 6^2 \cdot 7^1 = 36 \cdot (7) = 252$

YOUR TURN

Perform the indicated operation and express the result in exponential form if possible.

1 $3^8 \cdot 3^2$

2 $\dfrac{4^9}{4^3}$

3 $(7 \cdot 3)^2$

4 $4^3 - 4^2$

5 $(6^2)^3$

6 $(7^{-1})^3$

7 $(3 \cdot 2)^{(1+2)}$

8 $6^2 \cdot 6^8$

9 $5^{11} \cdot 5^2 \cdot 5^4$

10 $(5^3 \cdot 5^2)^3$

11 $\dfrac{16^{16}}{16^2} = ?$

   A 16^{14}

   B 16^8

   C 16^4

   D 16^2

12 $3^3 \cdot 3^7 = ?$

   F 3^{10}

   G 3^{21}

   H 9^{10}

   J 9^{21}

13 $3^7 \cdot 2^7 = ?$

   A 5^7

   B 6^7

   C 5^{14}

   D 6^{14}

14 $7^{-2} = ?$

   F -14

   G -7^2

   H $-\frac{1}{14}$

   J $\frac{1}{49}$

15 Which one of the following equalities is true?

   A $2^4 = 4^2$

   B $3^4 = 4^3$

   C $6^3 = 3^6$

   D $16^1 = 1^{16}$

16 Which one of the following is equivalent to $(1 + 2 + 3)^2$?

   F $1^2 + 2^2 + 3^2$

   G $(1 + 2)^2 + 3^2$

   H $1^2 + (2 + 3)^2$

   J 6^2

17 Which one of the following is equivalent to $4 \cdot 8^{-1}$?

   A -32

   B -12

   C 12^{-1}

   D $\frac{1}{2}$

18 $2^0 + 3^0 + 4^0 + 5^0 = ?$

   F 0

   G 1

   H 4

   J 14

19 Which one of the following is equivalent to 28^2?

   A 14^4

   B $14^2 + 2^2$

   C $14^2 \cdot 2^2$

   D 56

20 For what value of n does $7^n = 8^n$?

   F   0

   G   1

   H   10

   J   no value

21 Evaluate $x^0 + 4$, when $x = 7$

22 $3^0 \cdot 2^0 = ?$

23 $(3 \cdot 2)^0 = ?$

24 $-3^0 + (-3)^0 = ?$

25 Evaluate $3x^0 + (3x)^0$, when $x = 4$

3.5 Sets/Closure

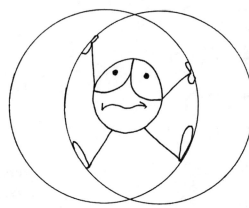

Sets/Closure

Symbol	Name	Definition	Sample
{item, item}	Set	A well defined collection	Set of even, positive integers from 1 to 10 inclusive $\{2, 4, 6, 8, 10\}$
{Element, element...}	Element	A member of a set	Given $\{1, 3, 5\}$ 1, 3, and 5 are each elements
	Venn Diagrams	A pictorial used to view sets and their overlap	A B 2, 6 / 4, 8 / 12, 16 Set $A = \{2, 4, 6, 8\}$ Set $B = \{4, 8, 12, 16\}$ the overlap is $\{4, 8\}$
Ø or { }	Null or Empty Set	A set with no elements	Set of odd numbers divisible by 2 or Ø
Closed	Closed Set	A set is closed if: when any elements of the set are used in an operation, the result is always part of the set.	Set of odd integers is **closed** under multiplication because: the multiplication of any 2 elements in the set yields a product which is always within the same set.

OUR TURN

Q:

1 Name 2 elements in the set of positive odd integers.

2 Give an example of an empty set.

3 Is the set of whole numbers closed under multiplication?

4 Is the set of whole numbers closed under subtraction?

A:

1 3 and 7 (Many other answers are possible)
Both numbers are in the set {1, 3, 5, 7, 9, 11...}.

2 The set of numbers which are both even and odd. No number is both even and odd.

3 Yes.
The multiplication of any 2 whole numbers is also a whole number, therefore the set is **closed** under multiplication.

4 No
The subtraction of 2 whole numbers does **not** always generate a whole number. For example: 2 – 6 = –4. Negative four is **not** a whole number.

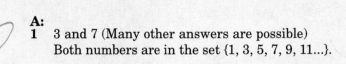

YOUR TURN

1 An element of the set of irrational numbers is:

A $\sqrt{0}$

B $\sqrt{1}$

C $\sqrt{2}$

D $\sqrt{4}$

2 The set of negative integers is closed under which one of the following operations?

F addition

G subtraction

H multiplication

J division

3 Which one of the following is a member of the set of odd integers?

A $\frac{3}{5}$

B $9 - 5$

C $\sqrt{19}$

D $\sqrt{25}$

4 Which of the following represents a member belonging to the set of never ending, repeating decimals?

F $\sqrt{2}$

G π

H 161661666...

J $\frac{2}{3}$

5 The integers and the fractions form which of the following sets?

A the counting numbers

B the whole numbers

C the rational numbers

D the irrational numbers

6 Which one of the following sets contains only whole numbers?

F {– 2, – 1, 0, 1, 2}

G {0, 1, 2, 3, 4}

H {1, 1$\frac{1}{2}$, 2, 2$\frac{1}{2}$}

J {.3, .4, .5, .6}

7 Multiplying any 2 elements in the set of odd integers gives which of the following sets?

A   integers

B   even integers

C   odd integers

D   positive integers

8 Which set represents the overlap of the set of perfect squares and the set of positive integers from 1 to 10 inclusive?

F   {1, 4, 9}

G   {2, 4, 6, 8, 10}

H   {1, 2, 3, 4}

J   {2, 4, 8}

9 How many elements belong to the set of prime numbers and the set of even integers?

A   none

B   one

C   two

D   three

10 The null set is also know as which one of the following?

F   closed set

G   empty set

H   integer set

J   irrational set

11 The set of odd integers is closed under which one of the following operations?

A   addition

B   subtraction

C   multiplication

D   division

12 The set of perfect squares is closed under which one of the following operations?

F   addition

G   subtraction

H   multiplication

J   division

3.6 LONG ANSWER QUESTIONS FOR CHAPTER 3

1 Given the following fraction:

$$\frac{6 + 2^2 - 3 \times 2}{10 - 4 \times 2}$$

PART A

What is the value of the above fraction?

Show all work or explain how you arrived at your answer.

Answer _____

PART B

The fraction is repeated here for you to use in Part B.

Insert one set of parentheses so the fraction below will now be equal to 4.

$$\frac{6 + 2^2 - 3 \times 2}{10 - 4 \times 2}$$

2 Dawn performed the following steps:

Given : $7(a + 0) + 3(b + 1)$

Step 1: $7(a) + 3(b + 1)$

Step 2: $7(a) + 3(1 + b)$

Step 3: $7(a) + 3(1) + 3(b)$

Step 4: $7(a) + 1(3) + 3(b)$

Step 5: $7(a) + 3 + 3(b)$

For each of the steps shown above, state which property/law of integers was used. Be as precise as possible. The first answer has been completed for you.

From Given to Step 1   <u>Additive Identity Property</u>

From Step 1 to Step 2   _____

From Step 2 to Step 3   _____

From Step 3 to Step 4   _____

From Step 4 to Step 5   _____

3   Given   Set A: {even integers}

          Set B: {prime numbers}

          Set C: {multiples of 7}

PART A

Give 2 examples of elements that are in Set A and Set C.

Answer : _____ and _____

PART B

What is the set of numbers that are in both Set A and in Set B?

Answer: _____

PART C

What is the set of numbers that are in both Set B and in Set C?

Answer: _____

Chapter Four
Ratios, Proportions, & Rates

4

Ratios/Proportions/Rates allow us to adjust size proportionally. How do we map a scaled drawing of a house or build a scale model of a train? How do we adjust a recipe for a different number of people? How do we represent a portion of a group? This chapter addresses these items.

Suppose Jodi's recipe for glazed carrots makes 8 servings. It calls for $\frac{3}{8}$ teaspoon of salt for each 32 ounces of baby carrots. How much salt is needed to make 12 servings? How many ounces of carrots are required?

A map of New York State is drawn to a scale of 1.5 cm = 10 miles. The map shows the distance between Johnstown and Saratoga to be approximately 5.5 cm. How many real miles are between the two cities?

This chapter deals with these issues.

4.1 TERMINOLOGY

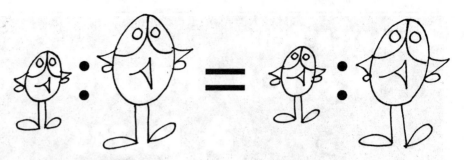

BASIC TERMINOLOGY

Terminology	Description	Sample
Ratio	a comparison of two quantities by division	$3 : 7$ the ratio of 3 to 7 3 is to 7 3 to 7 3 out of 7 $\quad\Big\}\ \dfrac{3}{7}$
Proportion	two ratios that are equal	$3 : 7 = x : 14$ 3 is to 7 as x is to 14 $\Big\}\ \dfrac{3}{7} = \dfrac{x}{14}$
Cross Multiplication	in a proportion, the cross-products are equal	$\dfrac{3}{7} = \dfrac{x}{14}$ $7 \cdot x = 3 \cdot 14$

DIRECT / INVERSE PROPORTIONS

Direct Proportion	two values whose quotient (ratio) remains constant	$\dfrac{x_1}{y_1} = \dfrac{x_2}{y_2}$ or $\dfrac{x}{y} = \text{constant}$
Inverse Proportion	two values whose product remains constant	$x_1 \cdot y_1 = x_2 \cdot y_2$ or $x \cdot y = \text{constant}$

OUR TURN

Q: Express the following ratios in fraction form.

1 5 is to 7

2 4 : 9

Express the following ratios using the same units.
Write your answer in fraction form.

3 1 second : 1 minute

4 4 ounce : 2 pounds

A:

1 $\dfrac{5}{7}$

2 $\dfrac{4}{9}$

3 $\dfrac{1}{60}$

$$\frac{1 \text{ second}}{1 \text{ minute}} = \frac{1 \text{ second}}{60 \text{ seconds}} = \frac{1}{60}$$

4 $\dfrac{1}{8}$

$$\frac{4 \text{ ounces}}{2 \text{ pounds}} = \frac{4 \text{ ounces}}{2 \cdot 16 \text{ ounces}} = \frac{4}{32} = \frac{1}{8}$$

Q: Express the following proportions in fraction form.

5 $3 : 7 = 2 : n$

6 3 is to 5 as 6 is to 10

7 If x varies directly as y and $x = 6$ when $y = 4$, how much is x when $y = 12$?

A:

5 $\frac{3}{7} = \frac{2}{n}$

6 $\frac{3}{5} = \frac{6}{10}$

7 18

$$\frac{x_1}{y_1} = \frac{x_2}{y_2} \Rightarrow \frac{6}{4} = \frac{x}{12}$$
$$4x = 72$$
$$x = 18$$

YOUR TURN

Express the following ratios in simplest fraction form.

1 3 to 12

2 6 boys to 4 girls

3 4 minutes to 12 minutes

4 2 gallons of lemonade to 7 people

5 $6 : 9$

6 The ratio of 2 to 5

7 The ratio of 5 to 2

8 6 out of 12

In a class of 30 students, there are 13 boys. Express the following ratios.

9 Boys to class

10 Boys to girls

11 Girls to class

Express the following ratios in simplest form. Adjust units for consistency.

12 $\frac{3 \text{ inches}}{1 \text{ feet}}$

13 $\frac{2 \text{ quarts}}{1 \text{ gallon}}$

14 $\frac{2 \text{ day}}{1 \text{ week}}$

15 $\frac{1 \text{ month}}{2 \text{ years}}$

16 $\frac{4 \text{ feet}}{1 \text{ yard}}$

17 $\frac{4 \text{ meters}}{1 \text{ kilometer}}$

18 $\frac{5 \text{ cents}}{1 \text{ dollar}}$

19 $\frac{1 \text{ quarter}}{1 \text{ dime}}$

Express the following proportions in fraction form.

20 $3 : 10 = a : b$

21 $x : 7 = 5 : 2$

22 3 is to 11 as x is to 3

23 3 out of 4 is the same as 8 out of n

4.2 SOLVING A PROPORTION

PROCEDURE TO SOLVE A PROPORTION

Step	Explanation	Example
Step 1	express as a proportion with fractions	Given: $3 : 8 = 6 : x$ or 3 is to 8 as 6 is to x $\Downarrow$ $\dfrac{3}{8} = \dfrac{6}{x}$
Step 2	cross multiply	$\dfrac{3}{8} = \dfrac{6}{x}$ $3x = 48$
Step 3	solve the equation for x	$\dfrac{3x}{3} = \dfrac{48}{3}$ $x = 16$

$3:7=X:14$

OUR TURN

Q: Solve the following proportion: $4 : 5 = 28 : x$

A:

$4 : 5 = 28 : x$	given
$\dfrac{4}{5} = \dfrac{28}{x}$	change to fraction form
$4x = 5(28)$	cross multiply
$4x = 140$	$5 \cdot (28) = 140$
$x = 35$	divide by 4

YOUR TURN

Solve the following proportions for n.

1 $\dfrac{3}{5} = \dfrac{9}{n}$

2 $\dfrac{6}{11} = \dfrac{24}{n}$

3 $\dfrac{n}{20} = \dfrac{6}{5}$

4 $\dfrac{6}{n} = \dfrac{4}{10}$

5 $\dfrac{15}{20} = \dfrac{n}{50}$

6 $n : 8 = 10 : 40$

7 6 is to 18 as n is to 12

8 $n : 2 = 5 : 8$

9 1 is to 60 as 6 is to n

10 $\dfrac{3}{7} = \dfrac{2}{n}$

11 If x varies directly as y, and y is 8 when x is 3, how much is x when $y = 18$?

12 If x varies directly as y, and $y = 4$ when $x = 9$, find y when $x = 27$.

13 For a given height, the base of a triangle and the area of a triangle vary directly. If the base is 6 when the area is 8, what is the base when the area is 12?

14 x varies directly as y. If y is doubled, then x _____.

  A is doubled

  B is increased by 2

  C remains the same

  D is halved

15 When rice is prepared, the amount of rice varies directly as the amount of water required. If 2 cups of rice requires 4.5 cups of water, what is the total number of cups of water needed to prepare 5 cups of rice?

4.3 RATES

RATE/UNIT RATE

Term	Definition	Sample
Rate	a ratio of two quantities with different units	$\dfrac{16 \text{ apples}}{3 \text{ dollars}}$ compares the number of apples to the amount of dollars
Unit Rate	a rate where the denominator is reduced to 1	$\dfrac{8 \text{ apples}}{2 \text{ dollars}} = \dfrac{4 \text{ apples}}{1 \text{ dollar}}$ unit rate is 4 apples per dollar

OUR TURN

Q:

1 A store carries 3 different sizes of grape juice, each for a different price. Using the table at the right, determine which is the best buy on cost.

Size	Cost
6 oz.	$1.20
11 oz.	$2.00
16 oz.	$3.25

It is estimated that for a particular recipe the following information at the right is available:

Using this data, answer the following questions:

2 To serve 18 people, how many cloves of garlic are necessary for the recipe?

3 If 1 cup of lemon juice is used, what is the corresponding quantity of beans necessary?

Item	Quantity
Serves	6 people
Pasta	1 pound
Olive Oil	1 tablespoon
Chickpeas	15 ounces
Garlic	4 cloves
Chicken Broth	2 cups
Tuna	6 ounces
Lemon Juice	$\frac{1}{4}$ cup
Beans	8 ounces

A:

1   The 11 oz. size is the best buy (value).
Compare the cost per ounce, to find the least expensive.

$$\frac{\text{cost}}{\text{ounce}} : \frac{1.20}{6} = .20 \Rightarrow 20 \text{ cents per ounce}$$

$$\frac{2.00}{11} = .18\overline{18} \Rightarrow \approx 18 \text{ cents per ounce}$$

$$\frac{3.25}{16} = .2031 \Rightarrow \approx 20 \text{ cents per ounce}$$

The 11 ounce size has the least cost per ounce and is the best buy.

2   12 cloves are necessary
6 people use 4 cloves as 18 people use x cloves.

$$\text{Make a proportion of } \frac{\text{people}}{\text{cloves}} : \frac{6}{4} = \frac{18}{x}$$

Cross Multiply $6x = 72$
Divide by 6 $x = 12$

3   32 ounces of beans are needed.
Make a proportion based on the recipe of lemon juice to beans.
$\frac{1}{4}$ cup of lemon juice goes with 8 oz. as 1 cup of lemon juice goes with n beans

$$\text{Make a proportion of } \frac{\text{cups of lemon juice}}{\text{ounces of beans}} : \frac{\frac{1}{4}}{8} = \frac{1}{n}$$

Cross Multiply $\frac{1}{4}n = 8$

Divide by $\frac{1}{4}$ $n = 32$

Your Turn

1   A metal pipe 3 ft. long weighs 2 pounds. At this rate, how much will a 12 ft. long pipe of the same material weigh?

2   A plane travels a distance of 2400 miles in 4 hours. At this rate, how many hours will it take the plane to travel 3000 miles?

3   A mushroom pizza requires 5 oz. of fresh mushrooms. At this rate, how many pizzas will 30 oz. of mushrooms cover?

4   Use the accompanying chart to determine which can of tuna is the better buy.

Size	Cost
6 oz.	$1.00
10 oz.	$1.60
24 oz.	$4.00

5   Four bars of soap cost $2.80. At this rate, what is the cost of 10 bars of soap?

6   Using one class of 30 students as a sample, it was found that 6 had cats as pets. Based on this data, how many students out of the 700 in the school would you expect to have a cat as a pet?

7 If 3 pages can be typed every 8 minutes, how long will it take to type 21 pages at this rate?

8 A car can travel 160 miles on 9 gallons of gasoline. At this rate, how many gallons are required for a trip of 560 miles?

9 Three teaspoons of sugar have 50 calories. At this rate, how many calories will 21 teaspoons of sugar have?

10 A stew recipe for 8 people used 3 pounds of potatoes and $1\frac{1}{2}$ pounds of carrots. At this rate, 6 pounds of carrots would be used in a recipe for how many people?

11 A 3-pound box of assorted hard candies contains 27 butterscotch flavored candies. At this rate, how many butterscotch candies would you expect in a 2-pound bag?

12 Three buses are required to take 105 students to the museum. At this rate, how many buses will be required for 420 students?

4.4 SIMILAR FIGURES

SIMILAR FIGURES

Term	Definition
Similar figures symbol: ~	Two figures with: same shapes, not necessarily the same size
Line ratio	The ratio of a polygon side to a corresponding side of a similar polygon
Properties of similar figures	• Corresponding angles are congruent • Corresponding sides are proportional and equal to the line ratio • Corresponding perimeters are proportional and equal to line ratio

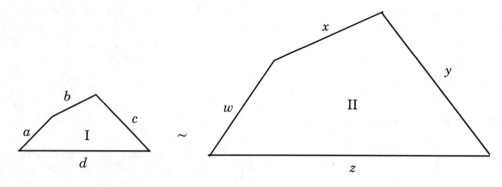

$$\text{Line Ratio} = \frac{a}{w} = \frac{b}{x} = \frac{c}{y} = \frac{d}{z} = \frac{\text{Perimeter Figure I}}{\text{Perimeter Figure II}}$$

$$\text{Area Ratio} = \frac{\text{Area Figure I}}{\text{Area Figure II}} = (\text{Line Ratio})^2$$

OUR TURN

Q:

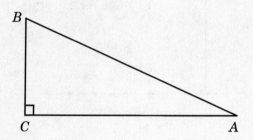

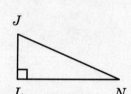

Triangle ABC is similar to triangle NJL and $m\angle B = m\angle J$. Based on this information, answer the following questions:

1 If $BC = 10$ and $JL = 5$, what is the line ratio of $\triangle ABC$ to $\triangle NJL$?

2 If $BC = 10$, $JL = 6$, and $CA = 8$, find LN.

3 If the ratio of BC to JL is $\frac{3}{2}$ and the perimeter of $\triangle ABC = 9$, what is the perimeter of $\triangle NJL$.

4 If $AB : NJ = 4 : 5$, what is the ratio of the area of $\triangle ABC$ to the area of $\triangle NJL$?

A:
1 $\frac{2}{1}$ or 2:1

$$\text{Line ratio} = \frac{\text{a side of } \triangle ABC}{\text{corresponding side of } \triangle NJL}$$

$$= \frac{10}{5} = \frac{2}{1}$$

2 4.8

Corresponding sides of similar triangles are proportional

$$\frac{\text{side } \Delta\,ABC}{\text{Corresponding side } \Delta\,NJL} : \quad \frac{10}{6} = \frac{8}{x}$$

$$x = 4.8$$

3 6

The perimeter of two similar triangles is the same ratio as their corresponding sides

$$\frac{\text{side } \Delta\,ABC}{\text{corresponding side } \Delta\,NJL} = \frac{\text{Perimeter } \Delta\,ABC}{\text{Perimeter } \Delta\,NJL}$$

$$\frac{3}{2} = \frac{9}{x}$$

$$3x = 18$$
$$x = 6$$

4 $\dfrac{16}{25}$ or $16 : 25$

$$\left(\frac{\text{side } \Delta\,ABC}{\text{corresponding side } \Delta\,NJL}\right)^{2} = \frac{\text{area } \Delta\,ABC}{\text{area } \Delta\,NJL}$$

$$\left(\frac{4}{5}\right)^{2} = \frac{\text{area } \Delta\,ABC}{\text{area } \Delta\,NJL}$$

$$\frac{16}{25} = \frac{\text{area } \Delta\,ABC}{\text{area } \Delta\,NJL}$$

YOUR TURN

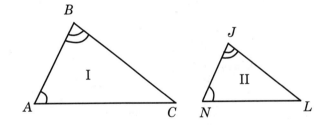

Note: The similar figures above are *not* drawn to scale and should only be used in conjunction with the formulas shown above as aids in calculating the answers to questions 1 through 6.

1 If $AB = 10$, $NJ = 2$, and $BC = 12$, find JL.

2 If $AB = 10$, $AC = 6$, $NJ = 5$, find NL.

3 If $BC = 10$, $JL = 15$, and the perimeter of Δ I is 30, what is the perimeter of Δ II ?

4 If the perimeter of Δ I is 20 and the perimeter of Δ II is 30, find AC if NL is 6.

5 The ratio of AB to NJ is 6 to 5. What is the ratio of JL to BC?

6 If $AB = 6$, $BC = 7$, $AC = 8$, and $NJ = 2$, what is the perimeter of Δ II?

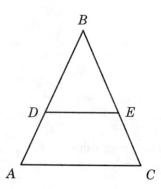

In the figure above, △ABC is similar to △DBE and $\overline{DE}$ is parallel to $\overline{AC}$. Base your answers to questions 7 through 10 on this figure.

7 If $BD : BA = 2 : 3$, find DE if AC is 12.

8 If $DE = 4$ and $AC = 16$, find BE if $BC = 20$.

9 If $BD = 2$ and $DA = 3$, what is the line ratio of △DBE to △ABC?

10 If $BD = 6$ and $DA = 6$, find BE, if $BC = 8$.

11

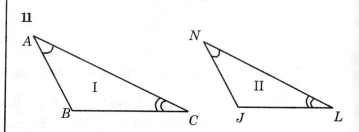

If △1 ~ △II, $AC = 12$, and $NL = 10$, find the measure of angle J if the measure of angle B is 120°.

12 If a 30 ft. tree casts a shadow of 9 ft., what shadow length would a 20 ft. tree cast?

13 A 5 ft. person casts a shadow of 6 ft. What length of shadow would a 3 ft. fence cast under the same conditions?

4.5 SCALE MODELS

SCALE MODELS/SCALE

Scale Model	an object similar to an actual object but of a different size
Scale	the ratio of the model size to the actual size

OUR TURN

Q:

1 On a map, 1 cm represents 30 miles. A trip which measures $4\frac{1}{2}$ cm on the map is how many actual miles?

2 A 3 inch x 5 inch photo is enlarged proportionally so that the smaller dimension becomes 8 inches. What size will the larger dimension become?

A:

1 135 miles

Make a proportion: $\dfrac{map}{real} \Rightarrow \dfrac{1 \text{ cm}}{30 \text{ mi.}} = \dfrac{4\frac{1}{2} \text{ cm}}{x \text{ mi.}}$

Cross Multiply: $x = 30 \cdot (4\frac{1}{2})$

$x = 135$ miles

2 $13\frac{1}{3}$ inches

Make a proportion: $\dfrac{\text{original size}}{\text{new size}} \Rightarrow \dfrac{3}{8} = \dfrac{5}{x}$

Cross Multiply: $3x = 40$

$x = 13\frac{1}{3}$ inches

YOUR TURN

1 A model of a car was made using a scale of 2 ft. = 1 in. If the model has a tire whose diameter measures $\frac{3}{4}$ in., what is the actual tire diameter?

2 An 8 in. x 10 in. photo is reduced proportionally so that the larger dimension becomes 8 in. What is the new size of the smaller dimension?

3 The distance from New York City to Riverhead is approximately 150 miles. On a map whose scale is 24 mi. = 2 inches, what is the distance between the two locations in inches?

4

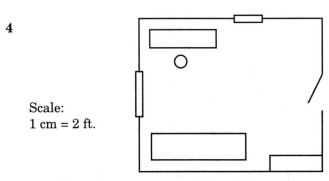

Scale:
1 cm = 2 ft.

The scale drawing above represents a room. Using a ruler and the provided scale, what is the perimeter of the actual room?

5
The scale on the map at the right is 1 inch = 60 mi. Using a ruler for measurement, what is the actual distance in miles from Binghamton to Syracuse?

Syracuse

Interstate 81

Interstate 88 to Albany

to Elmira

Binghamton

Interstate 86 to NYC

to Scranton

6
The scale of the map at the right is 1 cm = 5 mi. Using a ruler for measurement, what is the actual distance in miles from Pine Lake to Higgins Bay?

Higgins Bay

Memorial Highway

Sherman Mt
2650 ft

Pine Lake

7 N scale model trains use a scale of 1 : 160 with the actual size. An actual train car 60 ft. long will be how long in an N scale model?

4.6   PERCENT AND PROPORTIONS

Percent Symbol: **%**	A ratio that compares to the number 100 13% means 13 out of 100 or $\frac{13}{100}$	
Proportions and Percent	$\dfrac{\text{part}}{\text{whole}} = \dfrac{\text{percent}}{100}$ $\dfrac{\text{“is”}}{\text{“of”}} = \dfrac{\text{percent}}{100}$	
Useful Vocabulary	**English**	**Math**
	is	=
	of	times
	per	division
	cent	100
	percent (%)	division by 100
	out of	division
	ratio	division

PERCENTS AND PROPORTIONS

OUR TURN

Q:

1   In a class, 15 of the students are boys and 10 are girls. What percent of the class is boys?

2   A bookshelf has 5 mysteries, 2 science fiction, and 3 autobiographies. What percent of these are science fiction?

A:

1   60%

$$\frac{\text{part}}{\text{whole}} = \frac{\text{percent}}{100}$$

boys = 15, whole class = 25

$$\frac{15}{25} = \frac{x}{100}$$

$$25x = 1500$$
$$x = 60$$

2   20%

$$\frac{\text{part}}{\text{whole}} = \frac{\text{percent}}{100} \quad .$$

sci fi = 2, total = 10

$$\frac{2}{10} = \frac{x}{100}$$

$$10x = 200$$

$$x = 20$$

YOUR TURN

1   3 out of 12 is what percent?

2   2 music CDs out of 20 CDs is what percent?

3 At a concert, 200 people stood and 800 sat. What percent stood?

4 1 day is approximately what percent of a week?

5 1 second is approximately what percent of a minute?

6 Adam typed 6 pages of his 15 page report. What percent is still not typed?

7 Emmanuel had 5 hours of homework. After 3 hours, what percent had he done?

8 Three of the 30 people on the school bus brought their lunch to school in a paper bag. What percent brought their lunch in a paper bag?

The accompanying table shows the results of a survey about favorite colors.
Use this table for questions 9-11.

Color	Boys	Girls
Red	10	4
Blue	8	6
Green	3	5
Yellow	3	7
Brown	5	9

9 Approximately what percent of the survey were boys?

10 Approximately what percent of the girls liked blue as their favorite color?

11 Approximately what percent of those surveyed like red?

12 In a class of 30 students, 12 are girls. What percent of the class is boys?

13 Scott scored 3 of the 5 goals for the Roslyn soccer team. What percent of the goals did he score?

14 On an 80 mile hike, Dawn covered a distance of 20 miles. What percent of the hike remains to be walked?

15 Avi has $15.00. He spends $2.00 on a notebook and $4.00 for pens and pencils. What percent of his money did he spend?

16 A square is divided into 16 smaller squares of equal size and 6 of them are shaded. What percent of the original square is shaded?

17 What percent of the larger rectangle below is shaded if all the smaller rectangles are of equal size?

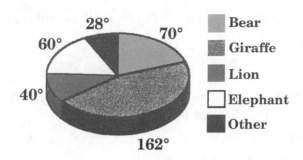

28° 70°
60°
40°
162°

Bear
Giraffe
Lion
Elephant
Other

18 The circle graph above shows a survey of the class' favorite zoo animals. The giraffes represent what percent?

19 Fourteen questions on a 25 question true or false test were true. What percent was false?

20 On a school trip, 12 students brought peanut butter and jelly sandwiches, 14 brought cheese sandwiches, 8 brought meat sandwiches, and the remaining 6 brought tuna. What percent of the group brought tuna sandwiches?

4.7 BASIC PERCENT PROBLEM

BASIC PERCENT PROBLEMS

$$\frac{\text{Part}}{\text{Whole}} = \frac{\text{Percent}}{100}$$

What to find	Word example	Proportion example
Find the percent	7 is what percent of 28	Part $\rightarrow$ $\frac{7}{28} = \frac{n}{100}$ $\leftarrow$ percent Whole $\rightarrow$ $\quad\quad\quad\quad$ $\leftarrow$ 100 $\frac{7}{28} = \frac{n}{100}$
Find the whole	6 is 20% of what number	Part $\rightarrow$ $\frac{6}{x} = \frac{20}{100}$ $\leftarrow$ percent Whole $\rightarrow$ $\quad\quad\quad\quad$ $\leftarrow$ 100 $\frac{6}{x} = \frac{20}{100}$
Find the part	What is 10% of 210	$\frac{\text{Part}}{\text{Whole}} \rightarrow \frac{x}{210} = \frac{10}{100}$ $\leftarrow$ percent $\quad\quad\quad$ $\leftarrow$ 100 $\frac{x}{210} = \frac{10}{100}$

OUR TURN

Q:

1 6 out of 10 is what percent?

2 What is 7% of 280?

3 8% of what number is 30?

4 Express 1000% without the % symbol.

A:

1 60%

$$\underset{\text{Whole} \rightarrow}{\overset{\text{Part} \rightarrow}{}} \frac{6}{10} = \frac{n}{100} \overset{\leftarrow \text{ percent}}{\underset{\leftarrow \text{ 100}}{}}$$

$10n = 600$ cross multiply
$n = 60$ divide by 100

2 19.6

$$\underset{\text{Whole} \rightarrow}{\overset{\text{Part} \rightarrow}{}} \frac{n}{280} = \frac{7}{100} \overset{\leftarrow \text{ percent}}{\underset{\leftarrow 100}{}}$$

$100n = 1960$ cross multiply
$n = 19.6$ divide by 100

3 375

$$\underset{\text{Whole} \rightarrow}{\overset{\text{Part} \rightarrow}{}} \frac{30}{n} = \frac{8}{100} \overset{\leftarrow \text{ percent}}{\underset{\leftarrow \text{ 100}}{}}$$

$8n = 3000$ cross multiply
$n = 375$ divide by 8

4 10

$$1000\% \Rightarrow \frac{1000}{100} = 10$$

YOUR TURN

1 What is 4% of 800?

2 What is 40% of 10?

3 What is 10% of 40?

4 8 is what percent of 40?

5 8 is what percent of 8?

6 3% of what number is 12?

7 10% of what number is 3?

8 16 is what percent of 2?

9 What is 4% of 4?

10 5% of what number is 1?

11 What is 50% of 2?

12 What is 2% of 50?

13 What is 80% of 70?

14 6 is what percent of 24?

15 4% of what number is 1?

16 4 is what percent of 400?

17 .4 is what percent of 100?

18 What is 300% of 9?

19 11 out of 55 is what percent?

20 What integer is the same as 200%?

21 What is 60% of 60?

22 15% of what number is 3?

4.8 PERCENT/DECIMALS/FRACTIONS

CONVERTING TO A PERCENT

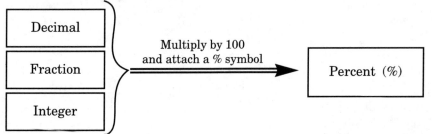

CONVERTING FROM A PERCENT

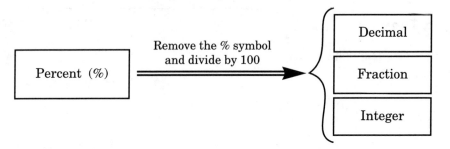

OUR TURN

Q: Convert the following to percents.

1 .35

2 $\frac{4}{5}$

3 27

Convert the following from percents, to an equivalent form.

4 80%

5 2000%

6 .4%

A:

1 35%

$$.35 \times 100 = 35 \Rightarrow 35\%$$

2 80%

$$\frac{4}{5} \times 100 = 80 \rightarrow 80\%$$

3 2700%

$$27 \times 100 = 2700 \Rightarrow 2700\%$$

4 .8 or $\frac{4}{5}$

$$80\% = \frac{80}{100}$$
.8
$$\frac{8}{10} = \frac{4}{5}$$

5 20

$$2000\% \Rightarrow \frac{2000}{100} = 20$$

6 .004 or $\frac{1}{250}$

$$.4\% = \frac{.4}{100}$$
.004
$$\frac{\frac{2}{5}}{100} = \frac{2}{500} = \frac{1}{250}$$

Your Turn

Convert the following to percent.

1 $\frac{1}{8}$

2 .42

3 1.49

4 $\frac{1}{80}$

5 $\frac{3}{4}$

6 4

7 $\frac{1}{9}$

8 $\frac{2}{3}$

9 .04

10 10

Convert the following from percents to an equivalent form.

11 3%

12 30%

13 300%

14 3000%

15 100%

16 28%

17 28.5%

18 $12\frac{1}{2}\%$

19 .6%

20 .004%

4.9 Applications of Percent

Applications of percent

To Find:	Calculation
Simple Interest	Interest = (principal) x (rate) x (time)
Commission	Commission = (percent) x (sales)
Change	(new value) − (old value)
Percent Change	$\left(\dfrac{change}{old\ value}\right)$ x 100
Tax	Tax = (tax rate) x (amount of sale)

OUR TURN

Q:

1   What is the total simple interest, if $2000 is deposited at 6% per year for 3 years?

2   A salesman sells $1000 worth of clothing; his commissions is 8%. What is the dollar amount of his commission?

3   A coat costs $85 and is on sale for $65. What is the decrease in price?

4   A suit costs $80 and is on sale $60. What is the percent change in price?

5   A $65 dress has how much sales tax added if the sales tax is 6%?

A:

1   $360

Simple Interest = (principal) × (rate) × (time)
= (2000) × (.06) × (3)
= 360

2   $80

Commission = (percent) × (sales)
= (.08) × (1000)
= 80

3   $20

Change = (new value) – (old value)
= |65 – 85| = 20

4   25%

$$\text{Percent Change} = \left(\frac{\text{change}}{\text{old value}} \right) \times 100$$

$$= \frac{|60 - 80|}{80} = \frac{20}{80} = 25\%$$

5   $3.90

Tax = (tax rate) × (amount of sale)
= (.06) × (65) = $3.90

YOUR TURN

1   Find the simple interest earned if $4000 is deposited for 2 years at 5% per year.

2   Find the simple interest earned if $3000 is deposited for 3 years at 4% per year.

3   If Bjorn invests $200 at 4% yearly simple interest for 2 years, how much money will he have after the 2 years are completed?

4   Eric earns 6% commission on his sales. If he sells $5000 worth of merchandise, what is his amount of commission in dollars?

5   This year it snowed on 8 days in January; last year it snowed on 6 days. What is the percent increase?

6   The number of public libraries in 1980 was approximately 8700. In 1990, there were approximately 9000. What was the percent increase?

7   Tina bought four items at the drug store: a comb for $1.00, deodorant for $2.75, toothpaste for $3.00, and floss for $2.00. If the tax rate is 8% and the items were taxable, how much tax does she pay?

8   In the New York City area, the median house price in 1999 was $203,200. In 2000, it was $221,500. What was the percent change, to the nearest percent?

Elaine receives 4% commission for her first $2000 of sales and 3% on any sales above that. What commission would she receive on the following sales amounts?

9 $1000

10 $2000

11 $3000

12 $10,000

4.10 SPECIAL RATIOS

The following ratios are mentioned here for completeness. Each is covered separately in another section and in more detail.

SPECIAL RATIOS

Probability	The ratio of: $\dfrac{\text{number of ways a particular event can happen}}{\text{total number of possible outcomes}}$	See Chapter 13 for more detail.
Trigonometric Ratios	$\sin A = \dfrac{\text{length of side opposite } \angle A}{\text{length of hypotenuse}}$ $\cos A = \dfrac{\text{length of side adjacent to } \angle A}{\text{length of hypotenuse}}$ $\tan A = \dfrac{\text{length of side opposite } \angle A}{\text{length of side adjacent to } \angle A}$	See Chapter 8 for more detail.
Average	The ratio of: $\dfrac{\text{sum of items}}{\text{quantity of items}}$	See Chapter 12 for more detail.

OUR TURN

Q:

$$A, B, C, D, E, F, G, H, I, J, K, L, M$$

1 Given the above letters, what is the probability of selecting a vowel?

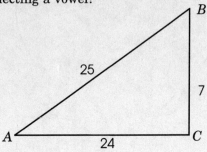

Figure not drawn to scale

Given the accompanying triangle, what are the values of:

2 $\sin A$

3 $\cos B$

4 $\tan A$

5 If the average of 12 items is 6, what is the sum of the items?

A:

1 $\frac{3}{13}$

There are 3 vowels (A, E, I)
There are 13 letters
$P(\text{vowel}) = \frac{3}{13}$

2 $\frac{7}{25}$

$\sin A = \dfrac{\text{length of side opposite } \angle A}{\text{length of hypotenuse}} = \dfrac{7}{25}$

3 $\frac{7}{25}$

$\cos A = \dfrac{\text{length of side adjacent to } \angle B}{\text{length of hypotenuse}} = \dfrac{7}{25}$

4 $\frac{7}{24}$

$\tan A = \dfrac{\text{length of side Opposite } \angle A}{\text{length of side adjacent to } \angle A} = \dfrac{7}{24}$

5 72

$\text{Average} = \dfrac{\text{sum of items}}{\text{quantity of items}}$

$12 = \dfrac{\text{sum}}{6}$ average = 12
                              number of items = 6

$\dfrac{12}{1} = \dfrac{\text{sum}}{6}$ place a 1 under the 12

sum = 72   cross multiply

YOUR TURN

1 Given the accompanying triangle, what is the value of tan W?

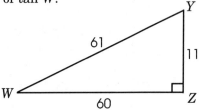

Figure not drawn to scale

2 In the accompanying diagram, if $\sin A = \frac{3}{5}$, what is the value of x?

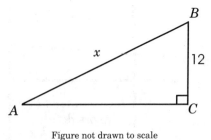

Figure not drawn to scale

Use the following information for question 3.

$\sin 37^\circ = \frac{3}{5}$

$\cos 37^\circ = \frac{4}{5}$

$\tan 37^\circ = \frac{3}{4}$

3 In the accompanying diagram, if $m\angle A = 37^\circ$ and $BC = 12$, what is the length of AB?

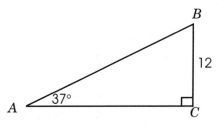

Figure not drawn to scale

4 In the accompanying diagram, $NJ = 5$, $LJ = 12$ and $NL = 13$. What is the value of tan L?

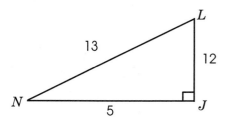

Figure not drawn to scale

5 If the probability of Mari getting a hit when she bats is $\frac{1}{6}$. How many hits would you expect if she was at bat a total of 180 times during the season.

6 A bag contains only red, white, and blue marbles. If the $P(\text{red}) = .4$ and $P(\text{white}) = .5$, what is the probability of selecting a blue marble?

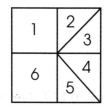

7 The square above is divided into four equal smaller squares and two of those smaller squares are each divided in half. If the six pieces are numbered as shown, what is the probability of selecting an even numbered piece?

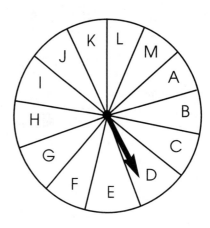

8 A spinner with equal divisions has letters as shown above. On a single spin, what is the probability of landing in a space with a letter that has a vertical line of symmetry?

9 Erin got an 80, 82, and 84 on her first three math tests. What score must she get on the fourth test to increase her average to 85 for the four tests?

10 Roy took two exams and averaged 85. He took three more exams and averaged 90. What was his combined average for all five tests?

11 If the average of four test grades is 86, what is the sum of the grades?

12 If eleven numbers have the same average as the first ten of these same numbers, what is the value of the eleventh number?

A zero

B the average of the first 10 numbers

C the median of the first 10 numbers

D the mode of the first 10 numbers

4.11 LONG ANSWER QUESTION FOR CHAPTER 4

1 Karen's mom had a doll made proportionally to look like Karen. The doll's height is one eighth of Karen's height and the doll's arm is 3 inches long.

PART A
Write a proportion to find Karen's real arm size. Place a box around your proportion.

PART B
Find Karen's real arm size.
Show all work.

Answer _____ inches

2 At 40 miles per hour, a 200 mile trip takes 5 hours. If the speed is increased by 25%, how much farther can be traveled in the same 5 hours?

Show all your work.

Answer _____ miles farther

3 A hitter's batting average is determined by the ratio of hits to the number of times at bat, rounded to 3 decimal places.

PART A

If Josh previously got 120 hits after 400 times at bat, what is his batting average?

Show your work.

Answer _____

PART B

If Josh expects to continue at this rate, how many hits should he expect to get in the next 70 times at bat?

Show your work.

Answer _____

4   In the accompanying figure, $\triangle ABC$ is similar to $\triangle NJL$ and $AB=12$ and $NJ=3$.

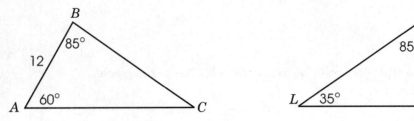

Figures not drawn to scale

PART A

Which side of triangle NJL corresponds with side BC in $\triangle ABC$?

Answer _____

Explain how you arrived at your answer.

_____

_____

_____

_____

PART B

If the perimeter of $\triangle NJL$ is 12, what is the perimeter of $\triangle ABC$?

Show your work.

Answer _____

PART C

The value of side AB is what percent of the value of side NJ?

Show your work.

Answer _____

CHAPTER FIVE

ALGEBRA

Algebra is a way to convert words into mathematical terms. We use algebra to help us solve problems in an efficient and time-saving manner. For example:

The price of shipping is $6.00 for the first pound and $2.00 for each additional pound. What is the heaviest package that can be shipped for $41.00.

Dawn has $63.00 and wants to buy a CD player for $127.00. If she baby-sits on Saturdays at $8.00 per hour, how many hours would she have to baby-sit to be able to afford the CD player?

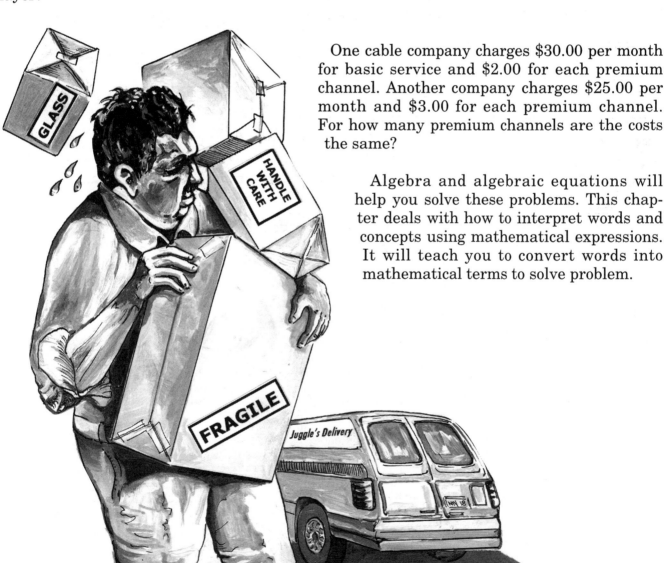

One cable company charges $30.00 per month for basic service and $2.00 for each premium channel. Another company charges $25.00 per month and $3.00 for each premium channel. For how many premium channels are the costs the same?

Algebra and algebraic equations will help you solve these problems. This chapter deals with how to interpret words and concepts using mathematical expressions. It will teach you to convert words into mathematical terms to solve problem.

5.1 BASICS

TERMINOLOGY

Term	Description	Example
Variable	A letter used to represent an numerical value.	x, n, y
Term	A grouping of a number and variables using only multiplication and division. (The variables may be raised to a power.)	$2x, xyz$ $$\frac{3xy^2}{5}$$
Coefficient	the numerical portions of the term	$3x^2$ The coefficient is 3. $\frac{7x}{5}$ The coefficient is $\frac{7}{5}$.
Like terms	terms with the same variables, raised to the same powers (regardless of coefficient)	$3x^2y$ and $7x^2y$ are like terms xyz and $12xyz$ are like terms x^2y and xy^2 are not like terms
Constant term	a term with no variable	$6, \ -7, \ \frac{3}{5}$
Polynomial term	the product of a number and single variable (The variable may be raised to an integer power.)	$3x, \quad 3x^2, \quad 7x^3, \quad 3x^{15}$
Combining like terms	Locate all the like terms in a mathematical expression and combine them by adding and /or subtracting according to the signs.	$6xy + 7xy \Rightarrow 13xy$ $7x^2y - 2x^2y \Rightarrow 5x^2y$ $\overline{7x + 2y \Rightarrow 7x + 2y}$ (not like terms)
Simplest form	when all like terms are combined	$2x + 3x + 4x^2 = 5x + x^2$ $x + 2x + 5x = 8x$

❽ A minus as a coefficient is equivalent to a -1. The coefficient of $-x^2$ is -1

❽ A constant is considered a polynomial term.

Anatomy of a Polynomial Term

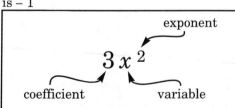

OUR TURN

Q:

1 What is the coefficient of the term $\dfrac{-3x^5}{7y}$?

2 Combine the terms: $2xy^2 + 3xy^2 + 7xy^2$

3 Express in simplest form: $6x^2 + 3x + 4 - 2x^2 - 5x + 2x - 1$

4 Is $\dfrac{3x^2}{y}$ a polynomial term?

A:

1 $-\dfrac{3}{7}$ The coefficient is the numerical component of the term.

2 $12xy^2$ Combine by adding and/or subtracting according to the signs.

3 $4x^2 + 3$ Combining like terms: $6x^2 - 2x^2 = 4x^2$
$$3x - 5x + 2x = 0$$
$$4 - 1 = 3$$

4 No   It is not of the form of a coefficient multiplied by a single variable. It has x and y.

YOUR TURN

1 What is the coefficient of the term $2x^3y$?

2 Which of the following is a polynomial term?

   A $2x^2$

   B $2xy$

   C xyz

   D $\dfrac{4}{x}$

3 What is the coefficient of the term $-2x^4y^5z^6$?

   F x

   G y

   H z

   J -2

4 Simplify: $2x + y + 3y$

5 Simplify: $3x - 4 + 6$

6 Which of the following is a constant term?

   A $\dfrac{1}{2}$

   B x

   C x^2

   D x^3

7 Express in simplest form:
$$3x^2 - 2x - 1 - x - 2$$

8 Express in simplest form:
$$4x^7 + 2x^5 - 3x^3 + 1 - x^5 - 2x^3$$

9 Express in the simplest form:
$$2xyz + 5ab + 4xyz - 2ab$$

10 Express in the simplest form:
$$x^2 + 2x^2 + x^3 + 3x^3$$

11 Express the perimeter of the rectangle in simplest form:

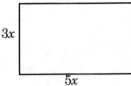

12 Express the perimeter of the equilateral triangle in simplest form:

13 In simplest form, which of the following represent s the perimeter of the accompanying quadrilateral?

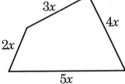

F   14

G $14x$

H $120x$

J $14x^4$

14 In simplest form, which of the following represents the perimeter of the accompanying pentagon?

A   15

B $15x$

C $8x + 15$

D $7x + 8$

15 What is the coefficient of $-xyz$?

16 Which of the following contains a pair of like terms?

F $2x$ and $2x^2$

G $3x$ and x^3

H x^2y and xy^2

J $3xyz$ and $\frac{1}{2}xyz$

5.2 POLYNOMIALS

A polynomial is one or more polynomial terms combined by addition or subtraction.

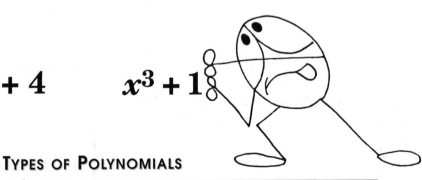

TYPES OF POLYNOMIALS

Number of Terms	Name	Examples
1	Monomial	$3x$, $4x^2$, $9x$
2	Binomial	$3x + 4$, $7x^2 + 7x$, $x^3 + 1$
3	Trinomial	$3x^2 + 4x + 4$, $7x^3 + x^2 + 1$
4 and more	Polynomial	$7x^{11} + 3x^2 + 2x - 1$ $2x^5 + 3x^4 - 7x^3 + 4x - 9$

ADDING POLYNOMIALS

To add Polynomials, combine their like terms

Example : $(6x^2 + 7x + 2) + (4x^2 - 2x - 4)$

Combine like terms: $6x^2 + 4x^2 = 10x^2$
$7x - 2x = 5x$
$2 - 4 = -2$

Answer: $10x^2 + 5x - 2$

MULTIPLYING A POLYNOMIAL BY A CONSTANT

To multiply a polynomial by a constant, use the distributive property.

Example : $5(x^2 + 3x - 2)$

$5(x^2 + 3x - 2) = 5(x^2) + 5(3x) - 5(2)$

$= 5x^2 + 15x - 10$

SUBTRACTING A POLYNOMIAL

- To subtract a polynomial, distribute the minus sign.
- It is as if you multiplied the polynomial by –1.
- Combine like terms.

Example: $(5x + 2) - (3x - 2)$

$(5x + 2) - (3x - 2)$ Distribute the minus sign.

$= 5x + 2 - (3x) - (-2)$

$= 5x + 2 - 3x + 2$ Combine like terms.

$= 2x + 4$

OUR TURN

Q:

1   Add : $x^2 - 3x + 2$ and $7x^2 + 4$

2   Simplify: $5(x + 2) + 2(x - 1)$

3   Add: $2x + 1$, $3x - 1$ and $6x + 3$

4   Find the perimeter of the accompanying triangle.

2x   x + 3

5x – 1

A:

1   $8x^2 - 3x + 6$ $(x^2 - 3x + 2) + (7x^2 + 4)$

Combine like terms: $x^2 + 7x^2 = 8x^2$
$2 + 4 = 6$

2   $7x + 8$ $5(x + 2) + 2(x - 1)$

Distribute: $5(x) + 5(2) + 2(x) + 2(-1)$
$5x + 10 + 2x - 2$

Combine like terms: $7x + 8$

3   $11x + 3$ $(2x + 1) + (3x - 1) + (6x + 3)$

Combine like terms: $2x + 3x + 6x = 11x$
$1 - 1 + 3 = 3$

4   $8x + 2$

Perimeter is the sum of the sides:
$(2x) + (x + 3) + (5x - 1)$

Combine like terms: $2x + x + 5x = 8x$
$3 - 1 = 2$

YOUR TURN

1 Which of the following is a binomial?

    A 2

    B $2x$

    C $2x + 2$

    D $2x^2 + 2x + 2$

For questions 2 through 10, perform the indicated operation and simplify.

2 $(6x + 1) + (3x + 2)$

3 $(4x^2 - 3x - 1) + (2x^2 + 2)$

4 $(3x - 2) + 2(x - 1)$

5 $4(x + 2) + 2$

6 $3(x + 2) + 2(x + 3)$

7 $- (x - 2) + 3$

8 $(x^2 + 2x) + 2(x + 1)$

9 $3(x - 1) - 2(x + 2)$

10 $7 - (3x + 4)$

11 In simplest form, what is the perimeter of the accompanying trapezoid?

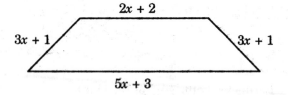

12 Express the perimeter of the accompanying triangle in simplest form.

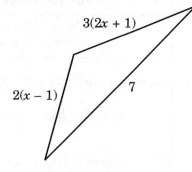

For questions 13 through 18, rewrite the expressions using the distributive property.

13 $2(x + y + z)$

14 $2(3x - 1)$

15 $- (7x + 2)$

16 $- (7x - 2)$

17 $- 2(7x - 2)$

18 $6(xy + yz)$

19 Add: $6x + 1$ to $3x - 4$

20 Add: $2(x + 3)$ to $3(x - 1)$

21 Find the sum of : $3(x - 2)$ and $2(x - 3)$

22 Subtract: $2x - 3$ from $x + 2$

23 Subtract: $2(x - 1)$ from $3(x - 2)$

5.3 English to Math

Operation Phrases

Addition Phrases	Subtraction Phrases
$x + y$	$x - y$
• Sum of x and y • x plus y • y added to x • x increased by y • y more than x • x exceeded by y	• Difference between x and y • x minus y • y subtracted from x • x diminished by y • y less than x • x reduced by y

Operation Phrases (continued)

Multiplication Phrases	Division Phrases
$x \cdot y$, xy , $x \times y$, $(x)(y)$	$x \div y$, $\frac{x}{y}$
• Product of x and y • x times y • x multiplied by y • "of" as in $x\%$ of y	• Quotient of x and y • x over y • ratio of x to y • $x : y$ • x divided by y • x parts "out of" y

Comparison Phrases

Verbal	Math
• is • equals	$=$
• is not equal	$\neq$
• is more than • is greater than	$>$
• is less than • is fewer than	$<$
• is more than or equal to • is greater than or equal to • a minimum of • no less than • at least	$\geq$
• is less than or equal to • a maximum of • no more than • at most	$\leq$

Our Turn

Q:

1 If x is the number, represent 2 less than three times the number.

2 If x is the number, represent the sum of the number squared and the square of 6.

3 If x is the number, represent the square of the sum of the number and three.

A:

1 $3x - 2$

2 $x^2 + 6^2$

3 $(x + 3)^2$

Your Turn

Represent each of the following expressions or equations using the letter x to represent "the number."

1 Two less than a number.

2 Twice a number decreased by 5.

3 The product of a number and a seven.

4 Two more than the quotient of a number and 6.

5 A number exceeds 3 by 2.

6 The sum of the square of a number and 3.

7 The square root of the product of seven and a number.

8 Twice a number decreased by the product of 4 and m.

9 Seven increased by three times a number.

10 The sum of twice a number and the square of the number.

11 The ratio of a number to 1 more than the number.

12 Five diminished by the product of a number and three.

13 The difference between a number and 6.

14 The product of a number increased by two and the number four.

15 The product of a number and one more than the number.

16 How many minutes are in h hours?

17 How many nickels are in d dimes?

18 How many feet are in i inches?

19 How many days are in w weeks?

20 Each week Leo adds $5 to his savings account. If the account is opened with P dollars, how many dollars are in the account after w weeks?

21 Henry weighs w pounds. For each of the next 3 weeks he loses n pounds per week. What is his weight after three weeks?

22 Zora is now d years old. How old was she 4 years ago?

23 Russ makes x dollars on his job. This year he will get a raise of 10%. In terms of x, what is his new salary?

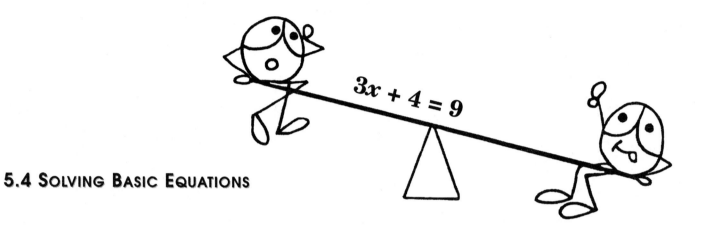

$$3x + 4 = 9$$

5.4 SOLVING BASIC EQUATIONS

TERMINOLOGY

Terminology	Description	Example	Comments
Equation	two quantities set equal	$2 + 3 = 5$ $3x + 4 = 9$	
Solution	the value of a variable which makes the equation true	$x + 7 = 9$ The solution is $x = 2$.	
Solve an equation	the directions to a student to find the solution	solve: $x + 7 = 9$ The solution is $x = 2$.	
Simplify	Put in simplest form.	$6x + 3x + 7 = 9x + 7$	Combine like terms.
Isolate the variable	Get the variable by itself (using adding and/or subtracting).	$\begin{array}{r} 3x + 6 = 7 \\ -6 \quad -6 \\ \hline 3x \quad\; = 1 \end{array}$	Subtract 6 from each side.
Make the variable coefficient equal to one	Create a 1 as the variable coefficient.	$\begin{array}{c} \dfrac{3x}{3} = \dfrac{9}{3} \\ x = 3 \end{array}$	Divide each side by 3.

❽ To maintain the balance in an equation, any mathematical process performed on one side of the equation must also be performed on the other side of the equal sign.

GENERAL PROCEDURE TO SOLVE AN EQUATION

Step	Description
1	Simplify each side of the equation.
2	Isolate the variable.
3	Create a coefficient of 1 for the variable.

HOW TO SOLVE BASIC ONE-STEP EQUATIONS

Equation Type	General Methodology applied to each side of the equation	Example
$x + 5 = 8$	Isolate the variable: subtract 5.	$\begin{array}{r} x + 5 = 8 \\ -5 \quad -5 \\ \hline x \quad\;\; = 3 \end{array}$
$x - 3 = 8$	Isolate the variable: add 3.	$\begin{array}{r} x - 3 = 8 \\ +3 \quad +3 \\ \hline x \quad\;\; = 11 \end{array}$
$2x = 8$	Create a coefficient of 1 for the variable: divide by 2.	$\begin{array}{c} \dfrac{2x}{2} = \dfrac{8}{2} \\ x = 4 \end{array}$
$\frac{1}{2}x = 8$	Create a coefficient of 1 for the variable: multiply by 2.	$\frac{1}{2}x = 8$ $(2)\,\frac{1}{2}x = 8\,(2)$ $x = 16$
$\frac{2}{3}x = 8$	Create a coefficient of 1 for the variable: multiply by $\frac{3}{2}$.	$\frac{2}{3}x = 8$ $(\frac{3}{2})\,\frac{2}{3}x = 8\,(\frac{3}{2})$ $x = \frac{24}{2} = 12$

HOW TO SOLVE BASIC TWO-STEP EQUATIONS

Step	Description
1	Isolate the variable, by removing addition or subtraction.
2	Create a variable coefficient of 1.

Equation	General Methodology applied to each side of the equation	Example
$2x + 6 = 10$	Isolate the variable: subtract 6.	$\begin{array}{r} 2x + 6 = 10 \\ -6 \quad -6 \\ \hline 2x \quad\;\; = 4 \end{array}$
	Create a variable coefficient of 1: divide by 2.	$\begin{array}{c} \dfrac{2x}{2} = \dfrac{4}{2} \\ x = 2 \end{array}$

How to Solve Equations with Variables on each side

Step	Description
1	Simplify each side of the equality.
2	Collect all the variable terms on to the side of the equation with the greater variable coefficient (use adding and/or subtracting).
3	Combine like terms.
4	Isolate the variable.
5	Create a variable coefficient of 1.

Equation Type	General Methodology applied to each side of the equation	Example
$x + 3x + 4 = x + 10$	Simplify each side.	$x + 3x + 4 = x + 10$ $4x + 4 = x + 10$
	Collect the variables: subtract x.	$\begin{array}{rcl} 4x + 4 &=& x + 10 \\ -x & & -x \\ \hline 3x + 4 &=& 10 \end{array}$
	Isolate the variable: subtract 4.	$\begin{array}{rcl} 3x + 4 &=& 10 \\ -4 & & -4 \\ \hline 3x &=& 6 \end{array}$
	Create a variable coefficient of 1: divide by 3.	$\dfrac{3x}{3} = \dfrac{6}{3}$ $x = 2$

A Special Equation

d = rt	
distance = rate × time	
d = distance	the distance traveled
r = rate	the average speed
t = time	the time spent traveling at the given speed

Our Turn

Q:

Solve the following equations:

1 $x - 3 = 11$

2 $2x = 64$

A:

1 $x = 14$

Add 3: $\begin{array}{rcl} x - 3 &=& 11 \\ +3 & & +3 \\ \hline x &=& 14 \end{array}$

2 $x = 32$

Divide by 2: $\dfrac{2x}{2} = \dfrac{64}{2}$
 $x = 32$

3 $\frac{1}{4}x = 5$

A:

3 $x = 20$ $\qquad$ $\frac{1}{4}x = 5$

Multiply by 4: $\quad$ $(4)\frac{1}{4}x = 5\,(4)$

$\qquad\qquad\qquad x = 20$

4 $2x - 1 = 7$

4 $x = 4$ $\qquad$ $2x - 1 = 7$

Add 1: $\qquad \dfrac{+1 \quad +1}{2x \qquad = 8}$

Divide by 2: $\quad \dfrac{2x}{2} = \dfrac{8}{2}$

$\qquad\qquad\qquad x = 4$

5 $2(x - 3) = 12$

5 $x = 9$ $\qquad$ $2(x - 3) = 12$

Distribute the 2: $2x - 6 = 12$

Add 6: $\qquad\qquad +6 \quad +6$

Divide by 2: $\qquad \dfrac{2x}{2} = \dfrac{18}{2}$

$\qquad\qquad\qquad x = 9$

6 $3x + 2 = x + 12$

6 $x = 5$ $\qquad$ $3x + 2 = x + 12$

Subtract x: $\dfrac{-x \qquad\quad -x}{2x + 2 = \qquad 12}$

Subtract 2: $\quad 2x + 2 = 12$

$\qquad\qquad\quad \dfrac{-2 \quad -2}{}$

Divide by 2: $\dfrac{2x}{2} = \dfrac{10}{2}$

$\qquad\qquad\qquad x = 5$

7 For the Smith family to make a 175 mile trip in 5 hours, at what average speed should they be traveling?

7 $\quad$ 35 mph

$\qquad\qquad$ d = r $\times$ t
$\qquad\qquad$ 175 = r (5)
$\qquad\qquad$ 35 = r

YOUR TURN

Solve each of the following equations:

1 $3x = 9$

2 $5x = 75$

3 $2x + 1 = 9$

4 $3x - 2 = 16$

5 $3x + 2 = x + 8$

6 $\frac{1}{4}x = 7$

7 $\frac{2}{5}x = 8$

8 $2(x - 1) = 12$

9 $3(2x + 1) = 21$

10 $5x + 6 = 96$

11 $2(x + 3) = x + 10$

12 $6x + 4 = 2(x - 10)$

13 $-(x - 1) = 9$

14 $5x + 3x - 2 = 22$

15 $2x - 1 = 5x - 10$

16 $2x + 5 - x = 3(x - 5)$

17 $\frac{1}{3}x + 4 = 9$

18 $\frac{1}{2}x - 6 = 4$

19 $(x + 1) + (2x + 1) = 17$

20 $4(x - 2) - 3(x + 1) = 1$

21 If each side of a square is represented by $2x + 3$ and the perimeter of the square is 92, what is the value of x?

22 If the perimeter of the accompanying rectangle is 32, what is the value of x?

$$2x - 1 \quad \boxed{}$$
$$3x + 2$$

23 Five packages have weights of x, $3x$, $2x + 4$, $5x - 10$, and $x + 5$. If their combined weight is 95 pounds, what is the value of x?

24 If 9 more than eight times a number is 41, what is the value of the number?

25 3 more than twice a number is equal to four times the number diminished by 7. Which of the following equations can be used to solve for the number?

   A $(2x + 3) + 4x = 7$

   B $2x - 4 = 7x + 3$

   C $2x + 3 = 7 - 4x$

   D $2x + 3 = 4x - 7$

26 If Harry travels 6 hours at 20 miles per hour, how many miles does he travel?

27 If Kay travels a distance of 24 km at an average speed of 8 km per hour, how long did it take her to make the trip?

28 If Adam travels at 10 miles per hour (mph) for 3 hours and then 3 mph for 10 hours, how many miles has he traveled?

29 Jodi travels from New York by plane. The flight lasts 6 hours and the plane averages 600 miles per hour. How many miles has she traveled?

5.5 SOLVING INEQUALITIES

HOW TO SOLVE BASIC INEQUALITIES
SIMILAR SOLUTION METHODS

Step	Description
1	Simplify each side.
2	Isolate the variable.
3	Create a variable coefficient of 1.

Equation Type	General Methodology applied to each side of the equation	Example
$6x - 1 \le 11$	Isolate the variable: add 1.	$\begin{array}{rcl} 6x - 1 & \le & 11 \\ +1 & & +1 \\ \hline 6x & = & 12 \end{array}$
	Create a variable coefficient of 1: divide by 6.	$\begin{array}{rcl} \dfrac{6x}{6} & \le & \dfrac{12}{6} \\ x & \le & 2 \end{array}$ x is the set of all real numbers less than or equal to 2

❽ Inequalities create solution sets rather than unique solutions.

❽ When creating the coefficient for the variable of 1:
   If you multiply or divide by a negative number, the inequality reverses.

OUR TURN

Q: Solve:

1   $3x \le 6$

2   $4x + 1 > 9$

A:

1   $x \le 2$ $\begin{array}{l} 3x \le 6 \\ \text{Divide by 3:} \quad x \le 2 \end{array}$

2   $x > 2$ $\begin{array}{rl} & 4x + 1 > 9 \\ \text{Subtract 1:} & \underline{-1 \;-1} \\ & 4x \quad > 8 \\ \text{Divide by 4:} & x \quad\;\; > 2 \end{array}$

YOUR TURN

Solve each of the following inequalities:

1   $7x > 21$

2   $3x \ge 21$

3   $3x < 24$

4   $8x \le 24$

5   $6x + 2 > 14$

6   $3x - 1 \le 8$

7   $3x + 2x + 1 > 11$

8   $3(x - 1) \ge 18$

9   $\frac{1}{2}x > 9$

10 $4(2x + 3) < 44$

Solve the following inequalities. Let n represent the number.

11 Six times a number is at least 54.

12 Two more than three times a number is at most 26.

13 A number decreased by 5 is no more than 35.

14 Twice a number increased by 6 has a maximum value of 20.

15 A number increased by twice the number is less than 27.

5.6 SOLVING BASIC x² (QUADRATIC) EQUATIONS

HOW TO SOLVE A BASIC x² EQUATION

Step	Description
1	Simplify each side.
2	Isolate the x^2 term.
3	Create a coefficient of 1 for the x^2 term.
4	Take the square root of each side.

Equation Type	General Methodology applied to each side of the equation	Example
$x^2 = 4$	Take the square root.	$x^2 = 4$ $\sqrt{x^2} = \pm\sqrt{4}$ $x = \pm 2$ $x = 2$ or $x = -2$
$x^2 + 9 = 25$	Isolate the x^2: subtract 9. Take the square root.	$x^2 + 9 = 25$ $\underline{-9 \quad -9}$ $x^2 \quad = 16$ $\sqrt{x^2} = \pm\sqrt{16}$ $x = \pm 4$

❽ $\sqrt{x^2} = x$ (if $x \geq 0$)

❽ ± 2 means $+2$ or -2, both are correct.

❽ In a real world problem, sometimes the negative solution must be rejected.

OUR TURN

Q:

Solve:

1 $x^2 = 16$

2 $x^2 - 1 = 24$

A:

1 $x \pm 4$ $\qquad$ $x^2 = 16$

Take the square root: $\sqrt{x^2} = \pm\sqrt{16}$

$x = \pm 4$

2 $x = \pm 5$ $\qquad$ $x^2 - 1 = 24$

Add 1: $\qquad \dfrac{+1 \quad +1}{x^2 \qquad = 25}$

Take the square root: $\sqrt{x^2} = \pm\sqrt{25}$

$x = \pm 5$

YOUR TURN

Solve each of the following equations:

1 $\quad x^2 = 121$

2 $\quad x^2 + 1 = 101$

3 $\quad x^2 + 20 = 101$

4 $\quad 2x^2 - 10 = x^2 + 390$

5 $\quad x^2 - 3 = 61$

6 $\quad 2x^2 = 8$

7 $\quad x^2 + 3^2 = 5^2$

8 $\quad x^2 = 5^2 + 12^2$

9 $\quad x^2 + 2x^2 + 3x^2 = 600$

10 $\quad 2(x^2 - 1) = 48$

11 $\quad x^2 = 1$

12 $\quad$ If three less than the square of a positive number is 46, what is the number?

5.7 LONG ANSWER QUESTIONS FOR CHAPTER 5

1

PART A

Simplify the following expression:

$\qquad 2(x - 3) + 3(2x + 5) - 2(2x - 4)$

Show all of your work.

Answer: _____

PART B

Simplify the following expression:
$$3(6x - 1) - (x - 1) - 2(5x - 2)$$

Show all of your work.

Answer: _____

PART C

If the expression in Part A is equal to the expression in Part B, what is the value of x?

Show all of your work.

Answer: _____

2 Five packages have weights (in pounds) of $2(x - 1)$, $3x - 1$, $2x - 5$, $x + 1$ and $x + 2$. They are to be stored on a shelf that can only hold 31 pounds without breaking.

PART A

Write a simplified expression for the combined weight of the five packages. Show all of your work.

Answer: _____

PART B

Write an inequality that can be used to find the maximum value of x. Show all of your work.

Answer: _____

PART C

What is the maximum value of x? Show all of your work.

Answer: _____

3 On a class trip, 4 adults accompanied the class of 28 students to the museum. The price of an adult ticket was four dollars less than three times the price of a student ticket. The amount spent for all the tickets was $184.

PART A

Write an equation that can be used to find the ticket prices. Show all of your work and let x represent the price of a student ticket.

Answer: _____

PART B

Solve the equation in Part A and determine the price of a student ticket. Show all of your work.

Answer: _____

4 Dawn would like to buy an MP3 music player which costs $142. She has only saved $14. Her baby-sitting job earns her $8 per hour.

PART A

Write an equation which can be used to determine the number of hours Dawn needs to baby-sit in order to have enough money to buy the MP3 player. Explain how you arrived at your answer.

Answer: _____

PART B

How many hours does Dawn need to work to be able to afford the MP3 player? Show all of your work.

Answer: _____

PART C

If Dawn doubles her hourly rate, how will this affect the number of hours she'll need to work to accumulate the amount she needs? Explain your answer below. Be as specific as possible.

_____

_____

_____

_____

_____

CHAPTER SIX

INTRO TO GEOMETRY

What do the items pictured here have in common?

What shapes do you see?

How are shapes used?

Shapes are everywhere. They exist in nature, in art, in everyday life. Architects and builders use geometry to design and build buildings. Artists incorporate geometry into their art work and sculpture. We need an understanding of geometry and space for home design.

Geometry is the language of shapes. Just as we communicate in verbal languages – English, Spanish, French, Chinese, etc. – so too we communicate using shapes. Shapes are universal; they cross language barriers and can be understood throughout the world.

To begin our study of the world of shapes, this chapter will identify the basic terms used in geometry. It includes an introduction to angles, lines and rays – complimentary, supplementary, parallel, perpendicular, similar and congruent.

6.1 TERMINOLOGY

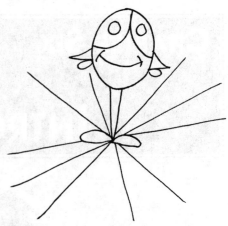

BASIC TERMINOLOGY - PART 1

Pictorial	Name	Representation	Description
•A	Point	Point A	represents a location
C ↔ D l	Line	Line CD ↔ CD Line l	a collection of points which extends without end in both directions
C → D	Ray	$\overrightarrow{CD}$ Ray CD	part of a line beginning at a defined point and extending in one direction
C • — • D	Line Segment	$\overline{CD}$ Segment CD	part of a line between two defined end points
A B 1 C	Angle	∠ABC ∠CBA ∠B ∠1 Angle B	two rays extending from a common endpoint

BASIC TERMINOLOGY - PART 2

Pictorial	Representation	Description
8 C • — • D	$m\,(\overline{CD}) = 8$	The length of line segment CD is 8 units.
A B 40° C	$m\angle B = 40°$ $m\angle ABC = 40°$	The measure of angle B is 40°. The measure of angle ABC is 40°.

BASIC TERMINOLOGY - PART 3

Pictorial	Name	Description
↔ CD	Double arrow	Line
→ CD	One way arrow	Ray
— CD	A horizontal line above the letters	Line segment
CD	No markings	Length of $\overline{CD}$
∠A	∠	Angle

Our Turn

Q :

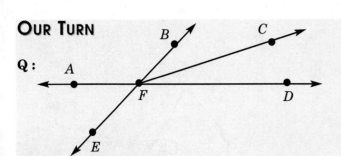

Using the diagram above,

1 Identify 2 angles.

2 Identify 2 rays.

3 Identify 2 lines.

4 Identify 2 line segments.

A:
Answers shown consist of a few examples. Other answers are possible.

1   $\angle AFB$; $\angle BFC$; $\angle CFD$; $\angle DFB$

2   $\vec{FA}$; $\vec{FD}$; $\vec{FB}$; $\vec{FC}$; $\vec{FE}$

3   $\overleftrightarrow{AD}$; $\overleftrightarrow{BE}$

4   $\overline{AD}$; $\overline{FC}$

Your Turn

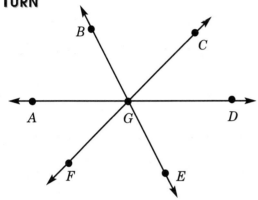

Using the diagram above:

1 Identify 8 angles.

2 Identify 3 lines.

3 Identify 4 rays.

4 Identify 3 lines segments.

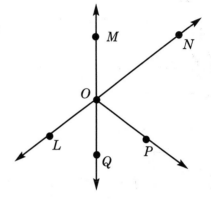

Using the diagram above:

5 Identify 6 angles.

6 Identify 3 rays.

7 Identify 4 line segments.

8 Identify 2 lines.

9 Identify 4 points.

10 Through points A, B, and C, which do not all lie on the same straight line, how many different lines can be drawn?

   A one

   B two

   C three

   D four

11 The notation $\vec{CD}$ represents which of the following?

   F line CD

   G segment CD

   H ray CD

   J angle DCD

6.2 THE BASIC ANGLE

ANGLE TERMINOLOGY

Pictorial	Representation
A *B* 2 *C* Side (Ray)	∠ *ABC* ∠ *CBA* ∠ *B* ∠ 2

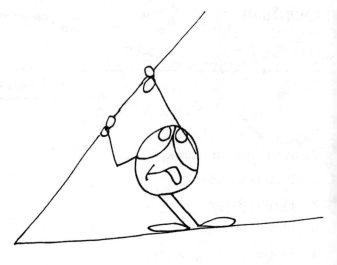

❽ Symbol: ∠ is the symbol for an angle

ANGLE SIZE

Name of Angle	Acute	Right	Obtuse	Straight	Reflex
Degree Measure	Between 0° and 90°	90°	Between 90° and 180°	180°	Between 180° and 360°
Diagram					

OUR TURN

Q: Identify the following angles by size.

1 89°

2 92°

3 141°

4 180°

A:

1 Acute — between 0° and 90°

2 Obtuse — between 90° and 180°

3 Obtuse — between 90° and 180°

4 Straight — 180° is a straight angle

YOUR TURN

Identify each angle according to size.

1 42°

2 1°

3 77°

4 193°

5 90°

6 100°

7 200°

Use the accompanying figure for questions 8 - 11

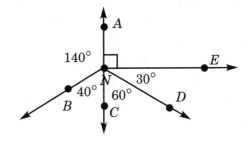

8 Identify 3 acute angles.

9 Identify 2 right angles.

10 Identify 3 obtuse angles.

11 Identify a straight angle.

12 A right angle has how many degrees?

    A exactly 180°

    B between 90° and 180°

    C between 0° and 90°

    D exactly 90°

6.3 MORE BASIC TERMS

BASIC TERMINOLOGY - PART 4

Pictorial	Name	Representation	Description
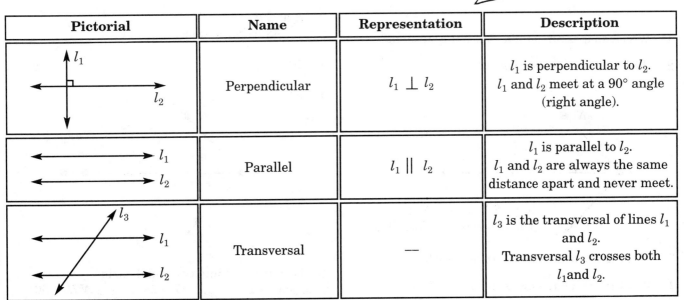 l_1 / l_2	Perpendicular	$l_1 \perp l_2$	l_1 is perpendicular to l_2. l_1 and l_2 meet at a 90° angle (right angle).
l_1 / l_2	Parallel	$l_1 \parallel l_2$	l_1 is parallel to l_2. l_1 and l_2 are always the same distance apart and never meet.
l_3 / l_1 / l_2	Transversal	—	l_3 is the transversal of lines l_1 and l_2. Transversal l_3 crosses both l_1 and l_2.

Pictorial	Name	Representation	Description
A W B B → A, D, C with 1, 2	Bisect	W bisects $\overline{AB}$ AW = WB _____ $\overrightarrow{BD}$ bisects $\angle B$ m $\angle 1$ = m $\angle 2$	To cut in half To divide into two equal parts
Area = 6 Area = 6	Equal	=	Same size, not necessarily same shape _____ Area of $\triangle$ = Area of $\square$
	Similar	~	Same shape, not necessary same size
	Congruent	≅	Same shape and same size _____ Identical

OUR TURN

Q:

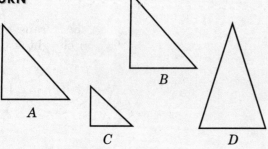

1   Which shapes are similar but not congruent?

2   Which shapes are congruent?

A:

1   A and C or B and C
     Same shape, different size.

2   A and B
     Exactly the same.

3   56°

4   28°

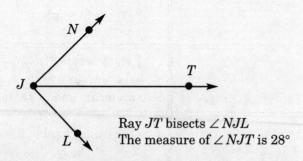

Ray JT bisects $\angle NJL$
The measure of $\angle NJT$ is 28°

3   What is the degree measure of $\angle NJL$

4   What is the degree measure of $\angle LJT$

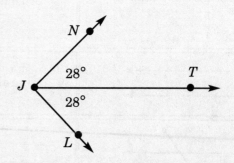

To bisect is to cut into two equal parts
Therefore $\angle LJT = \angle NJT = 28°$ and $\angle NJL = 56°$

YOUR TURN

1 Two parallel lines _____.

   A meet at 3 points

   B meet at 2 points

   C meet at 1 point

   D never meet

2 In the accompanying diagram, if ray *CF* bisects angle $\angle ACD$ and the measure of angle $\angle ACD$ is 50°, what is the measure of angle $\angle ACF$?

   F 25°

   G 50°

   H 75°

   J 100°

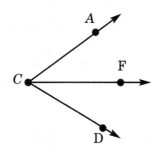

Figure not drawn to scale

Use the following diagrams for questions 3 - 5.

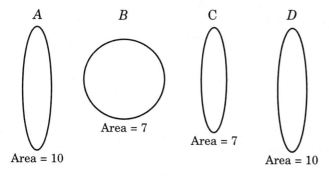

3 Name 2 congruent figures.

4 Name 2 figures that are similar but not congruent.

5 Name a set of figures that are equal in area but not congruent.

6 Jack buys a piece of lumber 12 feet long. He bisects the board and then bisects each of the pieces. What is the length of one of the smaller pieces?

   A 2 ft.

   B 3 ft.

   C 4 ft.

   D 6 ft.

Use the accompanying diagram for questions 7-10.

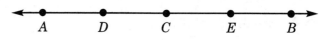

Point *C* bisects $\overline{AB}$ and points *D* and *E* bisect $\overline{AC}$ and $\overline{CB}$ respectively.

7 If *EB* = 4 cm, what is the length of *DE*?

8 If *AC* = 10 cm, what is the length of *DE*?

9 If *DE* = 8 cm, what is the length of *AB*?

10 If *DC* = 7 cm, what is the length of *CB*?

11 All circles are _____.

   F equal

   G congruent

   H similar

   J parallel

12 A film negative and the resulting photograph are examples of two items which are _____.

   A equal

   B congruent

   C similar

   D parallel

13 If two parallel lines are cut by a transversal, what is the greatest number of right angles that can be formed?

   F 2

   G 5

   H 6

   J 8

14 If the angle formed by two perpendicular lines is bisected, what is the measure of each of the smaller angles?

   A 25°

   B 35°

   C 45°

   D 55°

15 Two perpendicular lines form how many right angles?

   F 1

   G 2

   H 3

   J 4

6.4 Angle Pairs

Types of Angle Pairs

Pictorial	Name	Relationship	Formed by
	Adjacent Angles	$\angle 1$ is next to $\angle 2$	Two angles with a common vertex, sharing a common side and no overlap
	Complementary Angles	$m\angle 1 + m\angle 2 = 90°$	Two angles, the sum of whose measures is 90°
	Supplementary Angles	$m\angle 1 + m\angle 2 = 180°$	Two angles, the sum of whose measures is 180°

Pictorial	Name	Relationship	Formed by	What to look for
	Vertical Angles	$m\angle 1 = m\angle 2$	Two intersecting lines	an **X** shape
	Alternate Interior Angles	$m\angle 1 = m\angle 2$	Two parallel lines cut by a transversal	a **Z** shape
	Corresponding Angles	$m\angle 1 = m\angle 2$	Two parallel lines cut by a transversal	an **F** shape
	Interior Angles on the same side of the transversal	$m\angle 1 + m\angle 2 = 180°$	Two parallel lines cut by a transversal	a **⊏** shape

OUR TURN

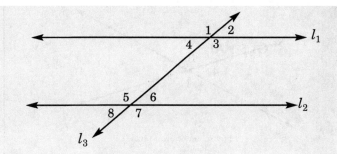

Q: As shown at the right, parallel lines l_1 and l_2 are cut by a transversal l_3.

1 Name 2 sets of vertical angles.

2 Name 2 sets of corresponding angles.

3 Name 2 sets of alternate interior angles.

4 If one of two complementary angles is 10° more than the other, how many degrees are in the measure of the smaller angle?

A:

1 ∠1 and ∠3
∠2 and ∠4
∠5 and ∠7
∠6 and ∠8
Look for an **X** shape.

2 ∠1 and ∠5
∠4 and ∠8
∠2 and ∠6
∠3 and ∠7
Look for an **F** shape

3 ∠3 and ∠5
∠4 and ∠6
Look for a **Z** shape

4 40°

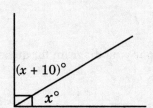

Two complimentary angles add to 90°

$$x + (x + 10) = 90$$
$$2x + 10 = 90$$
$$2x = 80$$
$$x = 40$$

YOUR TURN

Use the accompanying diagram for questions 1-8.

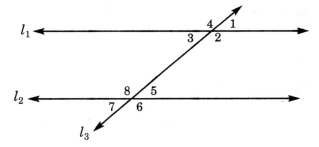

Figure not drawn to scale

l_1 and l_2 are parallel lines cut by a transversal l_3. If the measure of angle 4 is 100°, find the measure of each of the following angles.

1 ∠1

2 ∠2

3 ∠3

4 ∠5

5 ∠6

6 ∠7

7 ∠8

8 Using the diagram above ∠1 and ∠2 are _____ angles.

    A complementary

    B supplementary

    C corresponding

    D vertical

9

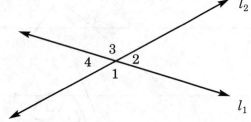

Figure not drawn to scale

The $m\angle 2 = 48°$, what is the measure of $\angle 4$?

F 28°

G 48°

H 62°

J 152°

Use the accompanying diagram for questions 10-15.

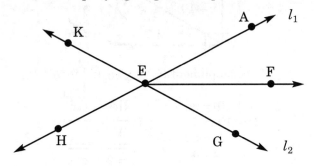

Figure not drawn to scale

Lines l_1 and l_2 intersect at E. Ray EF bisects angle AEG. If angle HEG measures 120°, find the measure of each of the following angles.

10 $\angle AEH$

11 $\angle AEF$

12 $\angle KEA$

13 $\angle KEH$

14 $\angle AEG$

15 $\angle HEF$

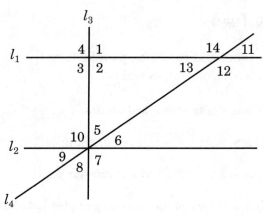

Figure not drawn to scale

In the figure above, parallel lines l_1 and l_2 are cut by a perpendicular transversal l_3 and a second transversal l_4. If the measure of $\angle 12$ is 110°, find the measure of each of the following angles.

16 $m\angle 6$

17 $m\angle 5$

18 $m\angle 2$

19 $m\angle 9$

20 $m\angle 11$

21 $m\angle 6 + m\angle 7 + m\angle 8$

22 $m\angle 1 + m\angle 3$

6.5 CONGRUENT/SIMILAR

CONGRUENT

If two figures are congruent...

- they are identical
- all corresponding sides and angles are equal

PROVING TWO TRIANGLES CONGRUENT

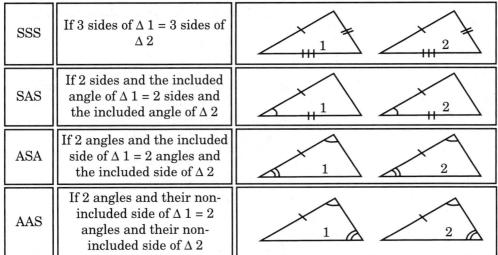

SSS	If 3 sides of Δ 1 = 3 sides of Δ 2	
SAS	If 2 sides and the included angle of Δ 1 = 2 sides and the included angle of Δ 2	
ASA	If 2 angles and the included side of Δ 1 = 2 angles and the included side of Δ 2	
AAS	If 2 angles and their non-included side of Δ 1 = 2 angles and their non-included side of Δ 2	

SIMILAR

If two figures are similar...

- the figures are the same shape, not necessarily the same size
- they are enlargements or reductions of each other
- all corresponding **angles** are equal
- all corresponding **sides** are proportional

PROVING TWO TRIANGLES SIMILAR

AA
If 2 angles of Δ 1 = 2 angles of Δ 2

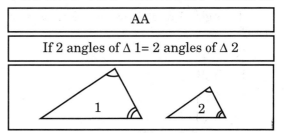

OUR TURN

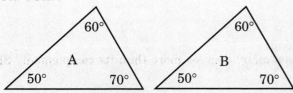

Figures not drawn to scale

Q:

1 Are ΔA and ΔB similar?

2 Are ΔA and ΔB congruent?

3 Are ΔC and ΔD congruent?

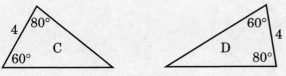

Figures not drawn to scale

A:

1 Yes
If two angles of one triangle are equal to two angles of a second triangle, then the two triangles are similar.

2 Maybe
The triangles are similar, however similar triangles are the same shape, not necessarily the same size. If the size matched, they would also be congruent.

3 Yes
If two angles and the included side of one triangle match two angles and the included side of a second triangle, the triangles are congruent.

YOUR TURN

Answer the following as *sometimes*, *always*, or *never*.

1 Two congruent triangles have the same area.

2 If two triangles are similar, their sides are equal.

3 If two sides and an angle of one triangle are congruent to two sides and an angle of a second triangle, the triangles are congruent.

4 If two triangles are similar, their corresponding sides are proportional.

5 If two angles of one triangle are congruent to two angles a second triangle, this is sufficient to prove congruence.

6

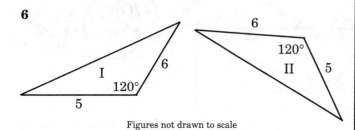

Figures not drawn to scale

Triangles I and II above are congruent by which rule?

    A SSS

    B SAS

    C ASA

    D AAS

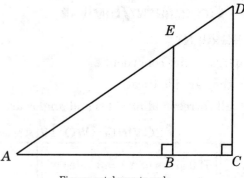

Figures not drawn to scale

7 In the diagram above, triangle ABE is similar to triangle ACD because $\angle EBA$ and $\angle DCA$ are both 90° and because:

    F EB is proportional to DC

    G $\angle A$ is in both triangles

    H angle BAE = angle ADC

    J AC is longer than BC

8 If two triangles are similar, which one of the following statements must be true?

    A corresponding sides are equal

    B they each contain a right angle

    C they each have the same area

    D the sum of their angles are equal

6.6 LONG ANSWER QUESTIONS FOR CHAPTER 6

1

PART A

If the measure of an angle is 27°, then its supplement is how many degrees more than its complement? Show your work.

Answer _____

PART B

If the measure of the angle in Part A is changed to 87°, then its supplement is how many degrees more than its complement? Show your work.

Answer _____

PART C

Come to a mathematical conclusion based on the previous examples and explain your conclusion in the space below.

_____

_____

_____

_____

_____

2 In the accompanying diagram, $\overline{DE}$ is parallel to $\overline{BC}$ and the the measure of angle B is 80°.

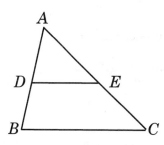

Figure not drawn to scale

PART A

What is the measure of angle ADE?

Answer _____

PART B
How many angles of $\triangle ABC$ are equal in measure to the angles of $\triangle ADE$?

Answer _____

PART C
What is the relationship between $\triangle ABC$ and $\triangle ADE$? Be as specific as possible.

Answer _____

PART D
If $AD = 3$, $DB = 3$, $AE = 5$, $EC = 5$ and $DE = 7$, find the value of BC. Show your work.

Answer _____

3 The measure of two complementary angles are represented by $4x - 30$ and $x + 70$.

PART A

Write an equation that can be used to solve for x.

Equation:

PART B

Solve the equation for x and write the degree measure of each angle. Show work.

Answers: x =

       Smaller angle = _____ degrees

       Larger angle   = _____ degrees

PART C

What is the difference between the supplement of the smaller angle in Part *B* and the supplement of the larger angle in Part *B*? Show your work and/or explain your reasoning.

Answer: _____ degrees

_____

_____

_____

_____

CHAPTER SEVEN
MEASUREMENT & CONSTRUCTION

7

Every field of study has its own tools. Art uses paints, brushes, canvasses and sculpting materials. Medicine uses stethoscopes, thermometers, lasers, etc. Cooking uses foods, spices and measuring tools. So too does Geometry. This chapter introduces the ruler, the protractor and the compass, as well as a few typical constructions.

Measurement units vary depending on cultures and evolution. Metric is used worldwide, while U.S. Customary Units are used in the United States. An American traveler to China may hear that it is 13° C outside. Since he is used to temperature measured in Fahrenheit, not Celsius, how should he dress? Similarly, if it is 5 kilometers from the hotel to the museum, can he walk or is a taxi a better option? If you just finished running 8 times around the track, would 3 hectoliters of water quench your thirst?

This chapter explains some basic measurement and construction tools. It also includes a reference set of conversion charts.

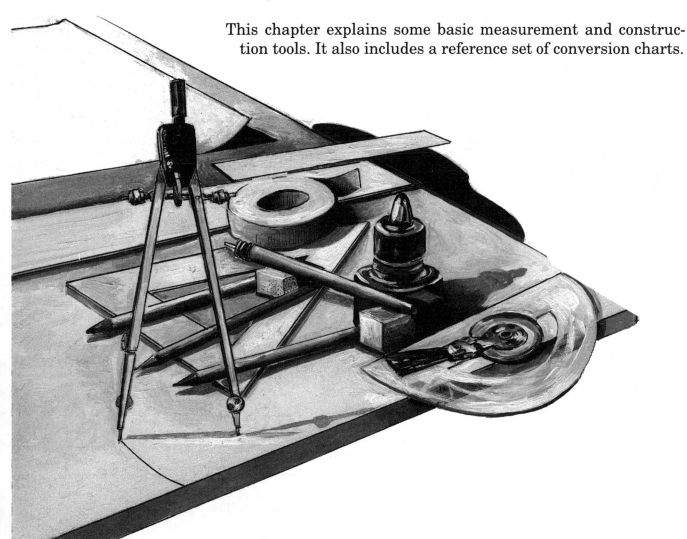

7.1 TOOLS/SIGNIFICANT DIGITS

TOOLS

Ruler	
	used to measure linear distance

Protractor	used to measure angles

Compass	used for geometric constructions and drawing circular arcs.

Straightedge	a ruler with no markings

Precision	The precision of an instrument is determined by the size of the smallest measurable unit.

	precision is 1 inch
	precision is $\frac{1}{4}$ inch
	precision is $\frac{1}{8}$ inch
	precision is $\frac{1}{16}$ inch

Significant Digits	• applies only the measured quantities • all the digits that are known exactly, plus one more digit which is estimated • the digits in the actual measurement

RULES TO DETERMINE SIGNIFICANT DIGITS

Rule	Number	Number of Significant Digits	Note
All non-zero digits are significant (1, 2, 3, 4, 5, 6, 7, 8, 9)	371.4 .671	4 3	All the digits are significant
All zeros between non-zero significant digits are significant	17.04 170.04	4 5	
Zeros used strictly as place holders are **not** significant	.003 .00405	1 3	The lead zeros are place holders
Trailing zeros that are part of the measurement are significant	.80 4.800	2 4	
A lone zero in front of a decimal point is cosmetic, and **not** significant	0.413	3	The zero is cosmetic only

CALCULATIONS WITH MEASURED QUANTITIES

+ /−   The result can have no more decimal digits than does the measured quantity with the least number of decimal places.

x / ÷   The result can not have more significant figures than the measurement with the fewest number of significant figures.

OUR TURN

Q :

1   What is the precision of the following ruler?

How many significant digits do each of the following have?

2   173.2

3   .0005

A:

1 $\frac{1}{8}$ inch   The smallest measurement mark on the ruler is one eighth.

2   4   All non-zero digits are significant.

3   1   Place holder zeros are not significant, only the 5 is significant.

YOUR TURN

1   To measure the length of a line, the instrument used is a:
   A   ruler
   B   straightedge
   C   compass
   D   protractor

2   To measure an angle, the instrument used is a:
   F   ruler
   G   straightedge
   H   compass
   J   protractor

3 The number 47.02 has how many significant digits?

A 1

B 2

C 3

D 4

4 A ruler is different from a straightedge because:

F it is longer

G it is shorter

H it has markings

J it has no markings

Identify the number of significant digits.

5 42.3

6 42.03

7 0.427

8 .049

9 .409

10 6.200

11 What is the precision of the protractor?

12 What is the precision of the ruler?

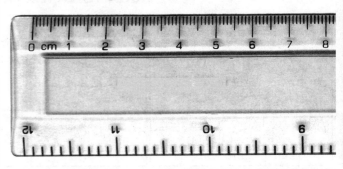

13 What is the precision of the scale on the clock?

QUARTZ

14 Which unit is most precise?

A second

B minute

C hour

D day

15 Which unit is most precise?

F kilometer

G meter

H centimeter

J millimeter

16 Compute the product and round your answer to match the rules for measured quantities.

.0431 x 13

17 Compute the difference and round your answer to match the rules for measured quantities.

27 − 15.7

7.2 RULER

Note: In this section there is no "Our Turn" needed to demonstrate how to complete the "Your Turn" questions.

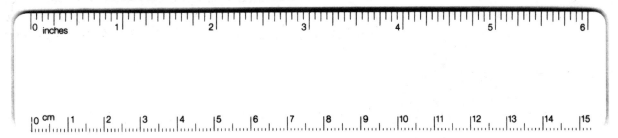

HOW TO MEASURE THE LENGTH OF A LINE SEGMENT

Step	Description	Pictures
0	Given: segment AB	$A \bullet \text{——————} \bullet B$
1	Using the desired unit, place the zero mark of the ruler at end point A and align the edge of the ruler with the line.	
2	Read the marking on the ruler which coincides with end point B. Be sure to use the same units.	AB is $1\frac{1}{2}$ inches

YOUR TURN

What is the length of each of these line segments in cm?

1 $\bullet$————$\bullet$

2 $\bullet$——————————$\bullet$

3 $\bullet$—$\bullet$

4 What is the perimeter of the triangle NJL measured in cm?

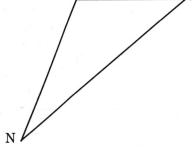

What is the length of each of these line segments in inches?

5 $\bullet$————————————$\bullet$

6 $\bullet$——————$\bullet$

7.3 PROTRACTOR

PROTRACTOR

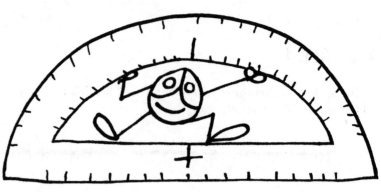

HOW TO FIND THE DEGREE MEASURE OF AN ANGLE

Step	Description	Pictures
0	Given: $\angle NJL$	❶ If necessary, extend the sides of the angle in length in order to fit over the scale on the protractor.
1	Place the center of the protractor at Vertex J and align the zero degree marking with one of the rays of the angle	Center of protractor
2	Using the scale that begins with 0, read the angle on the same scale where the other ray intersects the protractor _____ $m\angle NJL = 40°$	

YOUR TURN

What is the measure in degrees of each of the following angles?

1 _____ degrees

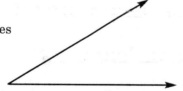

2 _____ degrees

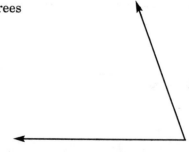

3 _____ degrees

4 _____ degrees

5 _____ degrees

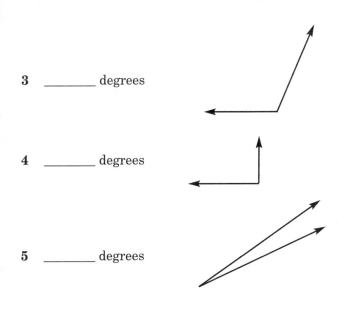

6 What is the measure of each angle of $\triangle NJL$?

7 What is the measure of each of the angles in triangle LMN?

7.4 DRAW AN ANGLE OF A GIVEN MEASURE

HOW TO DRAW AN ANGLE OF A GIVEN DEGREE MEASURE

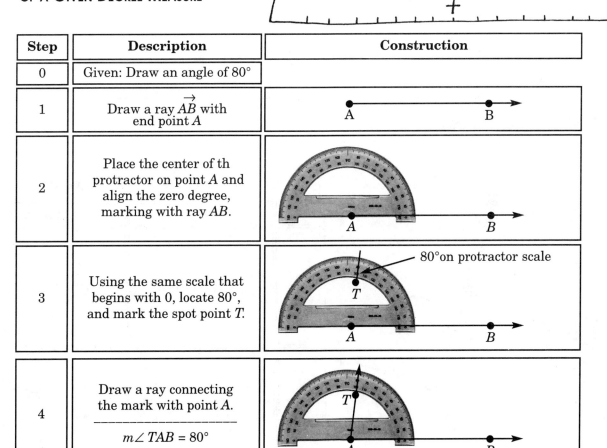

Step	Description	Construction
0	Given: Draw an angle of 80°	
1	Draw a ray $\overrightarrow{AB}$ with end point A	
2	Place the center of th protractor on point A and align the zero degree, marking with ray AB.	
3	Using the same scale that begins with 0, locate 80°, and mark the spot point T.	80°on protractor scale
4	Draw a ray connecting the mark with point A. <hr> $m\angle TAB = 80°$	

YOUR TURN

Using a protractor and straightedge, draw an angle equal to each of the following measures.

1 20°

2 120°

3 80°

4 95°

5 160°

6 55°

7.5 BISECTING AN ANGLE

HOW TO BISECT A GIVEN ANGLE

Step	Description	Drawing
0	Given: ∠NJL	
1	With compass point on J, swing an arc that intersects ray JN at T and ray JL at U	

2	With the compass point first at T and then at U, swing intersecting arcs of the same radius. Mark the intersection point Q.	
3	Draw $\overrightarrow{JQ}$ <hr> $\angle NJQ = \angle QJL$ and $\overrightarrow{JQ}$ is the angle bisector.	

YOUR TURN

Using a compass and straightedge, bisect each of the following angles.

1

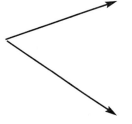

2

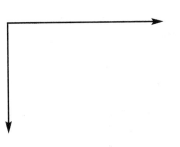

3

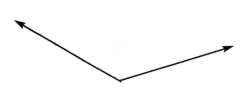

4

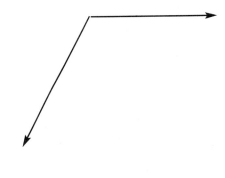

5

7.6 CONSTRUCT A PERPENDICULAR BISECTOR

HOW TO CONSTRUCT A PERPENDICULAR BISECTOR OF A GIVEN LINE SEGMENT

Step	Description	Construction
0	Given: line segment AB	
1	Place the compass point at A. With the compass opening more than half the length of AB, swing an arc above and below AB.	
2	With the same setting, place the compass point at B and swing an arc above and below line AB, intersecting the arc from step 1 at T and U respectively.	
3	Draw $\overleftrightarrow{TU}$, intersecting line segment AB at M. TU is the perpendicular bisector of line segment AB. M is the midpoint of segment AB.	

YOUR TURN

Using a compass and a straightedge, construct a perpendicular bisector of each of the following lines segments.

1

2

3

7.7 COPYING AN ANGLE

HOW TO CONSTRUCT AN ANGLE CONGRUENT TO A GIVEN ANGLE

Step	Description	Given Angle	Construction
0	Given: $\angle NJL$		
1	Draw line l through point A.		
2	Place the compass point on J and swing an arc intersecting ray JL at T and ray JN at U.		

How to Construct an Angle Congruent to a Given Angle (CONTINUED)

Step	Description	Given Angle	Construction
3	Without changing the compass setting, place the compass point on *A* and swing arc *RM*, intersecting line *l* at *M*.		*R* ⌒ arc, line *l* with points *A* and *M*
4	Place the compass point on *T* and adjust it to swing an arc through *U*.	*U*, *N* arcs; *J*, *T*, *L* on line	
5	Without changing the compass setting, place the compass point on *M* and swing an arc intersecting arc *RM* at *Q*.		*R*, *Q* arcs; line *l*, *A*, *M*
6	Draw $\vec{QA}$ ———————— ∠ *QAM* ≅ ∠ *NJL*		*R*, *Q*, ray; line *l*, *A*, *M*

YOUR TURN

Using a compass and straightedge, construct an angle congruent to the given angle.

1

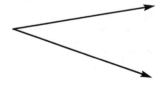

2

3

4

5

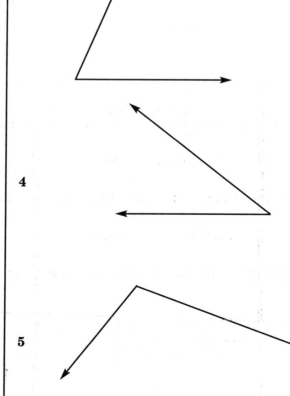

7.8 HOW TO CHANGE UNITS

GENERAL NOTES

1	Multiply and divide units as you would numbers.
2	When the same units appear in the numerator and denominator, they can be cancelled.
3	The "per" means division. Miles per hour $\Rightarrow \dfrac{miles}{hour}$
4	Changing a known conversion into fraction form, using a conversion factor: $3 \text{ ft} = 1 \text{ yd} \Rightarrow \left(\dfrac{3 \text{ ft}}{1 \text{ yd}}\right) \text{ or } \left(\dfrac{1 \text{ yd}}{3 \text{ ft}}\right)$ $\qquad$ $1 \text{ min} = 60 \text{ sec} \Rightarrow \left(\dfrac{1 \text{ min}}{60 \text{ sec}}\right) \text{ or } \left(\dfrac{60 \text{ sec}}{1 \text{ min}}\right)$

PROCEDURE

Step	Description	Example: change 6 ft to yds
1	List the item to be changed.	6 ft
2	Multiply by the conversion factor in fraction form. (Note: More than one conversion factor may be necessary.)	$6 \text{ ft} \left(\dfrac{1 \text{ yd}}{3 \text{ ft}}\right)$
3	The goal is to be able to cancel the units you wish to replace and insert the new units.	$6 \cancel{\text{ ft}} \left(\dfrac{1 \text{ yd}}{3 \cancel{\text{ ft}}}\right)$
4	After cancelling, multiply the remaining numbers and units.	$\dfrac{6 (1 \text{ yd})}{3} = \dfrac{6 \text{ yds}}{3} = 2 \text{ yds}$

OUR TURN

Q:

1 Convert 4 inches to cm, knowing 2.5 cm = 1 inch

2 Convert $3\,\dfrac{miles}{hr.}$ to $\dfrac{ft.}{min.}$, knowing 5280 ft. = 1 mile and 60 sec = 1 min.

A:

1 10 cm $4\ in\ \left(\dfrac{2.5\ cm}{1\ in}\right) = 10\ cm$

2 $264\,\dfrac{ft.}{min.}$ $3\,\dfrac{miles}{hr.}\ \left(\dfrac{5280\ ft.}{1\ mile}\right)\left(\dfrac{1\ hr.}{60\ sec}\right) = \dfrac{3(5280)}{60}\,\dfrac{ft.}{min.} = 264\,\dfrac{ft.}{min.}$

YOUR TURN

Convert each of the following to the units indicated

1 3 ounces to grams

2 2 days to hours

3 3 days to minutes

4 2 meters to inches

5 7 gallons to pints

6 2 tons to ounces

7 2 kilometers to miles

8 $2\,\dfrac{miles}{hour}$ to $\dfrac{miles}{minute}$

9 $3\,\dfrac{feet}{second}$ to $\dfrac{feet}{hour}$

10 $2\,\dfrac{inches}{second}$ to $\dfrac{feet}{minute}$

11 $3\,\dfrac{ounces}{foot}$ to $\dfrac{pounds}{yard}$

Note: For questions 12 and 13, it is necessary to use the following C° to F° (and F° to C°) conversion formulas:

$$F = \left(C \times \tfrac{9}{5}\right) + 32 \quad \text{or} \quad C = (F - 32) \times \tfrac{5}{9}$$

12 95° F to °C

13 55° C to °F

7.9 Measurement Reference Facts

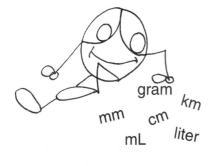

gram
km
mm cm
mL liter

Common Units

Measuring	Common Examples
Distance (linear units)	Meter Inches Feet Kilometers
Area (square units)	Square meters, m^2 Square inches, in^2 Square feet, ft^2
Volume (cubic units)	Cubic meters, m^3 Cubic inches, in^3
Time	Seconds, minutes, hours, years
Weight and Mass	Grams Pounds Tons
Liquid Measures	Liters Ounces Gallons
Temperature	Degrees Celisus, $°C$ Degrees Fahrenheit, $°F$

Metric Prefixes

Prefix	Amount of Basic Unit	Abbreviation
kilo-	1000	k
hecto -	100	h
deca-	10	da
basic unit	1	no prefix
deci-	$\frac{1}{10}$	d
centi-	$\frac{1}{100}$	c
milli-	$\frac{1}{1000}$	m

Most Common Metric Units

	Name	Abbreviation	Real World Size
Length	Kilometer	km	10 minutes of casual walking
	Meter	m	the height of a door knob
	Centimeter	cm	diameter of an AA battery or the length of a thumb-tack
	Millimeter	mm	the thickness of a dime
Weight (mass)	Kilogram	kg	the mass of 1 liter of water or skim milk, 4-6 pieces of fruit, a honeydew melon, or a bag of pasta
	Gram	g	the mass of a paper clip (large) or three medium size marshmallows
	Milligram	mg	an average size aspirin contains 160 milligrams
Capacity	Liter	L	the volume of a large milk carton or large plastic bottle of soda is in liters
	Milliliter	mL	the volume of a large drop of water

MOST COMMON U.S. CUSTOMARY UNITS

	Name	Abbreviation	Conversions
Length	Mile	mi.	12 in = 1 ft. 3 ft = 1 yd. 5280 ft = 1 mi.
	Yard	yd.	
	Foot	ft.	
	Inch	in.	
Weight (mass)	Ton	T.	16 oz = 1 lb. 2000 lb = 1 ton
	Pound	lb.	
	Ounce	oz.	
Capacity	Gallon	gal.	2 pts = 1 qt. 4 qts = 1 gal.
	Quart	qt.	
	Pint	pt.	

INTERSYSTEM CONVERSIONS

	US Customary to Metric	Metric to US Customary
Length	1 in ≈ 2.5 cm l ft ≈ .3 m 1 mi ≈ 1.6 km	1 cm ≈ .4 in. l m ≈ 40 in. 1 km ≈ .62 mi.
Weight (mass)	l oz ≈ 31 g 1 lb ≈ 453 g	l g = .035 oz. 1 kg = 2.2 lb.
Capacity	l qt ≈ .95 L 1 gal ≈ 4.5 L	1 L = 1.1 qts.

TIME

	Name	Abbreviation	Conversions
Time	Year	yr.	60 sec = 1 min. 60 min = 1 hr. 24 hr = 1 d. 28 - 31 d = 1 mo. 12 mo = 1 yr. 365 - 366 d = 1 yr.
	Month	mo.	
	Day	d.	
	Hour	hr.	
	Minute	min.	
	Second	sec.	

TEMPERATURE

	Name	Abbreviation	Conversions	
Temperature	Degrees Celsius	°C	Water Freezes: 0°C = 32°F Water Boils: 100°C = 212°F	
	Degrees Fahrenheit	°F	$F = \frac{9}{5}C + 32$	$C = \frac{5}{9}(F - 32)$

7.10 LONG ANSWER QUESTIONS FOR CHAPTER 7

1 Given angle *NJL*, bisect the angle using only a compass and a straightedge.

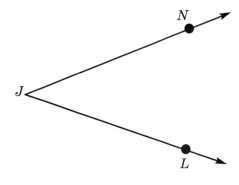

2 Maria's backyard has two trees that are 40 feet apart, as shown in the accompanying diagram. She wants to place lampposts so that the posts are 30 feet from both of the trees.

scale : 1 in. = 20 ft.

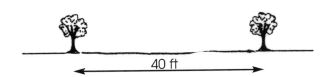

PART A
Using the above diagram, draw a sketch to show where the lampposts could be placed in relation to the trees.

PART B
How many locations for the lampposts are possible?

Answer _____

Explain how you arrived at your answer.

_____

_____

_____

_____

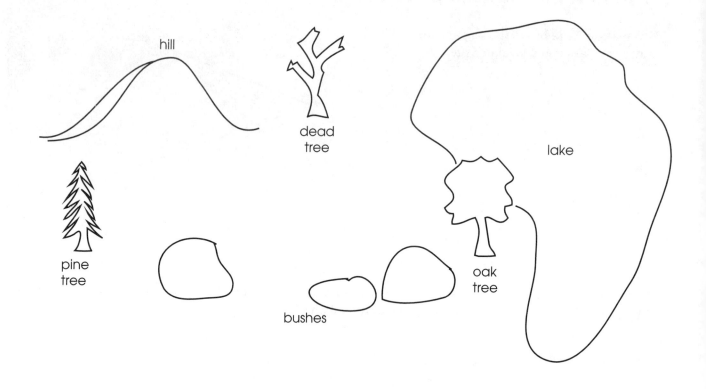

hill

dead
tree

lake

pine
tree

bushes

oak
tree

"The treasure is buried at the intersection of the perpendicular bisector of the line that would connect the pine and oak trees *and* with the angle bisector of the angle formed by connecting the dead tree, pine tree and oak tree in sequence."

3 On the treasure map above, construct the perpendicular bisector and angle bisector according to the directions and mark an **X** to indicate where the treasure is buried.

CHAPTER EIGHT
POLYGONS & CIRCLES

8

You're driving in a foreign country. You don't speak the language. What do the road signs mean?

Traffic symbols are *universal* – they are used throughout the world to mean the same thing. An octagonal shape in red means **STOP**, whether it says **PARE** (Spanish) or **ARRET** (French) or **STOP**. This is just one of the common uses of polygons and circles.

Polygons and circles are also used in building. The Egyptians built the pyramids thousand of years ago based on their knowledge of polygons. Buildings – homes, offices, stores, and factories – all use polygons and circles in their design. Landscapers use them to lay out gardens. Look around: polygons and circles are everywhere!

8.1 POLYGONS

DEFINITIONS

Polygon: a closed figure drawn only with line segments

Regular Polygon: a polygon with all angles equal and sides equal

POLYGON FAMILIES

Name	Triangle	Quadrilateral	Pentagon	Hexagon	Octagon	Decagon
Number of Sides	3	4	5	6	8	10
Example	△	▢	⬠	⬡	⯃	◯

Polygon ❽ Note - A polygon has the same number of interior angles as it does sides.

INTERIOR/EXTERIOR ANGLES

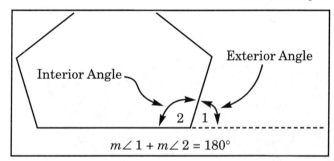

Interior Angle

Exterior Angle

$m\angle 1 + m\angle 2 = 180°$

	Interior Angles	**Exterior Angles**
Sum	$(n-2)(180)$	360
If regular, each angle	$\dfrac{(n-2)(180)}{n}$	$\dfrac{360}{n}$
	n = number of sides	

OUR TURN

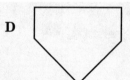

D

Q:

1 Which of the following is not a polygon?

A

B

C

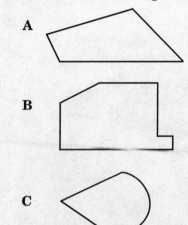

2 If a polygon has seven sides, what is the sum of the interior angles?

A:

1 C

A polygon is a closed figure drawn only with straight lines.

2 900°

Sum of interior angles = $(n-2) \times (180)$

$n = 7$

$= (7-2) \times (180)$

$= 5 \times (180)$

$= 900$

YOUR TURN

1 If each angle of a regular polygon is 135°, how many sides does the polygon have?

   A 5

   B 6

   C 7

   D 8

2 A stop sign, shown in the photo at the right, is what shape?

   F hexagon

   G octagon

   H pentagon

   J decagon

3 If one polygon is randomly selected from the group shown below, what is the probability of selecting a quadrilateral.

   A $\frac{1}{4}$

   B $\frac{1}{2}$

   C $\frac{3}{4}$

   D 1

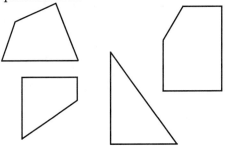

4 What is the sum of the exterior angles of a 24 sided polygon?

   F 360°

   G 500°

   H 1000°

   J 3960°

5 In the accompanying diagram, what is the value of x ?

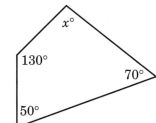

Figure not drawn to scale

   A 110°

   B 130°

   C 150°

   D 170°

6 From one vertex (corner) of an octagon, how many distinct diagonals can be drawn?

   F 2

   G 3

   H 4

   J 5

7 In the accompanying figure, the quadrilateral has been separated into which of the following?

   A two pentagons and a triangle

   B two quadrilaterals and a triangle

   C two triangles and a hexagon

   D two triangles and a quadrilateral

8 The accompanying figure shows a regular pentagon. What is the measure of each interior angle?

   F 90°

   G 100°

   H 108°

   J 128°

9 In the accompanying figures, the two triangles *ABC* and *NJL* overlap to form which of the following shapes?

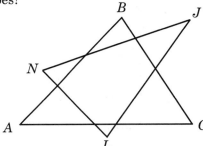

   A triangle

   B quadrilateral

   C pentagon

   D hexagon

10 In a triangle,what is the sum of one interior and its corresponding exterior angle?

   F 180°

   G 200°

   H 300°

   J 360°

8.2 TRIANGLES

CATEGORIZED BY SIDES

(scalene triangle)	Scalene	no equal sides
(isosceles triangle)	Isosceles	at least two equal sides
(equilateral triangle)	Equilateral	three equal sides

❸ Note:
- Equilateral: all sides = ; all angles =
- Each angle is $\frac{180}{3} = 60°$

❸ Note:
Sides vs Angles:
- Across from the largest side of a triangle is the largest angle and vice versa.
- Across from the smallest side of a triangle is the smallest angle and vice versa.

CATEGORIZED BY ANGLES

(acute triangle)	Acute	all acute angles
(right triangle)	Right	one right angle
(obtuse triangle)	Obtuse	one obtuse angle

GENERAL

(triangle ABC)	The sum of the measure of the three angle of a triangle is 180°.	$m\angle A + m\angle B + m\angle C = 180°$
(triangle ABC)	Across from equal angles are equal sides.	if $m\angle A = m\angle C$ then $BC = AB$
(triangle ABC)	Across from equal sides are equal angles.	if $AB = BC$ then $m\angle C = m\angle A$

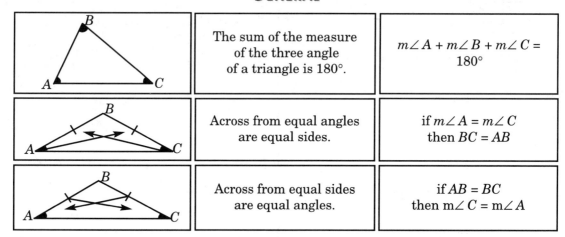

OUR TURN

Q:

1   What is the average value of the angle measures in a triangle?

2   In the figure at the right, which is the longest side?

3   In the accompanying figure, if $NJ = 4$ and $JL = 4$, which two angles must be equal?

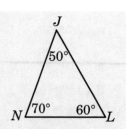

figure not drawn to scale

A:

1   60°

$$\text{Average } = \frac{\text{Sum of the angles}}{\text{Quantity of angles}} = \frac{180°}{3} = 60°$$

2   In a triangle, across (opposite) the largest angle, is the longest side.

3   ∠N and ∠L
   In a triangle, opposite equal sides are equal angles.

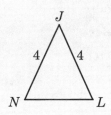

YOUR TURN

1   The accompanying triangle can be categorized as which of the following?

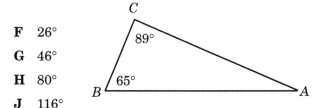

   A   scalene

   B   isosceles

   C   equilateral

   D   right

2   Find the measure of angle A, using the data in the accompanying triangle.

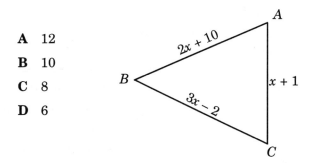

   F   26°

   G   46°

   H   80°

   J   116°

3   In △ ABC, the lengths of the sides are shown in the diagram. If AB ≅ BC, what is the value of x?

   A   12

   B   10

   C   8

   D   6

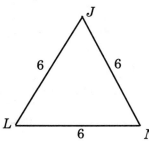

4   In △ NJL, what is the measure of ∠N?

   F   30°

   G   60°

   H   90°

   J   120°

5   What is the measure of an acute angle of an isosceles right triangle?

   A   45°

   B   60°

   C   75°

   D   90°

6   Given △ ABC below, which two sides must be equal in length?

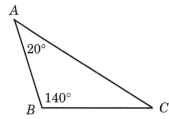

   F $\overline{AB}$ and $\overline{AC}$

   G $\overline{AB}$ and $\overline{BC}$

   H $\overline{AC}$ and $\overline{BC}$

   J $\overline{CB}$ and $\overline{BA}$

   Figure not drawn to scale

7   The three angles of a triangle are represented by 40°, x°, and y° as shown at the right. Which of the following can be used to represent the value of x?

   A   2y + 40

   B   180 – y

   C   140 – y

   D   y + 40

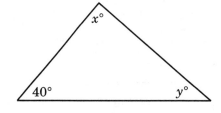

   Figure not drawn to scale

8   The measures of two angles of △ ABC are 57° and 64°, the measures of two angles of △ NJL are 64° and 59°. The two triangles must be which of the following?

   F   isosceles

   G   obtuse

   H   congruent

   J   similar

9 The measures of two angles of triangle *RST* are 42° and 96°. The triangle must be which of the following?

  A scalene

  B isosceles

  C equilateral

  D right

10 What is the sum of the measures of the angles of an acute triangle?

  F 60°

  G 90°

  H 150°

  J 180°

8.3 RIGHT TRIANGLES

PYTHAGOREAN THEOREM

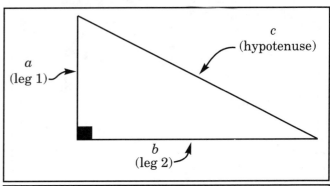

$$(\text{leg 1})^2 + (\text{leg 2})^2 = (\text{hypotenuse})^2$$
$$a^2 + b^2 = c^2$$

* Note - Hypotenuse: the hypotenuse is always the side opposite the right angle.

* Note - Adjacent: adjacent means "next to."

TRIGONOMETRY

❽Trigonometry: The branch of mathematics that deals with the relationships of the sides and angles of triangles.

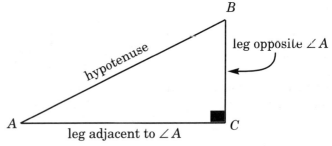

Trigonometric Function	Sine	Cosine	Tangent
Use	Sine of angle *A*	Cosine of angle *A*	Tangent of angle *A*
Abbreviation	sin *A*	cos *A*	tan *A*
Definition	sin *A* = $\dfrac{\text{length of leg } \textbf{Opposite} \angle A}{\text{length of } \textbf{Hypotenuse}}$	cos *A* = $\dfrac{\text{length of leg } \textbf{Adjacent to} \angle A}{\text{length of } \textbf{Hypotenuse}}$	tan *A* = $\dfrac{\text{length of leg } \textbf{Opposite} \angle A}{\text{length of leg } \textbf{Adjacent to} \angle A}$
Short Form	sin *A* = $\dfrac{\textbf{Opposite}}{\textbf{Hypotenuse}}$	cos *A* = $\dfrac{\textbf{Adjacent}}{\textbf{Hypotenuse}}$	tan *A* = $\dfrac{\textbf{Opposite}}{\textbf{Adjacent}}$
Mnemonic	SOH	CAH	TOA

❽ A table of trigonometric values is provided in the back of this book.

OUR TURN

Q:

1 A 100 ft. ladder is placed 60 ft. from a wall. How far up the wall will the ladder reach?

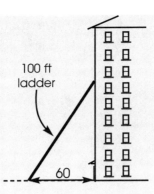

100 ft ladder

60

2 Norm walks along the perimeter of a rectangular park and Dawn takes the shortcut along the diagonal. How much shorter is Dawn's walk going from A to B?

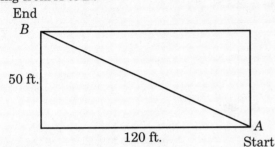

End
B

50 ft.

120 ft.

A
Start

A:

1 80 ft.

$$x^2 + 60^2 = 100^2$$
$$x^2 + 3600 = 10000$$
$$x^2 = 6400$$

$$x = \sqrt{6400}$$
$$x = 80$$

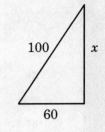

100   x

60

2 40 ft. shorter
Norm's walk 50 + 120 = 170 ft.
Dawn's walk:

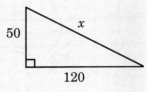

50   x

120

$$x^2 = 50^2 + 120^2$$
$$x^2 = 2500 + 14400$$
$$x^2 = 16900$$

$$x = \sqrt{16900}$$
$$x = 130$$

170 ft. − 130 ft. = 40 ft. shorter

YOUR TURN

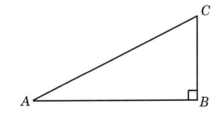

C

A   B

Figure not drawn to Scale

1 In the figure above, $AB = 6$ and $BC = 8$. Find the length of AC.

A 10

B 12

C 14

D 16

2 From a point 8 ft. from a tree it is a 65° angle to the top of the tree (diagram below). Find the height of the tree to the nearest foot.

F 3 ft.

G 7 ft.

H 14 ft.

J 17 ft.

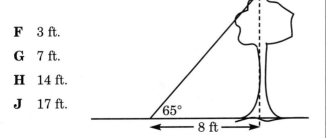

65°

8 ft

3 A ramp to the back of a truck is at a 15° angle and rises 3 ft. to line up with the truck's floor (see diagram below). How long is the ramp to the nearest foot?

15°
3

Figure not drawn to scale

A 11 ft.

B 12 ft.

C 14 ft.

D 15 ft.

4 The length of a rectangle is 10. The diagonal makes a 40° angle with the length. Find the length of the diagonal to the nearest integer (see diagram below).

F 8

G 12

H 13

J 16

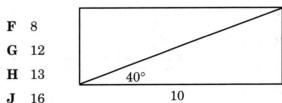

Figure not drawn to scale

40°

10

5 Triangle ABC is shown in the accompanying diagram. Which one of the following sets represents $\sin A$ and $\tan B$ respectively?

A $\{\frac{8}{15}, \frac{8}{17}\}$

B $\{\frac{15}{8}, \frac{15}{17}\}$

C $\{\frac{8}{17}, \frac{15}{17}\}$

D $\{\frac{8}{17}, \frac{15}{8}\}$

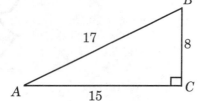

Figure not drawn to scale

6 To the nearest integer, how long is the diagonal of a square with side 12?

F 14

G 15

H 16

J 17

7 A car travels 5 miles east and then 12 miles north. How far is it from the starting point? (See accompanying diagram.)

A 12 mi.

B 13 mi.

C 14 mi.

D 15 mi.

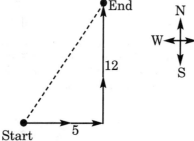

Figure not drawn to scale

8 Two legs of a right triangle are 8 and 13. If x represents the length of the hypotenuse, which equation can be used to find the value of x?

F $8^2 + 13^2 = x^2$

G $8^2 + x^2 = 13^2$

H $x^2 + 13^2 = 8^2$

J $8^2 + 13^2 = x$

9 In trapezoid $ABCD$, what is the height "h" to the nearest tenth? (See accompanying diagram.)

A 4.2

B 4.4

C 4.6

D 4.8

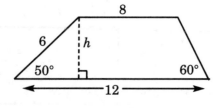

Figure not drawn to scale

10 A wall is supported by a brace 10 feet long as shown in the accompanying diagram. If one end of the brace is placed 6 feet from the base of the wall, how many feet up the wall does the brace reach?

F 6 ft

G 7 ft.

H 8 ft.

J 9 ft.

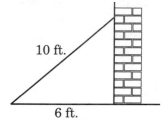

Figure not drawn to scale

11 Use the information in the diagram below to find the measure of angle A.

A 30°

B 45°

C 60°

D 90°

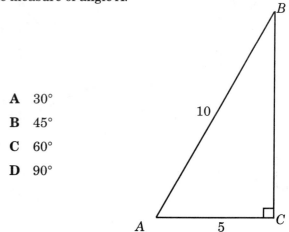

Figure not drawn to scale

12 Which statement regarding the accompanying diagram is true?

F $\sin 53° = \frac{8}{10}$

G $8^2 - 6^2 = 10^2$

H $\tan 37° = \frac{8}{10}$

J $\cos 37° = \frac{6}{10}$

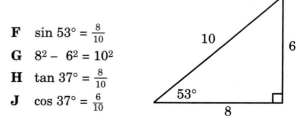

Figure not drawn to scale

8.4 QUADRILATERALS

❽ Symbol – The arrows indicate parallel sides.

❽ Trapezoid – The non-parallel sides are called legs.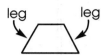

FAMILY MEMBERS

Pictures	Types	Descriptions
	Quadrilaterals	A four sided polygon ——————————— The sum of the interior angles is 360°
Parallelogram	Parallelogram	a quadrilateral with two pairs of parallel sides
Rectangle	Rectangle	a parallelogram with a right angle
Rhombus	Rhombus	a parallelogram with all four sides equal
Square	Square	both a rectangle and a rhombus with all sides and angles equal
Trapezoid	Trapezoid	a quadrilateral with only one pair of parallel sides
Isosceles Trapezoid	Isosceles Trapezoid	a trapezoid with two equal legs
Right Trapezoid	Right Trapezoid	a trapezoid with two right angles

Properties

Name	Picture	Sides	Angles	Diagonals	Area	Special Area Formulas
General Parallelogram	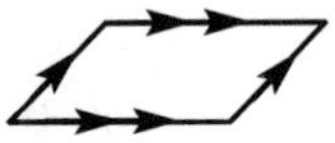	Opposite sides equal 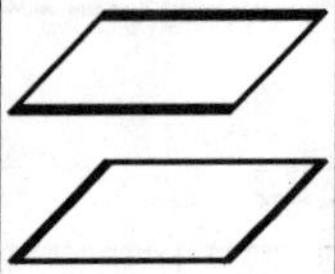	Opposite angles equal 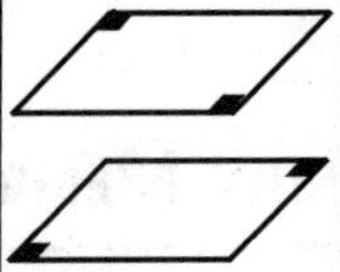	Not equal	$A = bh$ 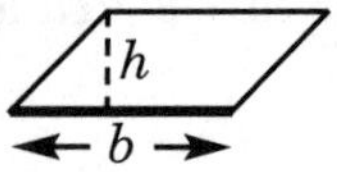	---
Rhombus	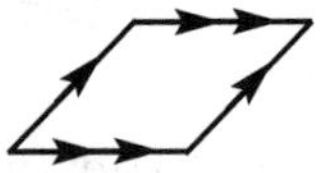	All sides equal 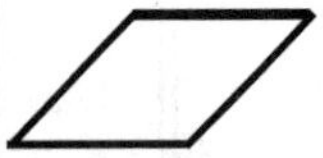	Opposite angle equal 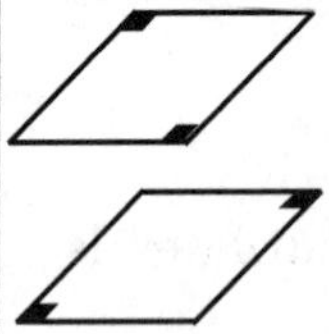	Not equal	$A = bh$ 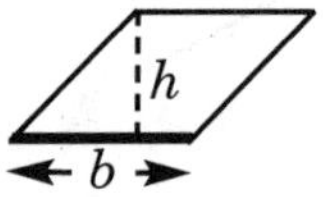	$A = \frac{d_1 d_2}{2}$ 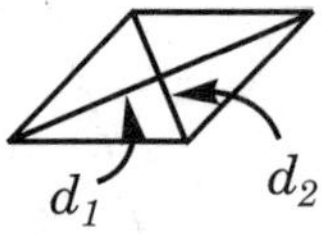
Rectangle	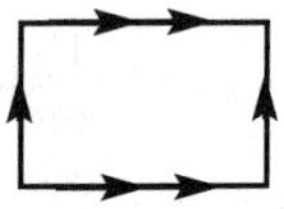	Opposite sides equal 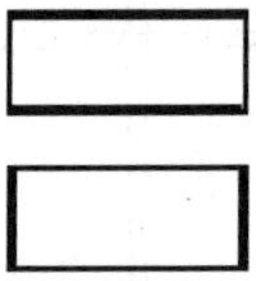	All angles equal 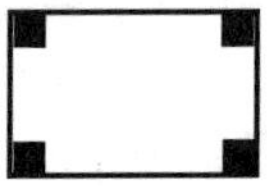	Diagonals are equal 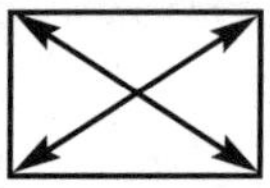	$A = bh$ 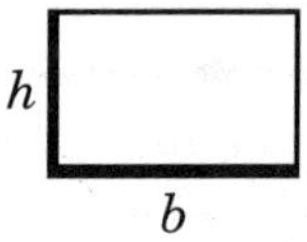	$A = lw$ 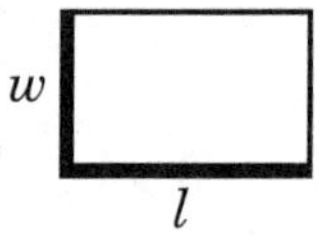
Square	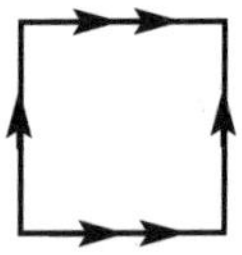	All sides equal	All angles equal	Diagonals are equal 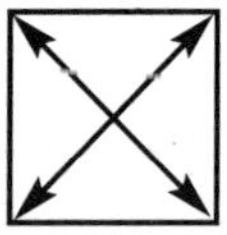	$A = bh$ 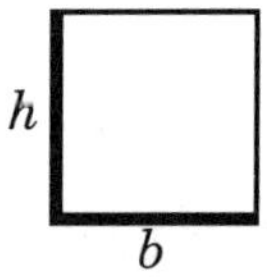	$A = s^2$ 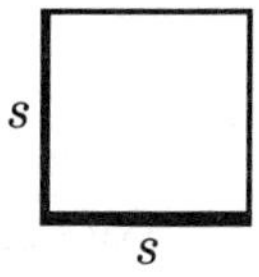
General Trapezoid	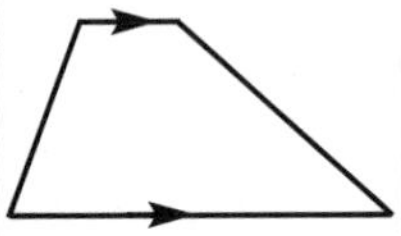	No sides equal	No angles equal	Not equal	$A = \frac{1}{2}h(b_1 + b_2)$ 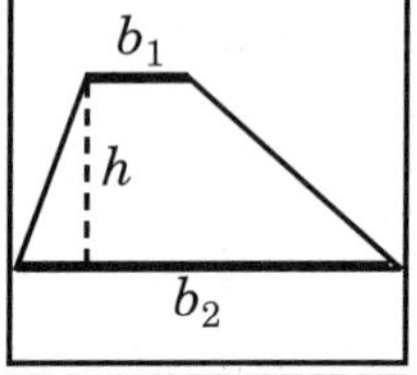	
Isosceles Trapezoid	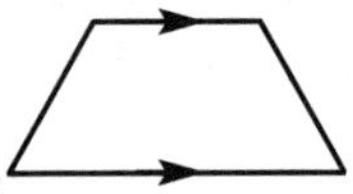	Legs are equal 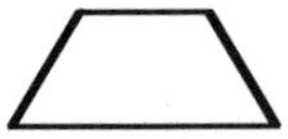	Base angles are equal 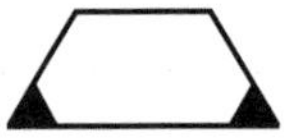	Diagonals are equal 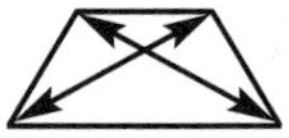	$A = \frac{1}{2}h(b_1 + b_2)$ 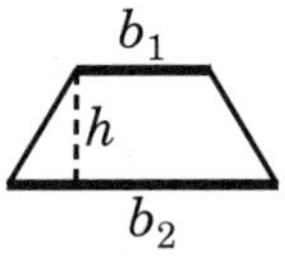	
Right Trapezoid	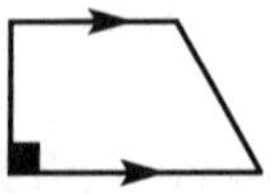	No sides equal	Two angles equal 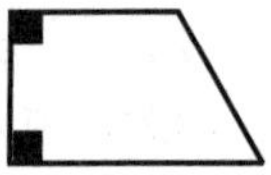	Not equal	$A = \frac{1}{2}h(b_1 + b_2)$ 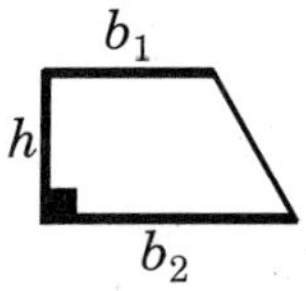	

Legend

- ***A*** is area
- ***b*** is base
- ***h*** is height
- ***d*** is diagonal
- ***l*** is length
- ***s*** is side
- ***w*** is width

OUR TURN

Q:

1 A rhombus is sometimes, always, or never a rectangle.

2 If the opposite sides of a parallelogram are represented by $4x - 17$ and $3x - 9$, what is the value of x?

3 The diagonals of an isosceles trapezoid are which of the following?

  A parallel

  B equal

  C unequal

  D shorter than either base

A:

1 Sometimes a rhombus is a rectangle if it is a square.

2 The opposite sides of a parallelogram are equal.

$$4x - 17 = 3x - 9$$
$$x - 17 = -9 \quad \text{(subtract } 3x)$$
$$x = 8 \quad \text{(add 17)}$$

3 B

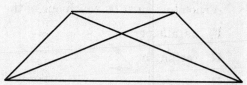

The diagonals of an isosceles trapezoid are always equal in length.

YOUR TURN

1 If the length of a rectangle is 12 cm and the length of the diagonal is 13 cm, what is the width of the rectangle?

  A 1 cm

  B 3 cm

  C 5 cm

  D 7 cm

2 The triangle formed by a diagonal of a square and 2 of its adjacent sides is:

  F equilateral

  G acute and scalene

  H obtuse and isosceles

  J right and isosceles

3 A right trapezoid has how many right angles?

  A 1

  B 2

  C 3

  D 4

4 The side of a square is 12. To the nearest integer, what is the length of its diagonal?

  F 17

  G 18

  H 19

  J 20

5 The length of a rectangle is 15 and the angle formed between the length and the diagonal is 60° (see diagram below). What is the length of the diagonal?

  A 20

  B 25

  C 30

  D 35

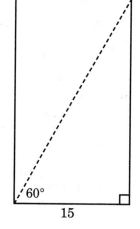

Figure not drawn to scale

6 In the diagram below, right trapezoid *ABCD* has the dimensions shown. What is the length of diagonal *BD*?

  F 10

  G 12

  H 14

  J 16

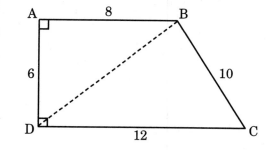

Figure not drawn to scale

7 Two adjacent sides of a rhombus are represented by $7x - 22$ and $4x + 20$. What is the value of x?

A 8

B 10

C 12

D 14

8 A rhombus must be which one of the following?

F parallelogram

G rectangle

H square

J trapezoid

9 In the figure below, what is the value of x?

A 160°

B 141°

C 131°

D 121°

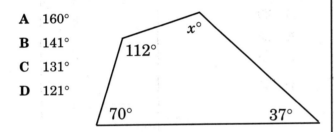

Figure not drawn to scale

10 In the diagram below, the measure of angle D is 50°. What is the measure of angle C?

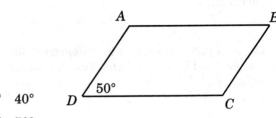

Figure not drawn to scale

F 40°

G 50°

H 130°

J 140°

11 In the diagram below, trapezoid ABCD is cut by intersecting line l. If the measure of angle 1 is 37°, what is the measure of angle 5?

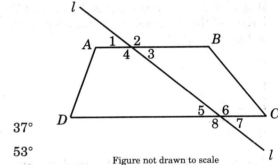

Figure not drawn to scale

A 37°

B 53°

C 74°

D 143°

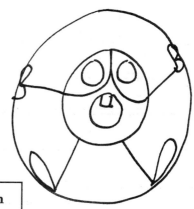

PARTS OF A CIRCLE

Picture	Name	Definition
	Center	the middle of the circle
	Circumference	the distance around the circle
	Radius (*r*)	the distance from the center to the circumference
	Diameter (*d*)	the distance from circumference to circumference, through the center
	Chord	the distance from circumference to circumference, through the circle
	Arc	the distance or degree measure from one part on the circumference to another, along the circumference
	Area of a circle	the space inside the circle

CIRCLE FACTS

A circle has 360° of arc

diameter formula: $d = 2r$

circumference formula: $C = 2\pi r$ or $C = \pi d$

area formula: $A = \pi r^2$

Every time a wheel turns around once, it travels a distance equal to its circumference.

$\leftarrow$ distance = $C = 2\pi r$ $\rightarrow$
$\leftarrow$ 1 rotation of the wheel $\rightarrow$

Legend	**Pi**
r = radius d = diameter C = circumference A = area	π is the Greek letter pi ———————————————— π is approximately equal to 3.14 or $\frac{22}{7}$

OUR TURN

Q:

1   A wheel with a radius of 4 rotates five times. To the nearest integer, how far does it travel ? (Use π = 3.14)

2   What is the degree measure between two consecutive numbers on a clock?

3   A semicircle is what part of a circle?

A:

1   126
Each turn a wheel travels $2\pi r = 2 \times (3.14) \times (4)$
$\qquad\qquad\qquad = 25.12$
In 5 turns, it travels: $5 \times (25.12) = 125.6$

2   30° Between the numbers there are 12 equal spaces around the clock.

$\dfrac{360°}{12} = 30°$

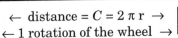

3   $\frac{1}{2}$

A semicircle is half of a circle.

YOUR TURN

1   Of the following, which is the best fractional estimate of π ?

    A $\frac{27}{2}$

    B $\frac{22}{5}$

    C $\frac{27}{7}$

    D $\frac{22}{7}$

2   If the length of the circumference of a circle is divided by the length of the circle's diameter, the result is which of the following?

    F   5.00

    G   3.14

    H   1.75

    J   2.00

3 What is the degree measure of the smaller angle formed by the hands of a clock at 7:00

A   120°

B   150°

C   180°

D   210°

4 If the radius of a circle is doubled, then what happens to the diameter?

F   it is also doubled

G   it is multiplied by 4

H   it is multiplied by 8

J   it is halved

5 If two radii of a circle are separated by a 30° angle and the points where the radii intersect the circumference are connected, what type of triangle is formed?

A   right triangle

B   equilateral triangle

C   isosceles triangle

D   scalene triangle

6 In the diagram below, the arcs have the degree measures: x, $2x$, $5x - 30$, and $3x - 10$ as indicated in the drawing. What is the value of x?

F   10

G   20

H   30

J   40

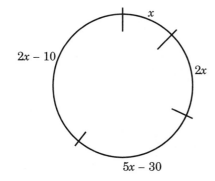

Figure not drawn to scale

7 A spinner is marked with degrees measures as shown in the diagram below. What is the probability of landing in the area marked C?

A   90°

B   80°

C   60°

D   50°

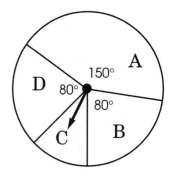

8 The smaller angle formed by the hands of clock is 120° at which one of the following times?

F   2:00

G   4:00

H   6:00

J   10:00

9 In the accompanying diagram, how many radii are shown?

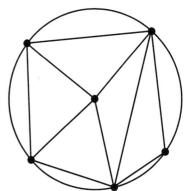

A   2

B   3

C   4

D   5

10 What is another name for the longest chord in a circle?

F   radius

G   diameter

H   diagonal

J   circumference

1   Given isosceles triangle *NJL* as shown in the accompanying
diagram (the degree measures are shown in the diagram):

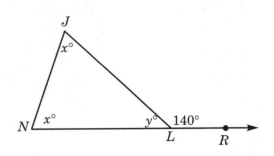

Figure not drawn to scale

PART A

Which sides of the isosceles triangle *NJL* are equal?

Answer: Side _____ and Side _____

Explain how you arrived at your answer.

_____

_____

_____

_____

_____

_____

PART B

If the measure of angle *JLR* is 140°, what is the value of x and what is the value of y?

Show your work.

Answer: $x =$ _____

$y =$ _____

2 The figure to the right shows three squares. The side of each square is twice the size of the square to its left. The perimeter of square II is 16.

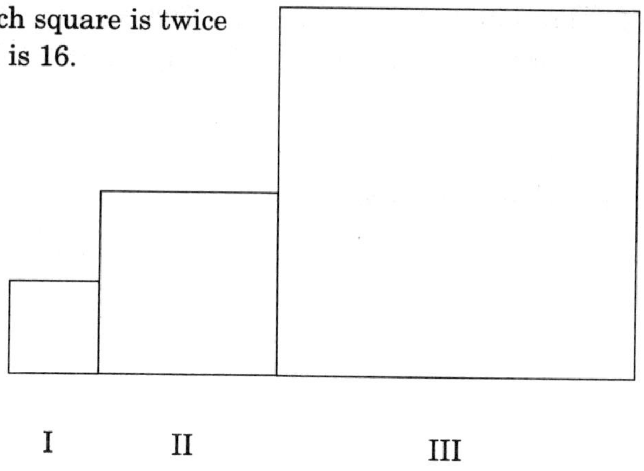

What are the lengths of the sides of square I, square II and square III?

Show your work.

I   II   III

Length of a side of square I   = _____

Length of a side of square II = _____

Length of a side of square III = _____

3 From a point on the ground, 700 ft from the base of a building, the angle of elevation to the top of the antenna on the roof of the building is 30° (see diagram below).

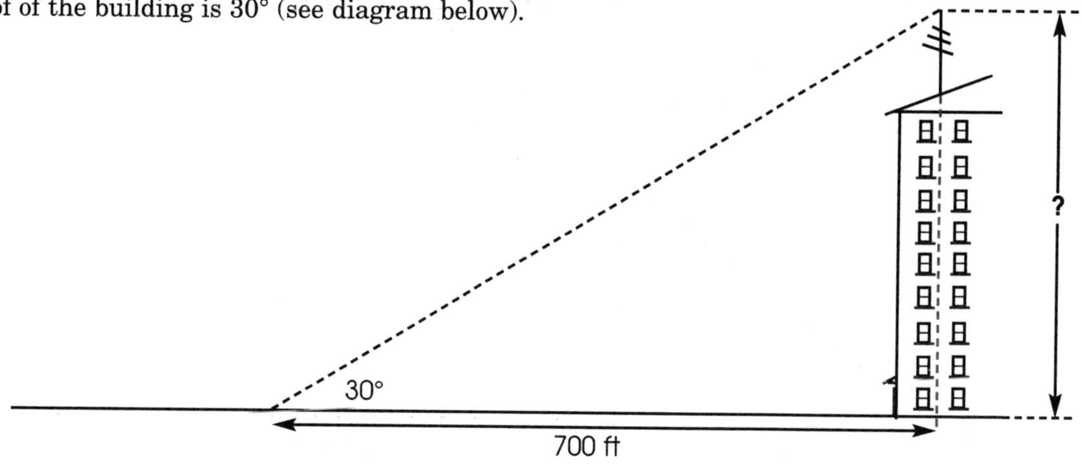

30°

700 ft

Figure not drawn to scale

PART A

To the nearest foot, how high is the top of the antenna from the ground? Show all of your work.

Answer: _____ feet

PART B

One foot is equivalent to .3 meters. How high, to the nearest meter, is the top of the antenna from the ground? Show all of your work.

Answer: _____ meters

4 Barry and Janis travel 25 yards due east and then 20 yards due north (see the diagram below). To the nearest yard, how far are they from where they started?

Show all of your work.

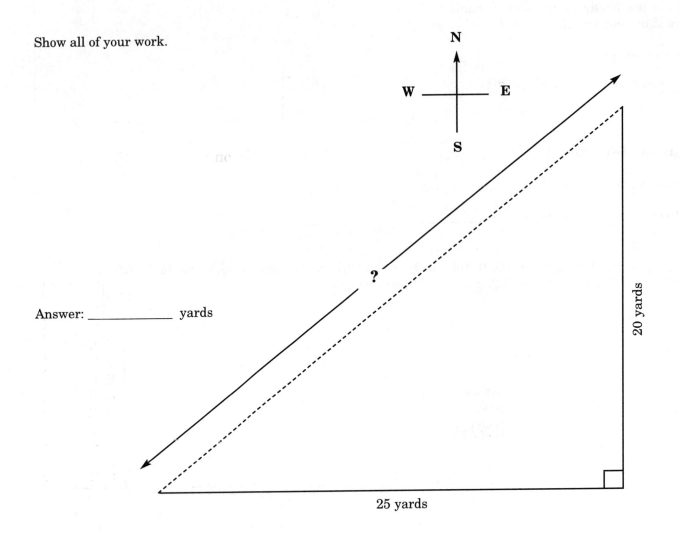

Answer: _____ yards

CHAPTER NINE
PERIMETER, AREA, & VOLUME

9

How many cans of paint are required to paint the front of a house? How many square yards of carpet are needed to cover a floor? How many cups of juice can be filled by the contents of my thermos? How many miles do I run if I jog three laps on the school track?

These are questions of:

- Perimeter – the distance around the outside of a shape
- Area – the space inside a flat shape
- Volume – the space inside a three-dimensional object

For example, Juanita wants to redo her room. She has a budget and needs to figure out what she can afford to do. Should she use wallpaper or paint on the walls? Should she re-carpet the room or will she leave the floors bare? What size dresser will fit in an appropriate space? Or, suppose Joan has a 12 inch by 8 inch photo which she will mat and frame. If the mat is 1 inch on each side and the oak frame is 2 inches on each side, how much space will be needed to hang the framed picture?

These are all questions related to perimeter, area and volume.

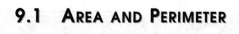

9.1 AREA AND PERIMETER

BASIC TERMINOLOGY

Pictorial	Name	Description	Units
	Perimeter	the distance around the figure	linear units ─────────── centimeters, inches, feet, miles cm, in., ft., mi.
	Area	the space enclosed in the figure	square units ─────────── square feet, square millimeters ft.^{2}, mm^2

❽ Circumference - the perimeter of a circle is called the circumference

PERIMETER FORMULAS

Pictorial	Shape	Perimeter Formula
	Polygon	add up the lengths of the sides around the figure
	Circle	$C = 2\,\pi\,r$ or $C = \pi\,d$

C = circumference
r = radius
d = diameter
π = 3.14 or $\frac{22}{7}$

Legend

A is area	**r** is radius
b is base	**s** is side
h is height	**w** is width
l is length	

AREA FORMULAS

	Shape	Formula
	Triangle	$A = \dfrac{bh}{2}$
	Rectangle	$A = bh$ or $A = lw$
	Parallelogram	$A = bh$
	Rhombus	$A = bh$
	Square	$A = bh$ or $A = s^2$
	Trapezoid	$\frac{1}{2} h(b_1 + b_2)$
	Circle	$A = \pi r^2$

OUR TURN

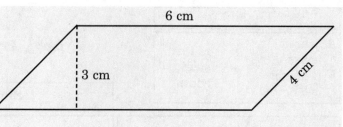

6 cm

3 cm

4 cm

Q:

1 Find the perimeter and area of the accompanying parallelogram.

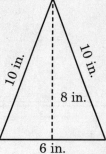

10 in.   10 in.

8 in.

6 in.

2 Find the perimeter and area of the accompanying triangle.

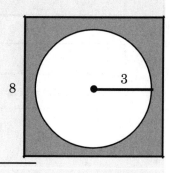

3

8

3 Find the shaded area between the circle and the square (all measurements are in cm). (Use $\pi = 3.14$)

A:

1 $P = 20$ cm
  $A = 18$ cm^2

Perimeter is the sum of the lengths of the sides.
$$4 + 6 + 4 + 6 = 20$$

Area = base × height
    = 6 × 3
    = 18

2 $P = 26$ in.
  $A = 24$ in.^{2}

Perimeter is the sum of the lengths of the sides.
  $P = 10 + 10 + 6 = 26$

$A = \frac{1}{2}$ × (base) × (height) = $\frac{1}{2}$ × (6) × (8) = 24

3 35.74 cm^2

The shaded area is the area of the square, less the area of the circle.

s

s

Area of square = s^2 = 8^2 = 64

Area of circle = $\pi r^2 = \pi$ × (3)^2
    = 9 π
    = 9 × (3.14)
    = 28.26

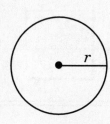

r

The shaded area =
64 − 28.26 = 35.74

YOUR TURN

1 Find the perimeter and area of the accompanying rectangle.

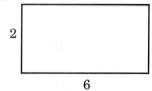

2

6

2 Find the perimeter and area of the accompanying triangle.

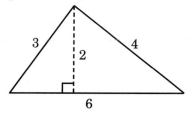

3   2   4

6

3 Find the perimeter and area of the accompanying parallelogram.

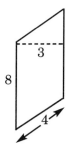

4 Find the perimeter and area of the accompanying square.

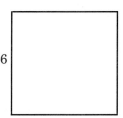

5 Find the perimeter and area of the accompanying trapezoid.

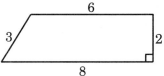

6 Find the circumference and area of the accompanying circle. (Use $\pi = \frac{22}{7}$)

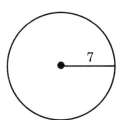

7 In the accompanying figure, find the shaded area to the nearest integer. (Use $\pi = 3.14$)

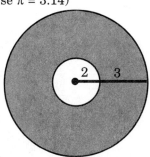

8 Find the shaded area between the circle and the square to the nearest tenth. (Use $\pi = 3.14$)

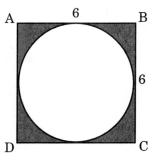

9 Find the area of the hexagon below. (All intersection are right angles.)

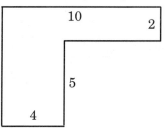

10 Find the perimeter of the figure below. (All intersections are right angles.)

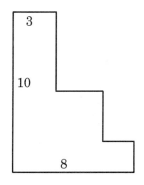

11 Find the perimeter of the figure below. (All intersections are right angles.)

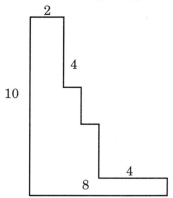

12 The figure at right shows the 16th hole of a miniature golf course. Using the given dimensions in feet and all intersections are right angles, find the enclosed area.

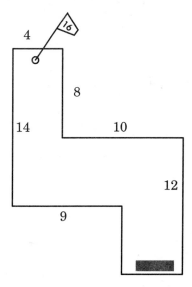

13 In the figure below, all intersections are at right angles. Find the shaded area.

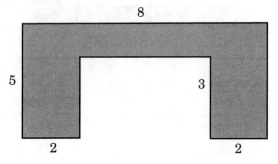

14 A hockey rink is formed by 2 semicircular areas adjacent to a rectangular area as shown below. To the nearest tenth, what is the perimeter of the rink? (Use $\pi = 3.14$)

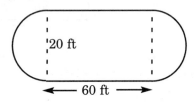

20 ft

60 ft

15 Four identical triangles are cut from the corners of a 5 x 9 rectangle as shown. What is the area of the shaded portion?

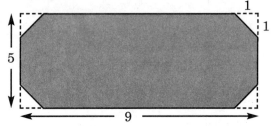

16 Find the area and perimeter of rhombus *ABCD* shown below.

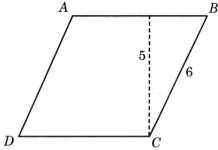

17 Find the perimeter and area of right triangle *NJL* shown below.

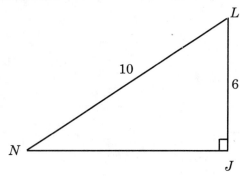

18 Find the area, to the nearest tenth, of triangle *NJL* shown below.

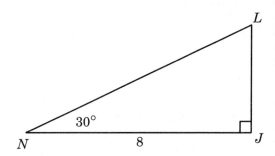

19 The figure below consists of a square and four identical circles. To the nearest tenth, find the shaded area. (Use $\pi = 3.14$)

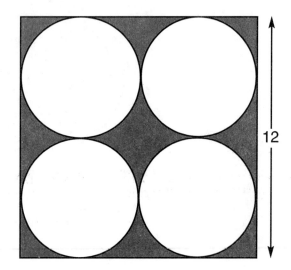

12

9.2 THREE DIMENSIONAL OR SPACE FIGURES

THREE DIMENSIONAL FIGURE BASICS

Pictorial	Shape	Description
bases / lateral face	Prism	Has two parallel and congruent bases. ──────── Lateral faces are parallelograms. ──────── Named for the shape of its base.
lateral face / base	Pyramid	Has one base. ──────── Lateral faces are triangles. ──────── Named for the shape of its base.
bases / lateral face	Cylinder	Has two parallel and congruent circular bases.
lateral face / base	Cone	Has one circular base.
(sphere)	Sphere	No faces, edges, or vertices and all points on the surface are the same distance from the center.

OUR TURN

Q: Identify the following shapes as precisely as possible.

1 Wedge of Cake

2 Pencil

3 Egyptian Pyramid

A:

1 Triangular Prism

2 Hexagonal Prism

3 Square Pyramid

YOUR TURN

Identify each of the following shapes as precisely as possible.

1 Cheese

2 Earth

3 Can

4 Dice

5 Basketball

6 Stack of Dimes

7 Oatmeal Container

8 Flour Box

9 Construction Warning Marker

10 Nut

11 Barn

12 Cracker Box

9.3 SURFACE AREA/VOLUME

BASIC TERMINOLOGY

Pictorial	Shape	Description	Units
	Net	pattern that can be folded into a three dimensional figure	——
	Surface Area	the sum of all the areas of the outside surface	Square units — in.², square inches cm², square centimeters
the space inside	Volume	total amount of space inside a three dimensional figure	Cubic units — in.³, cubic inches cm³, cubic centimeters

VOLUME AND TOTAL SURFACE AREA

Pictorial	Name	Volume	Total Surface Area
	Cylinder	$\pi r^2 h$	$2\pi r^2 + 2\pi rh$
	Cone	$\frac{1}{3}\pi r^2 h$	$\pi r^2 + \pi rl$
	Sphere	$\frac{4}{3}\pi r^3$	$4\pi r^2$
	Prism	Bh	$2B + ph$
	Pyramid	$\frac{1}{3}Bh$	$B + \frac{1}{2}pl$
	Cube	e^3	$6e^2$

OUR TURN

Q:

1 Draw a possible net for a square pyramid.

2 Find the total surface area and volume of the cone shown below. (Use $\pi = 3.14$.)

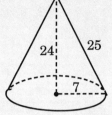

3 Find the total surface area and volume of a ball whose radius is 3 inches. (Use $\pi = 3.14$.)

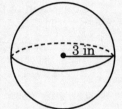

A:

1

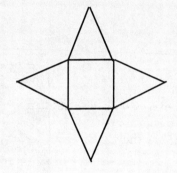

2 Surface Area = 703.36
Volume = 3692.64

The total surface area of a cone is

$\pi r^2 + \pi r l$

$r = 7$, $l = 25$, and $h = 24$

Total S.A. = $(3.14) \times (7)^2 + (3.14) \times (7) \times (25)$

= 703.36

$V = \pi r^2 h$

= $(3.14) \times (7)^2 \times (24)$

= 3692.64

3 Surface Area = 113.04 in^2
Volume = 113.04 in^3

Given: $r = 3$

S.A. = $4\pi r^2$

= $4 \times (3.14) \times (3)^2 = 113.04$

$V = \frac{4}{3}\pi r^3 = \frac{4}{3} \times (3.14) \times (3)^3 = 113.04$

YOUR TURN

Identify the space figure formed by the given net.

1

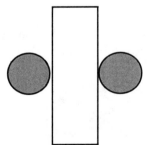

2

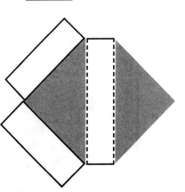

3

4

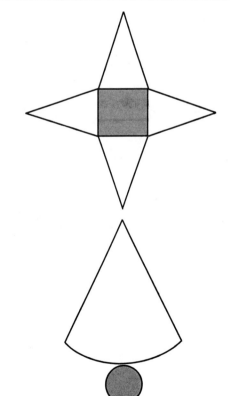

5

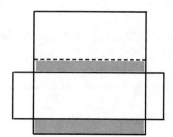

Find the total surface area and volume of each of the following space figures. (Use π = 3.14.) Round your answer to the nearest integer.

6 Cube:

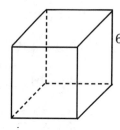

7 Sphere:

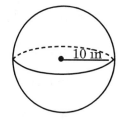

8 Triangular Prism:

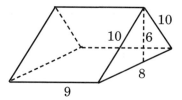

9 Cylinder:

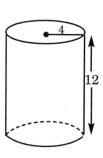

10 Cone:

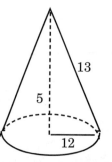

11 Find the volume of the square pyramid.

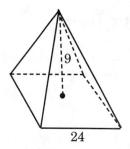

12 A rectangular prism has dimensions of 2, 8, and 2x – 1. Which of the following represents an expression of the volume?

A 2 + 8 + (2x – 1)

B 12x – 1

C 2 (8) (2x – 1)

D 10 (2x – 1)

13 A closed cylindrical can of balls has a diameter of 4 inches. If the can contains 3 balls stacked so that they touch the top and bottom inside covers of the can as shown, what is the volume of space in the can not filled by balls? (Use π = 3.14)

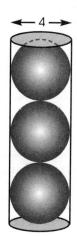

If the volume of each cube = 1, what is the volume of each of the following figures?

14

Figures not drawn to scale

15

16

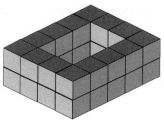

Figure not drawn to scale

17

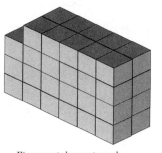

Figure not drawn to scale

9.4 LONG ANSWER QUESTIONS FOR CHAPTER 9

1   Two plans for a new vegetable garden are being considered. Joan's plan is a rectangle whose dimensions are 12 feet by 6 feet. Norm's plan is a circular garden whose radius is 5 feet.

PART A

Which garden plan, Joan's or Norm's, has the *most* space for planting? (Use $\pi = 3.14$). Show all of your work.

Answer _____

PART B

Which garden design requires the *least* amount of fencing to enclose the garden? (Use $\pi = 3.14$). Show all of your work.

Answer _____

2   Each time the wheel of a bicycle rotates once, it travels a distance equal to one circumference.

PART A

If the diameter of each wheel is 21 inches, what is the length of the wheel's circumference to the nearest inch? (Use $\pi = 3.14$). Show all of your work.

Answer _____ inches

PART B

How far does the bicycle travel if the wheel rotates 120 times? Show all of your work.

Answer _____ inches

PART C

If the bicycle traveled a distance of 132 feet, how many times did the wheel turn around? Show all of your work.

Answer _____

3 In the accompanying figure, *ACDH* and *BCEF* are rectangles. $AH = 2, GH = 3, GF = 4, FE = 5$

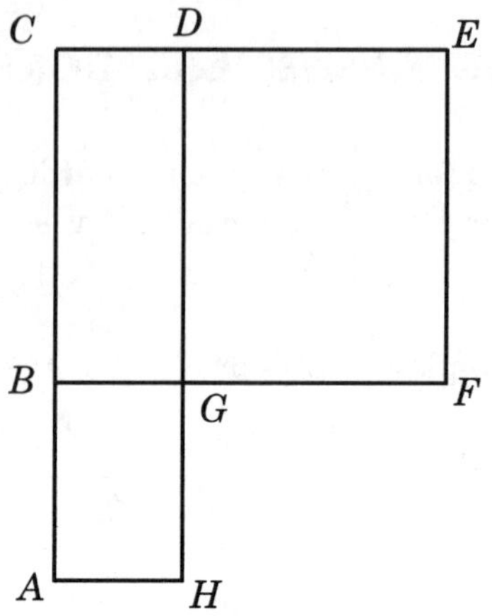

Figure not drawn to scale

PART A

What is the perimeter of hexagon *ACEFGH*?
Show all of your work.

Answer _____

PART B

Construct a diagonal line between *A* and *G*.
Question: The length of the diagonal *AG* is between which two consecutive integers? Show all of your work.

Answer _____

PART C

To the nearest integer, the area of rectangle *CBGD* is what percent of the area of hexagon *ACEFGH*? Show all of your work.

Answer _____ %

CHAPTER TEN
GRAPHS & COORDINATES

10

You are planning a trip and want to locate a town or a road on a map. Road maps are designed with coordinate grids, The index might say something like **K8**. This means: Go to where the grid line **K** crosses the grid line **8**. At the intersection of **K** and **8**, the town or road will be found.

Here are two more examples on a computer:

- When a computer technician wants to isolate non-functioning pixels on a monitor screen, she must describe the position using a grid-location formula.

- Hae Jin and her mother want to go to a local ball game for Hae Jin's birthday.

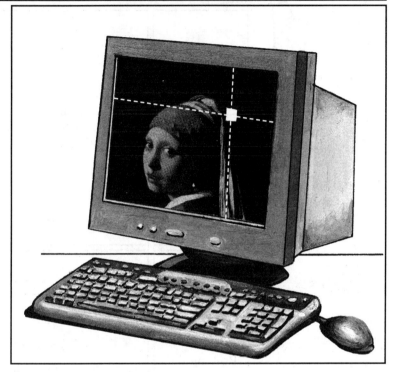

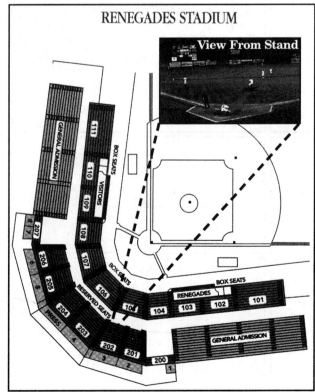

RENEGADES STADIUM

View From Stand

The box office provides a stadium plan of the seats. In what section would Hae Jin sit to be just behind the home team's dugout?

An example of the use of functions is:

You have $100 saved. Each week you expect to add an $3 additional to your saved money. How much will you have in 52 weeks? This relationship can be graphed and you can watch your money grow. We can graph the money we have (*y*-axis) against the number of weeks (*x*-axis).

In math, we graph lines and other functions on an *x-y* coordinate grid. This chapter explains the graphical relationships of equations and inequalities.

TERMINOLOGY

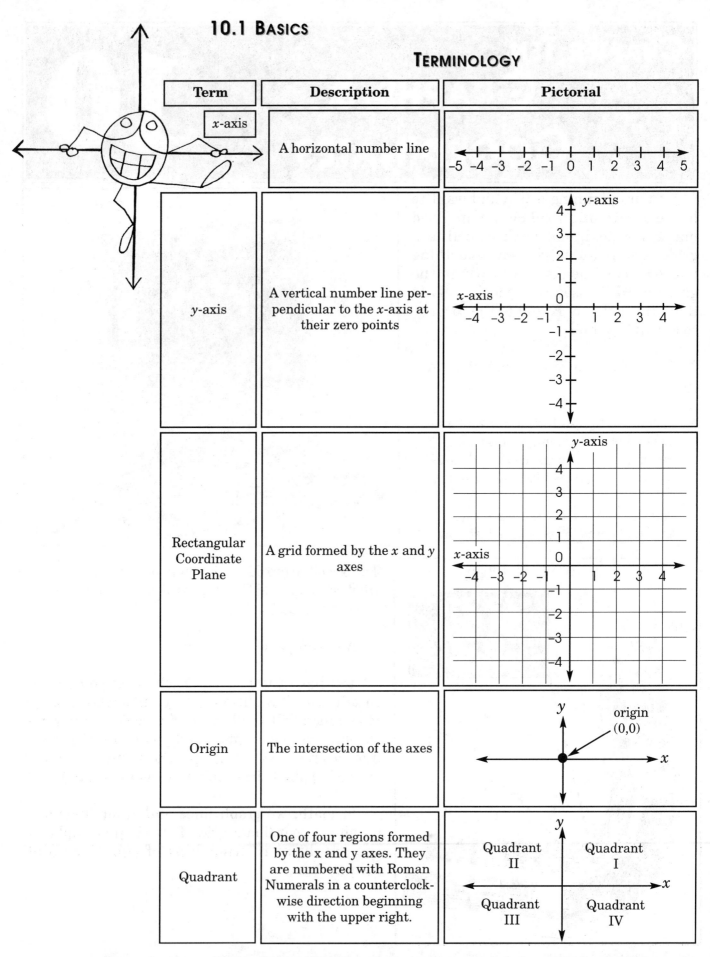

Term	Description	Pictorial
x-axis	A horizontal number line	← −5 −4 −3 −2 −1 0 1 2 3 4 5 →
y-axis	A vertical number line perpendicular to the x-axis at their zero points	(coordinate plane showing y-axis and x-axis)
Rectangular Coordinate Plane	A grid formed by the x and y axes	(gridded coordinate plane showing y-axis and x-axis)
Origin	The intersection of the axes	origin (0,0)
Quadrant	One of four regions formed by the x and y axes. They are numbered with Roman Numerals in a counterclockwise direction beginning with the upper right.	Quadrant II, Quadrant I, Quadrant III, Quadrant IV

Ordered Pair	An ordered pair in reference to the rectangular coordinate plane is written as: (*x*-coordinate, *y*-coordinate)
x-coordinate *y*-coordinate	The directed number of horizontal units from 0 The directed number of vertical units from 0
The point (x, y)	Located at the intersection of the indicated *x*-coordinate and *y*-coordinate values

ALL-IN-ONE TERMINOLOGY

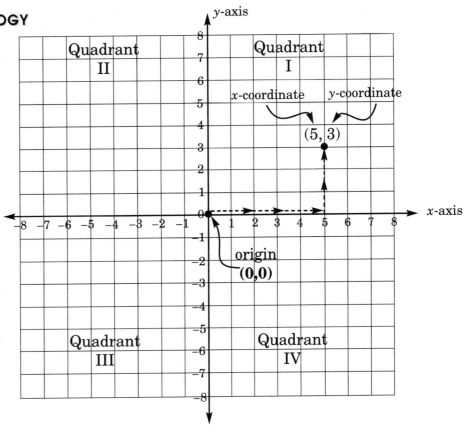

OUR TURN

Q:

1 In which quadrant is the point (– 3, 2) ?

A:

1 Quadrant II

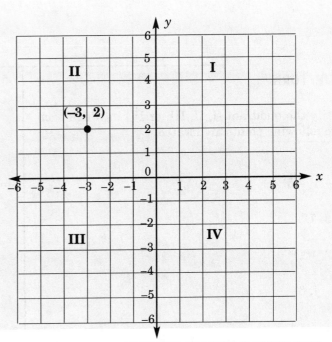

2 Locate the points $A(2, 5)$, $B(6, 5)$, and $C(3, -2)$. Draw AB and BC. What should be the coordinates of point D, such that $ABCD$ is a parallelogram?

A:

2 $(-1, -2)$

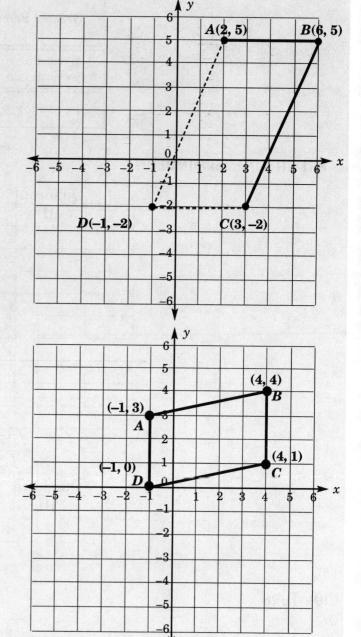

3 Locate the points $A(-1, 3)$, $B(4, 4)$, $C(4, 1)$, $D(-1, 0)$. Draw AB, BC, CD, DA. Identify the most specific name for the figure.

A:

3 Parallelogram

YOUR TURN

Identify the quadrant (I, II, III, or IV) in which each of the following points are located.

1 $(-1, -5)$

2 $(3, 7)$

3 $(2, -1)$

4 $(-4, 6)$

5 In the diagram below, isosceles triangle NJL has coordinates $N(-4, 0)$, $J(0, 4)$, $L(4, 0)$. Find the area of triangle NJL.

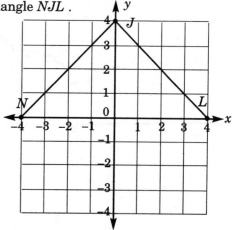

6 The coordinates of the point of intersection of the x and y axes is which of the following?

A $(0, 0)$

B $(1, 1)$

C $(2, 2)$

D $(3, 3)$

7 The origin has the coordinates represented by which of the following?

F $(0, 0)$

G $(1, 1)$

H $(2, 2)$

J $(3, 3)$

8 Using the diagram below, points $A(-3, 3)$, $B(-1, 3)$, $C(-1, -1)$, and $D(-3, -1)$ are connected as shown. What is the perimeter the rectangle?

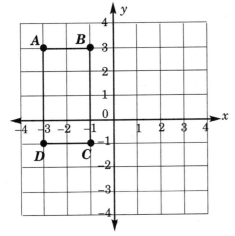

9 Using the grid below, plot the points $A(-4, 4)$, $B(-4, -2)$, and $C(2, -2)$. Find the area of triangle ABC.

A 12

B 18

C 24

D 36

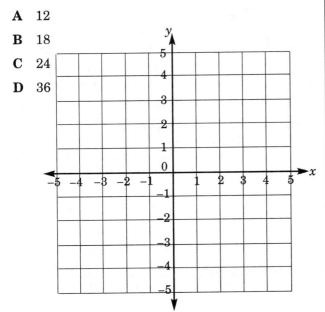

10 Using the grid below, plot the points: $A(-2, 3)$, $B(2, 3)$, $C(4, 0)$, and $D(-4, 0)$. What is the area of a quadrilateral $ABCD$?

F 9

G 12

H 15

J 18

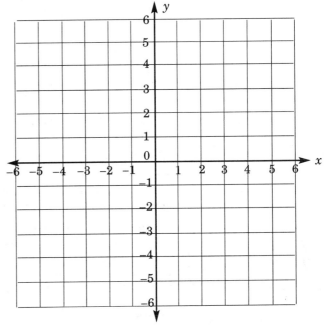

11 In the diagram below, a circle has been drawn on the coordinate grid. What are the coordinates of the center of the circle?

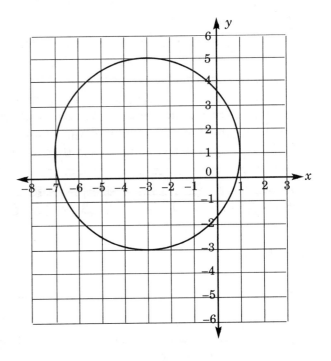

LINE GRAPHS - EQUALITY

Graph $x = 5$	
Step 1	Locate 5 on the number line
Step 2	Make a small dark circle ($\bullet$) at the 5

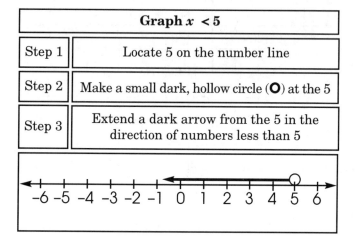

❽ Note
o vs $\bullet$
with > or < use **o**
with = , ≥ , ≤ use $\bullet$

LINE GRAPHS - INEQUALITY

Graph $x < 5$	
Step 1	Locate 5 on the number line
Step 2	Make a small dark, hollow circle (**O**) at the 5
Step 3	Extend a dark arrow from the 5 in the direction of numbers less than 5

Graph $x > 5$	
Step 1	Locate 5 on the number line
Step 2	Make a small dark, hollow circle (**O**) at the 5
Step 3	Extend a dark arrow from the 5 in the directions of numbers greater than 5

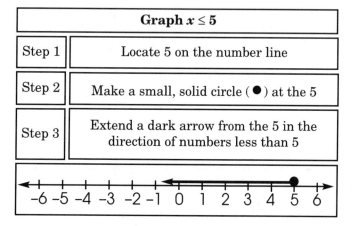

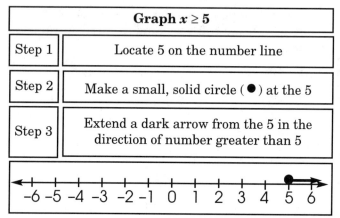

LINE GRAPHS - INEQUALITY (CONTINUED)

Graph $x \leq 5$	
Step 1	Locate 5 on the number line
Step 2	Make a small, solid circle ($\bullet$) at the 5
Step 3	Extend a dark arrow from the 5 in the direction of numbers less than 5

Graph $x \geq 5$	
Step 1	Locate 5 on the number line
Step 2	Make a small, solid circle ($\bullet$) at the 5
Step 3	Extend a dark arrow from the 5 in the direction of number greater than 5

OUR TURN

Q:

1 Graph the accompanying inequality on a number line.

$$2 < x \leq 5$$

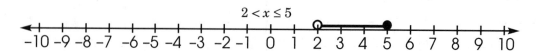

A:

YOUR TURN

Graph the following inequalities on a number line.

1 $x \leq 5$

2 $x > 4$

3 $x < 1$

4 $x \geq -2$

5 $-1 \leq x \leq 3$

6 $1 < x < 4$

7 $2 < x < 7$

8 $6 \leq x \leq 10$

9 $-3 \leq x$

10 Which graph represents the inequality $-1 \leq x < 4$?

A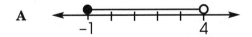

B

C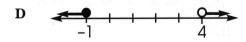

D

11 Which expression is represented in the graph below?

    F $-3 \leq x \leq 2$

    G $-3 \leq x < 2$

    H $-3 < x \leq 2$

    J $-3 < x < 2$

12 Which expression is represented by the graph below?

    A $2 > x$

    B $2 \geq x$

    C $2 < x$

    D $2 \leq x$

13 Which inequality is represented by the graph below?

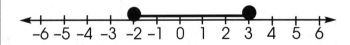

    F $-2 < x \leq 3$

    G $-2 < x < 3$

    H $-2 \leq x < 3$

    J $-2 \leq x \leq 3$

10.3 TWO VARIABLE EQUATIONS AND TABLES

X	1	2	3	4
Y	5	7	9	11

TABLE VS. EQUATION

A table of values compares two different quantities in order to define a relationship.
The same is true for an equation.

- A table has discrete points.
- An equation is continuous.

Table

x	1	2	3	4	5
y	5	7	9	11	13

Equation

$$y = 2x + 3$$

With the table, we have to look for the pattern.
With the equation, we have the pattern given to us.

GRAPHS FROM TABLES OR EQUATIONS

From Tables: Plot the (x, y) coordinate pairs.

From Equations: Make a table of values. Select x values and determine
the corresponding y values. Plot the (x, y) coordinate pairs.

READING A GRAPH

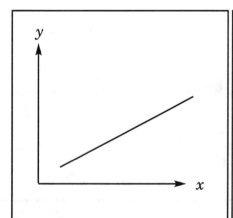

Increasing:
- y increases as x increases
- positive slope

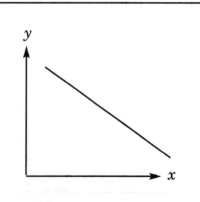

Decreasing:
- y decreases as x increases
- negative slope

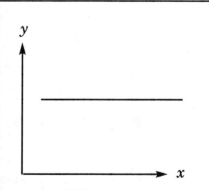

Constant:
- y remains constant as x increases
- zero slope

LINEAR FUNCTIONS

❽ Linear functions relate to straight lines.

Properties	Equations	Graphs
• None of the variables are squared. • The graph is a line.	$y = 2x + 3$ $y = 3$ $3x + 2y = 7$ $x - y - 3 = 0$ $x = 5$ * * linear, but not a function	

QUADRATIC FUNCTIONS

❽ Quadratic functions involve equations in which one of the x-terms (variables) is squared.

Properties	Equations	Graphs
• One of the x-terms (variables) is squared • Graph is a parabola	$y = x^2$ $y = x^2 + 2$ $y = x^2 + 3x - 1$	

OUR TURN

Q:

1 Complete the following table to correctly represent the equation $y = x + 3$

x	y
1	
2	
	8
	11

A:

1

x	y
1	4
2	5
5	8
8	11

$$y = x + 3$$

Replace x with 1 and solve for y $\Rightarrow$ $y = 1 + 3$
$y = 4$

Replace x with 2 and solve for y $\Rightarrow$ $y = 2 + 3$
$y = 5$

Replace y with 8 and solve for x $\Rightarrow$ $\begin{array}{r} 8 = x + 3 \\ -3 = -3 \\ \hline 5 = x \end{array}$

Replace y with 11 and solve for x $\Rightarrow$ $\begin{array}{r} 11 = x + 3 \\ -3 = -3 \\ \hline 8 = x \end{array}$

2 Which equation is represented by the accompanying table?

A $y = x + 3$

B $y = 2x + 3$

C $y = x^2 + 3$

D $y = x^2 - 1$

x	y
0	3
1	4
2	7
3	12

2 C

Only $x^2 + 3$ satisfied all 4 of the given data points.

YOUR TURN

1 Accurately complete the following table to reflect the equation $y = 2x - 3$.

x	y
-3	
1	
	5
	11

2 Accurately complete the following table to reflect the equation $x + 2y = 8$.

x	y
4	
	3
0	
	-1

3 Complete the following table of values to reflect the equation $x = 2y - 1$.

x	y
-3	
	5
	-3
5	

For the following questions (4-7), indicate which equation is represented by the respective accompanying table.

4

A $2x - y = 3$

B $4x + y = 5$

C $3x + 2y = 5$

D $3x + y = 5$

x	y
0	5
1	1
2	-3
3	-7

5

F $y = 2x^2$

G $y = 2x^2 + 1$

H $y = x^2 - x$

J $y = x^2 + x$

x	y
-1	0
0	0
1	2
2	6

6

A $y = 3x + 2$

B $y = 3(x + 1)$

C $y = 2(x + 1)$

D $y = 3(x - 1)$

x	y
-2	-3
-1	0
1	6
2	9

7

F $y = 2x^2 - 1$

G $y = 2x^2 + 1$

H $y = x^2 - 1$

J $y = x^2 + 1$

x	y
-1	1
0	-1
1	1
2	7

For questions 8-12, find the area of the figure represented by sequentially connecting the given coordinates.

8   N(0, 0),   J(0, 5),   L(4, 0)

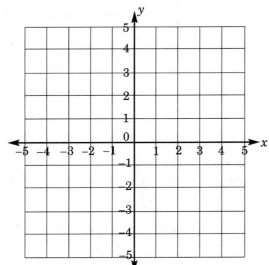

9   N(– 2, 2),   O(2, 2),   R(0, – 2),   M(– 4, – 2)

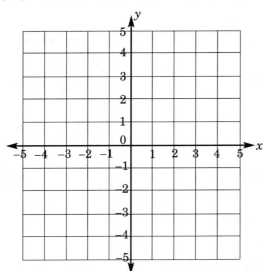

10   A(0, 5),   B(5, 0),   C(0, – 5),   D(– 5, 0)

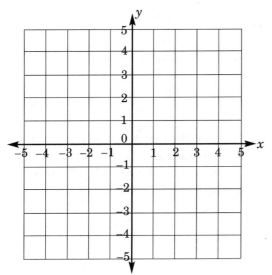

11   A(– 1, 4),   B(3, 4),   C(5, 2),   D(– 1, 2)

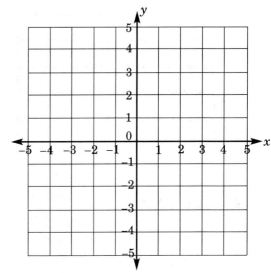

12   A(– 3, 0), B(0, 3), C(3, 0), D(3, – 4), E(– 3, – 4)

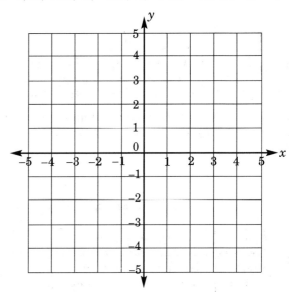

For questions 13-15, make a table of values for each equation and determine if the resulting graph would have a positive, negative, or zero slope.

13 $y = 3x + 4$

x	y

14 $y + x = 5$

x	y

15 $y = 4 - x$

x	y

10.4 FUNCTIONS

DEFINITION

Function	A relationship in which each input is paired with exactly one output according to a known rule.

Note: X is usually the input and y is usually the output. The output is usually expressed in terms of the input.

THREE WAYS TO EXPRESS FUNCTIONS

Type	Example
Equation	$y = 2x + 1$
Graph	*(graph showing lines through origin, axes labeled x and y)*
Table of Values	**x** **y** 0 2 1 4 2 6

TWO SPECIAL TYPES OF FUNCTIONS

Type	Description	Symbol	Example
Direct Variation	The quotient of x and y is always the same value.	$\dfrac{x}{y}$ = constant value	$\dfrac{x}{y} = 2$ $\dfrac{x}{y} = 3$
Inverse Variation	The product of x and y is always the same value.	xy = constant value	$xy = 7$ $xy = \dfrac{1}{3}$

OUR TURN

x	y
2	3
6	1
12	$\frac{1}{2}$

1 Does the table at the right represent a direct or inverse variation?

2 Which of the following equations represents the function rule for the table at the right?

  A $y = x + 4$
  B $y = 2x - 3$
  C $y = x - 2$
  D $y = 2x + 3$

x	y
–1	1
0	3
1	5
2	7

A:

1 Inverse Variation. The product $xy = 6$.

2 D By substituting the given x and y values into the answer choices, only choice D always expresses the correct value of y for the given x.

3 If y varies inversely as x, and $y = 6$, when $x = 2$, find the value of y when $x = 1$.

3 12 The product of x and y remains a constant when $x = 2$, $y = 6$, the product $= 12$. To have a product of 12 when $x = 1$, y must equal 12.

YOUR TURN

1 Which of the following equations represents an inverse variation?

   A $xy = 7$

   B $\frac{x}{y} = 7$

   C $x + y = 7$

   D $x - y = 7$

2 Which of the following equations represents a direct variation?

   F $xy = \frac{1}{2}$

   G $\frac{x}{y} = \frac{1}{2}$

   H $x + y = \frac{1}{2}$

   J $x - y = \frac{1}{2}$

3 Which of the following tables represents a direct variation?

A

x	y
1	4
2	6
3	8

B

x	y
1	4
3	12
5	20

C

x	y
1	3
2	2
3	1

D

x	y
2	6
4	4
6	2

4 Which of the following tables represents the function: $y = -x + 1$?

A

x	y
0	1
1	0
2	-1

B

x	y
1	0
2	3
3	4

C

x	y
0	1
2	-1
3	4

D

x	y
0	1
1	0
3	-3

5 If y varies directly as x, and $y = 7$ when $x = 2$, find the value of y when $x = 6$.

6 If y varies directly as x, and $y = 2$ when $x = 10$, find the value of x when $y = 10$.

7 If y varies inversely as x, and $y = 3$ when $x = 5$, find the value of y when $x = 15$.

8 If y varies inversely as x, and $y = 4$ when $x = 6$, find the value of x when $y = 3$.

9 The weight of a wooden board varies directly as its length. If a 6 ft. board weighs 12 pounds, how much will a 15 ft. board of the same type of wood weigh?

10 The table below displays distance (d) as a function of time (t). Which one of the following equations represents this function?

t	1	2	3	4
d	30	60	90	120

A d = 20t + 10

B d = 10t + 20

C d = 30t

D d = 20t – 10

11 The table below displays y as a function of x. Which one of the following equations represents this function?

x	1	2	3	4
y	2	5	8	11

F $y = 3x - 1$

G $y = 2x + 2$

H $y = 2x + 3$

J $y = x + 3$

10.5 Long Answer Questions for Chapter 10

1 Kim and Marie were playing a game. Marie had to walk blindfolded a certain number of steps according to Kim's directions. Marie's walk can be shown on a grid. She started at the point with coordinates A (4, 3). Her first turn was at B (4, 8); her second turn was at C (7, 8); her third turn was at D (7, 10), and finally, her walk ended at E (9, 10).

Part A

On the grid below, plot the path that Marie took and connect the points in the order that they occurred. Label each point with appropriate coordinates and letters.

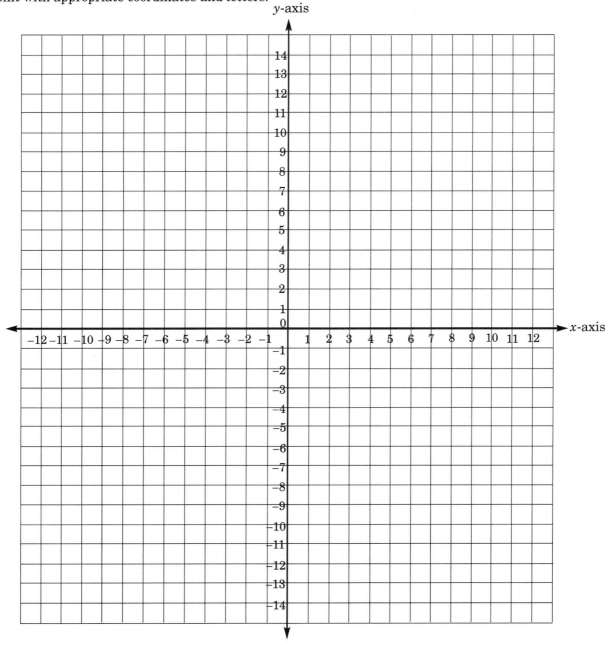

Part B

If Marie walked a total of 36 feet following the path from A to E, how many feet was the walk from C to D? Show your work or explain your answer in words.

Answer: _____ feet

2

PART A

Complete the accompanying table using the function: $y = -3x + 2$

x	y
-2	
-1	
	-1
	2
	-4

PART B

Use the coordinate grid below to graph the five points from the table.

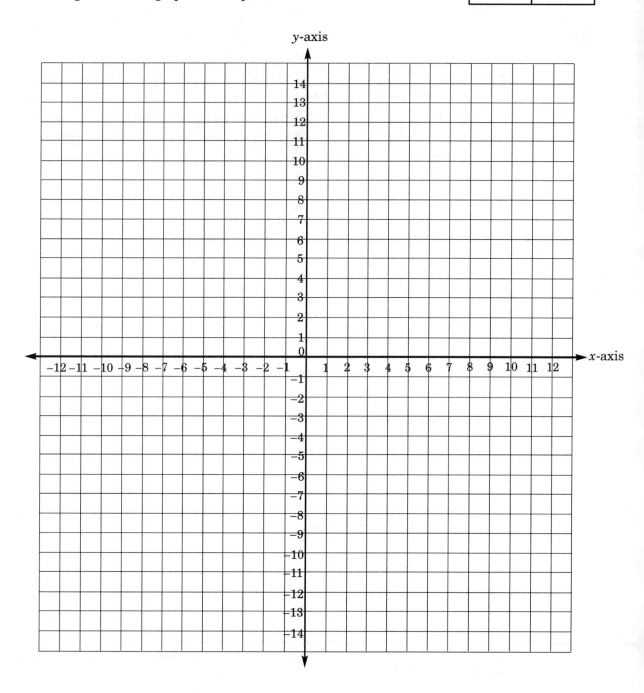

PART C

Does the point (– 4,14) lie on the graph in Part B (yes or no)?

Answer _____

Explain how you arrived at your answer.

_____

_____

_____

_____

_____

_____

3
PART A

Write the algebraic inequality for the sentence:

"Twice a number increased by 1 is greater than 9." Use n to represent the number.

Answer _____

PART B

Find three possible values for n which make the inequality true.

Answer 1 _____

Answer 2 _____

Answer 3 _____

Part C continues on the following page.

How do all the possible values of n which make the inequality true compare to the number 4?

_____

_____

_____

_____

_____

_____

What do these items have in common? Symmetry, an eye-appealing pattern that occurs both in nature and by design. Symmetry is a pattern that makes one side look like the other in either color or shape or both.

Transformations are movements according to a defined rule. They encompass rotation, reflection, translation, and/or dilation. That is, they are movements according to a defined rule. Examples of transformations include enlarging a photograph, dilation of the pupil of an eye, and a reflection in the mirror.

This chapter discusses the different forms of symmetry and how we apply them.

11.1 BASICS OF SYMMETRY AND TRANSFORMATIONS

TERMINOLOGY

Term	Description	Pictorial
Line of Symmetry	A line which splits the picture into 2 halves which are mirror images.	Line of Symmetry
Clockwise	Turns in the same direction as the hands of a clock.	
Counterclockwise	Turns in the opposite direction to that of the hands of a clock.	

SYMMETRY

Type of Symmetry	Description	Pictorial
Line Symmetry	If folded on the line of symmetry, the figures on each side will exactly overlap.	
Rotational Symmetry	If a figure can be rotated about an imaginary point A and rotates to look the same as the original in less than 360°, it has rotational symmetry about point A.	After a rotation of 90° clockwise, the figure looks like the original.
Point Symmetry	A figure with 180° rotational symmetry about a point For every point in the figure, if a line is drawn through an imaginary point A and extended the same distance, there will be a corresponding point.	

TRANSFORMATIONS

Type	Description	Pictorial	Type	Description	Pictorial
Line Reflections	FLIPS the given image over a defined line		**Translation**	SLIDES the image a defined distance (up, down, right, left)	
Rotation	TURNS the image a defined number of degrees about a point		**Dilation**	ENLARGES or DECREASES the image size proportionately	

OUR TURN

Q:

1 In the diagram below, Figure B is the image of Figure A under which transformation?

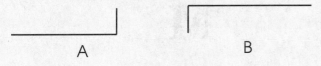

    A   B

A line reflection

B rotation

C translation

D dilation

2 Which letter(s) have vertical line symmetry?

A, B, C, D, E

3 Which letter(s) have horizontal line symmetry?

C, D, E, F, G

A:

1 Rotation (B)

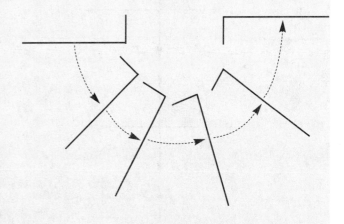

2 A only

3 C, D, E

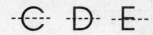

YOUR TURN

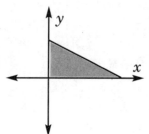
$$A \rightarrow A$$

1 Which transformation is represented by the figure above?

   A reflection

   B dilation

   C translation

   D rotation

2 The accompanying diagram shows a right triangle.

If the triangle is rotated 90° counter-clockwise about the origin, which of the following diagrams would be the result?

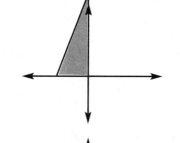

F

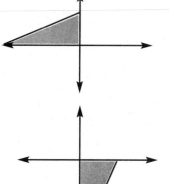

G

H

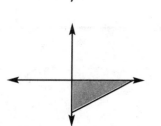

J

3 Which letter has point symmetry?

   A E

   B C

   C H

   D T

4 In the accompanying diagram, which transformation makes triangle 2 the image of triangle 1?

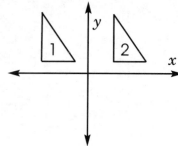

   F reflection in the *y*-axis

   G dilation

   H translation

   J rotation centered at the origin

5 Which transformation for letter M is shown in the accompanying diagram?

   A line Reflection

   B transformation

   C rotation

   D dilation

6 Which one of the following letter combinations has horizontal line symmetry?

   F HOP

   G POP

   H HOW

   J HOE

7 A square has rotational symmetry of how many degrees?

A 60°

B 90°

C 120°

D 150°

8 Which of the following represents a line reflection of the ↑ in the accompanying diagram?

F

G

H

J

9 Which of the following letter combinations has vertical line symmetry?

A ATE

B LATE

C MOM

D DAD

10 Which type of symmetry, if any, does regular hexagon ABCDEF have?

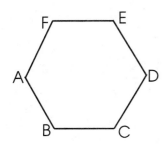

F point symmetry, only

G line symmetry, only

H point and line symmetry

J no symmetry

11 In the accompanying diagram, which point may be the image of point W after a reflection in the x-axis?

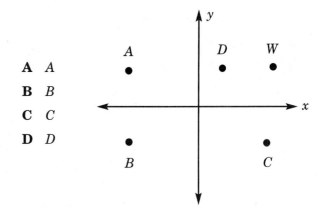

A A

B B

C C

D D

12 Which of the following 4 digit numbers has horizontal line symmetry?

F 5055

G 6066

H 8388

J 9699

13 If point A has coordinates (3,7), what will be the coordinates of point L, the reflection of point A in the x-axis?

A (7, 3)

B (− 3, 7)

C (3, − 7)

D (− 3, − 7)

14 If point N has coordinates (− 1, 4), what will be the coordinates of point J, the reflection of point N in the y-axis?

F (− 1, − 4)

G (1, − 4)

H (1, 4)

J (4, − 1)

15 The trapezoid shown in the accompanying diagram has what type of symmetry?

A vertical line

B horizontal line

C point symmetry

D vertical and horizontal

16 Which type of symmetry do all four of the accompanying symbols have?

    F vertical line

    G horizontal line

    H point symmetry

    J rotational symmetry

17 Which of the following diagrams has 120° rotational symmetry?

    A

    B

    C

    D

18 Which one of the following letters has point symmetry but not horizontal line symmetry?

    F S

    G C

    H I

    J M

19 In the accompanying diagram, *K* is the image of *A* after a translation. Under the same translation, which point is the image of *J*?

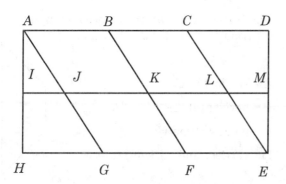

20 In which figure is △ *NJL* a reflection of △ *ABC* in line *l* ?

    A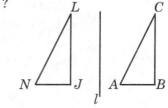

    B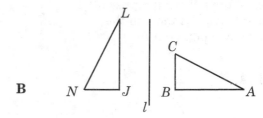

    C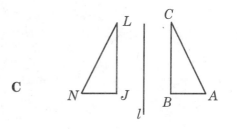

    D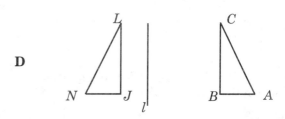

21 Triangle *NJL* is drawn in Quadrant III. If △*NJL* is reflected in the *y*-axis, its image will be in which quadrant?

    F I

    G II

    H III

    J IV

22 What is the total number of lines of symmetry for a rectangle that is not a square?

    A 0

    B 1

    C 2

    D 4

11.2 Long Answer Questions for Chapter 11

1 Given the following coordinates for $\triangle NJL$

$N\,(4,\ 6),\quad J\,(7,\ 3),\quad L\,(1,\ 2)$

Part A
Graph $\triangle NJL$ on the grid:

Part B
Reflect $\triangle NJL$ across the x-axis to become $\triangle RST$. What are the coordinates of points R, S and T?

Answer: $R\ ($, $)$

           $S\ ($, $)$

           $T\ ($, $)$

Part C
Reflect $\triangle NJL$ across line l, shown on the grid to become $\triangle UVW$. What are the coordinates of points U, V, and W?

Answer: $U\ ($, $)$

           $V\ ($, $)$

           $W\ ($, $)$

2
Part A
In the space below, draw 2 different figures that have vertical line symmetry but not horizontal line symmetry. Show the lines of symmetry.

Answers:

Part B
In the space below, draw 2 figures that have horizontal line symmetry but not vertical line symmetry. Show the line of symmetry.

Answers:

PART C

In the space below, draw 2 figures that have both horizontal and vertical line symmetry. Show the lines of symmetry.

Answers:

3

PART A

On the grid, plot A (2, 3) and B (7, 5). Connect these points to form line segment AB.

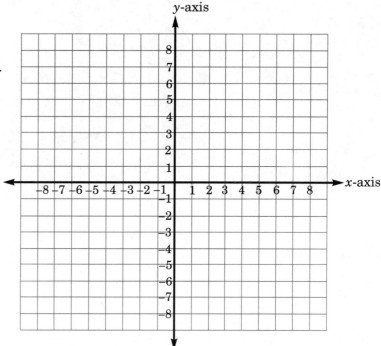

PART B

Reflect AB across the y-axis and label it RS. What are the coordinates of R and S?

Answer: R (,   )

   S (,   )

PART C

Reflect line segment RS across the x-axis and label it TU. What are the coordinates T and U?

Answer: T (,   )

   U (,   )

CHAPTER TWELVE

DATA & STATISTICS

12

Caitlin came home from her 8th grade math class and told her mom that she learned about quartiles, stems and leaves, and boxes and whiskers. Of course, her mom knew that she must be learning statistics.

Statistics and different graphical representations help us understand data which may be confusing or complicated. The following is a set of data which represents (to the nearest minute) the length of time each student in Dawn's class spends on the school bus in the morning: 3, 12, 14, 6, 10, 17, 4, 10, 9, 4, 7, 12, 16, 18, 19, 15, 3, 6, 15, 5, 7, 13, 11, 11, 9.

Wouldn't it be easier if this data were organized into a chart or a picture? Wouldn't it be more useful to have just a few numbers represent the whole group of data and still convey the same information? Statistics and graphics help us understand and interpret data.

Here is another example: The Chang family went on vacation. As they were coming home, they heard on the radio that it had snowed all week in their town. The average snowfall was $\frac{1}{2}$ inch per day. The Changs arrived at their house and could not get into their driveway. It was covered with 36 inches of snow! How could this be, if the average snowfall was $\frac{1}{2}$ inch?

Statistics helps us grasp and interpret information. In this chapter, we will learn the language of statistics and some of its presentations.

12.1 MEAN/MODE/MEDIAN

DESCRIPTION OF MEAN/MODE/MEDIAN

Terminology	Casual Terminology	Description
Mean	the average	$\text{Average} = \dfrac{\text{Sum of the data items}}{\text{Quantity of data items}}$
Mode	the most frequent number	• The value that occurs most. • If two values occur equally but more than all the others, there are 2 modes. • If all the values occur the same amount of times, there is no mode.

Median	the middle number when placed in increasing or decreasing order	Odd number of values:
		    median is the middle number.
		
		Even number of values:
		    median is the average of
		    the two middle numbers.

OUR TURN

Q: Answer the following questions using the given data: 4, 7, 3, 3, 4, 4, 4, 9

1   What is the mean (average)?

2   What is the mode?

3   What is the median?

A:

1   4.75

$$\frac{4 + 7 + 3 + 3 + 4 + 4 + 4 + 9}{8} = 4.75$$

2   4

The most frequent number is 4. There are four of them.

3   4

To find the median, sequence the numbers in numerical order. If the number of elements is even, the median is the average of the two middle numbers.

3, 3, 4, **4, 4**, 4, 7, 9

The median is $\dfrac{4 + 4}{2} = 4$

YOUR TURN

1   The accompanying chart shows how the cost of a specific notebook varied over a 5-week period. Based on the chart, which statement is true about the cost of this notebook over this period?

Week	Cost
1	$5.00
2	$5.25
3	$3.00
4	$3 50
5	$4.75

A   The mode was $3.00

B   The mean was $4.30

C   The median was $4.50

D   The median was $3.00

Given △ *NJL* with the angle measures as shown, calculate the following items about the three angles.

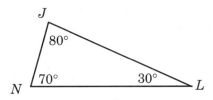

Figure not drawn to scale

2   the median

3   the mean

The table shown at right lists the football scores for Team A after 5 games and the scores of their opponents.

Game	Team A Score	Opponent Score
1	28	7
2	6	15
3	30	35
4	30	28
5	25	24

4   What is the mean score of Team A?

5   What is the median score of Team A?

6   What is the mean score of the opponents?

7   What is the median score for the opponents?

Given the following set of data: {6, 7, 10, 6, 7, 10, 6} Calculate the following items about the data.

8   the median

9   the mode

10   the average (mean) to the nearest hundredth

Use the accompanying table for Questions 11-16. Round all answers to the nearest hundredth.

Student	Test 1	Test 2
Norm	80	80
Joan	90	80
Dawn	95	80
Jessica	85	90
Josh	85	75
Seth	85	80
Lynne	100	90

11   What is the mean test score for Test 1?

12   What is the mean test score for Test 2?

13   What is the median test score for Test 1?

14   What is the median test score for Test 2?

15   What is the mode of the Test 1 scores?

16   What is the mode of the Test 2 scores?

17   In which set of data is the mean greater than the median?

   F   {2, 5, 6, 8, 8}

   G   {2, 3, 5, 6, 7, 8}

   H   {2, 4, 5, 6, 6, 7}

   J   {2, 4, 4, 5, 6, 7, 8}

12.2 FREQUENCY

DESCRIPTION OF FREQUENCY TERMS

Term	Description
Frequency	based on a tally, how often a particular data item or group appears
Cumulative Frequency	the number of data elements at that data value/data group or lower ————————————————— cumulative totals of the frequencies at the data value/data group or lower
Relative Frequency	Relative Frequency = $\dfrac{\text{frequency for the interval}}{\text{total observations}}$
Cumulative Relative Frequency	cumulative totals of the relative frequency at the data value/data group or lower

ILLUSTRATIVE EXAMPLE OF FREQUENCY OF TERMS

Data: 11, 22, 33, 44, 13, 23, 33, 43, 25, 35, 45, 27, 47, 49, 41

Data Interval	10 – 19	20 – 29	30 – 39	40 – 49	Data Interval
Tally	| |	| | | |	| | |	‖‖‖ |	Tally
Frequency	2	4	3	6	Total = 15, same as tally
Cumulative Frequency	2	2 + 4 = 6	2 + 4 + 3 = 9	2 + 4 + 3 + 6 = 15	Cumulative totals of the frequency
Relative Frequency	$\dfrac{2}{15} \approx .13$	$\dfrac{4}{15} \approx .27$	$\dfrac{3}{15} \approx .2$	$\dfrac{6}{15} \approx .4$	$\dfrac{\text{frequency of data interval}}{\text{total data items}}$
Cumulative Relative Frequency	.13	.13 + .27 = .4	.13 + .27 + .2 = .6	.13 + .27 + .2 + .4 = 1	Cumulative totals of relative frequencies

OUR TURN

Q: Given the following data set, complete the table and answer the questions.

Data: 9, 10, 12, 9, 10, 10, 8, 5, 10, 5

Value	Tally	Frequency	Cumulative Frequency	Relative Frequency	Cumulative Relative Frequency
5					
8					
9					
10					
12					

1 What is the mean of the data?

2 What is the median of the data?

3 What is the mode of the data?

A:

Value	Tally	Frequency	Cumulative Frequency	Relative Frequency	Cumulative Relative Frequency
5	||	2	2	$\frac{2}{10} = .2$	.2
8	|	1	2 + 1 = 3	$\frac{1}{10} = .1$	.2 + .1 = .3
9	||	2	2 + 1 + 2 = 5	$\frac{2}{10} = .2$	.2 + .1 + .2 = .5
10	||||	4	2 + 1 + 2 + 4 = 9	$\frac{4}{10} = .4$	.2 + .1 + .2 + .4 = .9
12	|	1	2 + 1 + 2 + 4 + 1 = 10	$\frac{1}{10} = .1$	.2 + .1 + .2 + .4 + .1 = 1

1 8.8

$$\text{mean} = \frac{\text{Sum of data items}}{\text{Number of data items}}$$

$$= \frac{9 + 10 + 12 + 9 + 10 + 10 + 8 + 5 + 10 + 5}{10} = \frac{88}{10} = 8.8$$

or

$$= \frac{5 \cdot (2) + 8 \cdot (1) + 9 \cdot (2) + 10 \cdot (4) + 12 \cdot (1)}{10} = \frac{88}{10} = 8.8$$

2 9.5

There were 10 numbers. The middle two, when listed in numerical order are 9 and 10.

5, 5, 8, 9, <u>9, 10</u>, 10, 10, 10, 12

$$\text{median} = \frac{9 + 10}{2} = 9.5$$

3 10

There are more tens than any other value.

YOUR TURN

Given the following data set, complete the table and answer the questions.

Data: 3, 3, 4, 4, 4, 7, 3, 3, 7

1

Data Value	Tally	Frequency	Cumulative Frequency	Relative Frequency
3				
4				
7				

2 To the nearest hundredth, what is the mean of the data?

3 What is the mode of the data?

4 What is the median of the data?

5 Given the following data set, complete the table using the data group shown.

Data: 26, 19, 35, 39, 8, 15, 7, 19, 9, 25, 33, 18, 14, 21, 6, 35, 39, 28, 7, 6, 13, 9, 11

Data Group	Tally	Frequency	Cumulative Frequency
0 – 10			
11 – 20			
21 – 30			
31 – 40			

The accompanying frequency table shows the ages of the first group of persons entering a restaurant. Use this table for questions 6 - 8.

Ages	Frequency
0 – 9	8
10 – 19	7
20 – 29	4
30 – 39	11
40 – 49	5
50 – 59	3
60 – 69	2

6 How many people are in the group?

7 What is the median age range?

8 What age range is the mode?

Description of Data Presentation

Data for this page: 6 cats, 7 dogs, 2 fish, 10 other

Terminology	Use	Example
Frequency Table or Quantity Chart	shows how many times a piece of data occurs	Students' Pets Total 25 **Items / Tally / Quantity** Cat — ＨＨＴ I — 6 Dog — ＬＨＴ II — 7 Fish — I I — 2 Other — ＨＨＴＨＨＴ — 10
Bar Graph	compares quantity by type, graphically	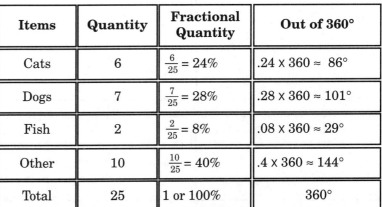 Students' Pets
Circle Graph	compares frequency as a fraction or percent of 360°	*(table and circle graph below)*

Bar Graph — Students' Pets
(Quantity axis: 0, 2, 4, 6, 8, 10; Categories: Cat, Dog, Fish, Other; Legend: Cat, Dog, Fish, Other)

Circle Graph table:

Items	Quantity	Fractional Quantity	Out of 360°
Cats	6	$\frac{6}{25} = 24\%$	.24 x 360 ≈ 86°
Dogs	7	$\frac{7}{25} = 28\%$	.28 x 360 ≈ 101°
Fish	2	$\frac{2}{25} = 8\%$	.08 x 360 ≈ 29°
Other	10	$\frac{10}{25} = 40\%$	.4 x 360 ≈ 144°
Total	25	1 or 100%	360°

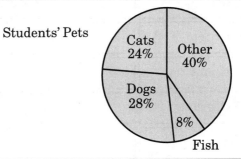

Students' Pets — Cats 24%, Other 40%, Dogs 28%, Fish 8%

Data for pages 208-209: 60, 61, 64, 67, 69, 71, 71, 72, 73, 73, 74, 74, 81, 81, 81, 82, 83, 92, 93, 93, 94

Terminology	Use	Example
Stem and Leaf Plots	Displays the front digits in numerical order as the stem. The units digits are in sequence as the leaves.	Stem | Leaf 6 | 0 1 4 7 9 7 | 1 1 2 3 3 4 4 8 | 1 1 1 2 3 9 | 2 3 3 4
Histogram	Displays data frequency. (usually for grouped data)	
Cumulative Histogram	Displays frequency on a cumulative basis. (usually for grouped data)	

Terminology	Use
Median	The middle number when data is listed in numerical order. It splits the data into two equal parts: half below the median and half above it.
1st Quartile	the median of the values in the lower half of the data.
3rd Quartile	the median of the values in the upper half of the data.
Lower Extreme	the lowest data value
Upper Extreme	the highest data value
Range	upper extreme minus lower extreme

BOX AND WHISKER PLOT

Terminology	Use
Box and Whisker Plots	Displays the median, 1st and 3rd Quartile, and Upper and Lower Extremes

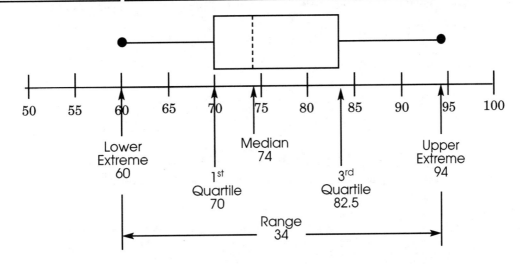

Note: The numbers in the above Box and Whisker Plot are based on the data from the previous page.

OUR TURN

Q:

1 Draw a stem and leaf plot using the following data.

Data: 14, 28, 36, 39, 15, 27, 16, 40, 19, 39, 16

2 Given the following data, identify the lower extreme, upper extreme, range, median, 1st Quartile, and 3rd Quartile.

Data: 15, 9, 17, 26, 3, 15, 30, 17, 20, 10, 5

3 Use the results from question 2 to draw a box and whisker plot.

4 Group the following data.
Data: 18, 23, 31, 33, 32, 31, 37, 19, 17, 10, 24, 17, 30, 13, 28, 26

A:

1 Stems are the lead digits.
Leaves are usually the units digits in ascending order, separated by spaces.

Stem	Leaf
1	4 5 6 6 9
2	7 8
3	6 9 9
4	0

2 Lower Extreme: 3
Upper Extreme: 30
Range: 27
Median: 15
1st Quartile: 9
3rd Quartile: 20

2 (continued)

First, list the numbers in ascending order:

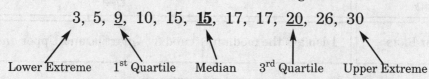

3, 5, <u>9</u>, 10, 15, **<u>15</u>**, 17, 17, <u>20</u>, 26, 30

Lower Extreme   1st Quartile   Median   3rd Quartile   Upper Extreme

range = upper extreme – lower extreme
= 30 – 3
= 27

3

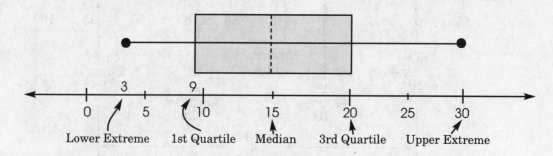

Lower Extreme   1st Quartile   Median   3rd Quartile   Upper Extreme

4

Data Group	Tally	Frequency
10 – 15	||	2
16 – 20	||||	4
21 – 25	||	2
26 – 30	|||	3
31 – 35	||||	4
36 – 40	|	1

YOUR TURN

Using the data below, identify the value of the requested data items.

Data: 4, 7, 15, 6, 18, 9, 7

1 Lower Extreme

2 Upper Extreme

3 Median

4 Range

5 1st Quartile

6 3rd Quartile

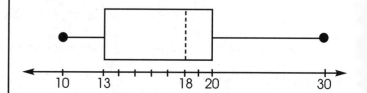

Using the box and whisker plot shown above, identify the value of the requested data item.

7 Lower Extreme

8 Upper Extreme

9 1st Quartile

10 Median

11 3rd Quartile

12 Range

MATH – BIG 8 REVIEW   N&N©

BAR GRAPH

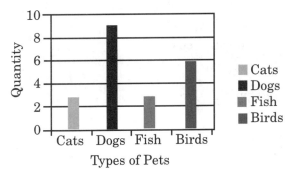

Using the bar graph above, answer the following questions.

13 What is the quantity of birds?

14 How many animals are referenced in the entire bar graph?

Stem	Leaf
0	1 3 4 7 7
1	2 6 6 7 8 9
2	4 5 5 3 9
3	0 0 1 1 1

Using the stem and leaf plot above, answer the following questions.

15 What is the median value?

16 What is the lower extreme?

17 What is the range of the data?

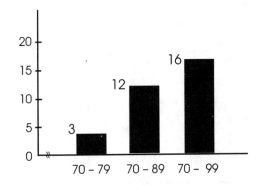

Using the cumulative frequency histogram above, answer the following questions.

18 How many data entries are there in total?

19 How many data entries are in the 80 - 89 group?

20 Which data group contains the median?

21 There are exactly 4 entries in which of the following groups?

A 70 - 79

B 80 - 89

C 70 - 99

D 90 - 99

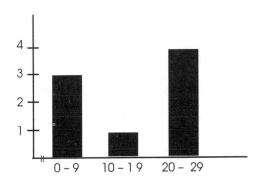

22 The frequency histogram above reflects which of the following stem and leaf plots?

F

Stem	Leaf
0	3 5 9
1	6 8
2	1 2 3

G

Stem	Leaf
0	1 1 4 4
1	2
2	3 3 3

H

Stem	Leaf
0	1 2 3
1	1 2 3
2	1 2

J

Stem	Leaf
0	1 1 1
1	2
2	3 3 3 3

12.4 COMPREHENSIVE EXAMPLE

Given the test score data shown below, calculate, display, or identify the following items as appropriate.

1 Draw a table showing:

   Data Value
   Tally
   Frequency
   Cumulative Frequency
   Relative Frequency

2 Display the data in a stem and leaf plot.

3 What is the value of each of the following:

   • Mean

   • Mode

   • Median

   • Lower Extreme

   • Upper Extreme

   • 1st Quartile

   • 3rd Quartile

4 Display the data with a box and whisker plot.

5 Group the data, using the intervals: 79 - 75, 76 - 80, 81 - 85, 86 - 90. Complete a frequency and cumulative frequency table for these groupings.

6 Draw a frequency histogram and cumulative frequency histogram using the given intervals.

1 Test Score Data:

80, 78, 85, 84, 85, 71, 78, 85, 80, 90

Value	Tally	Frequency	Relative Frequency	Cumulative Frequency
71	|	1	$\frac{1}{10} = 10\%$	1
78	||	2	$\frac{2}{10} = 20\%$	3
80	||	2	$\frac{2}{10} = 20\%$	5
84	|	1	$\frac{1}{10} = 10\%$	6
85	|||	3	$\frac{3}{10} = 30\%$	9
90	|	1	$\frac{1}{10} = 10\%$	10
Total	10	10	100%	10

2 Stem and Leaf Plot:

Stem	Leaf
7	1 8 8
8	0 0 4 5 5 5
9	0

3 Mean:

$$\frac{80 + 78 + 85 + 84 + 85 + 71 + 78 + 85 + 80 + 90}{10} = \frac{816}{10} = 81.6$$

Mode: 85 because it occurs three times

Median: 71, 78, 78, 80, **80, 84**, 85, 85, 85, 90

80 and 84 are the two middle numbers

$$\text{Median} = \frac{80 + 84}{2} = 82$$

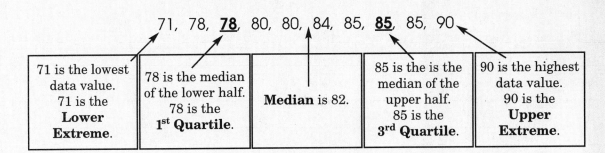

71, 78, **78**, 80, 80, 84, 85, **85**, 85, 90

| 71 is the lowest data value. 71 is the **Lower Extreme**. | 78 is the median of the lower half. 78 is the **1st Quartile**. | **Median** is 82. | 85 is the is the median of the upper half. 85 is the **3rd Quartile**. | 90 is the highest data value. 90 is the **Upper Extreme**. |

4 Box and Whisker Plot:

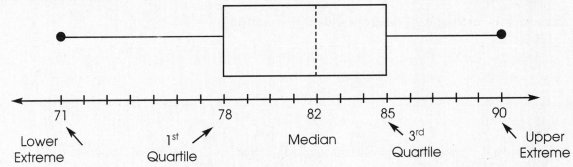

5 Grouping the data

Interval	Frequency	Cumulative Frequency
71 – 75	1	1
76 – 80	4	5
81 – 85	4	9
86 – 90	1	10

6 Histograms

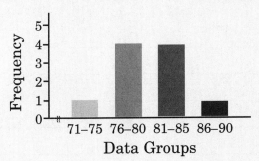

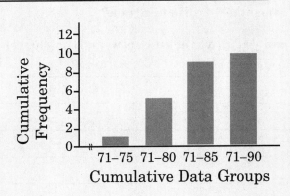

12.5 Long Answer Questions for Chapter 12

1 The mean, mode, and median of five numbers is 6. How many of these numbers must be 6?

Part A

Answer _____

Explain how you arrived at your answer.

_____

_____

_____

_____

_____

Part B

Give an example of the five numbers used to validate your answer.

2 Samantha's math test grades for the current marking period are: 72, 90, 82, 87, and 84.

Part A

What is Samantha's average for the five tests? Show all of your work.

Answer _____

Part B

What is Samantha's median test grade?

Explain how you arrived at your answer and/or your calculations.

_____

_____

_____

_____

_____

PART C

If Samantha would like to raise her average to 85, what grade does she need on her next test? Show all of your work.

Answer _____

3 On a science quiz, 20 students received the following scores:

100, 95, 95, 90, 85, 85, 80, 80, 80, 80, 75, 75, 75, 70, 70, 65, 65, 60, 55, 55

PART A

Use the space marked "Answer" to construct a stem and leaf plot to display the data:

Answer:

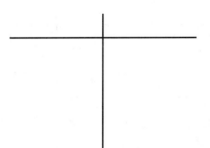

PART B

Use the grid on the next page to construct a histogram to display the data. Be sure to title the graph and label all axes and choose an appropriate scale.

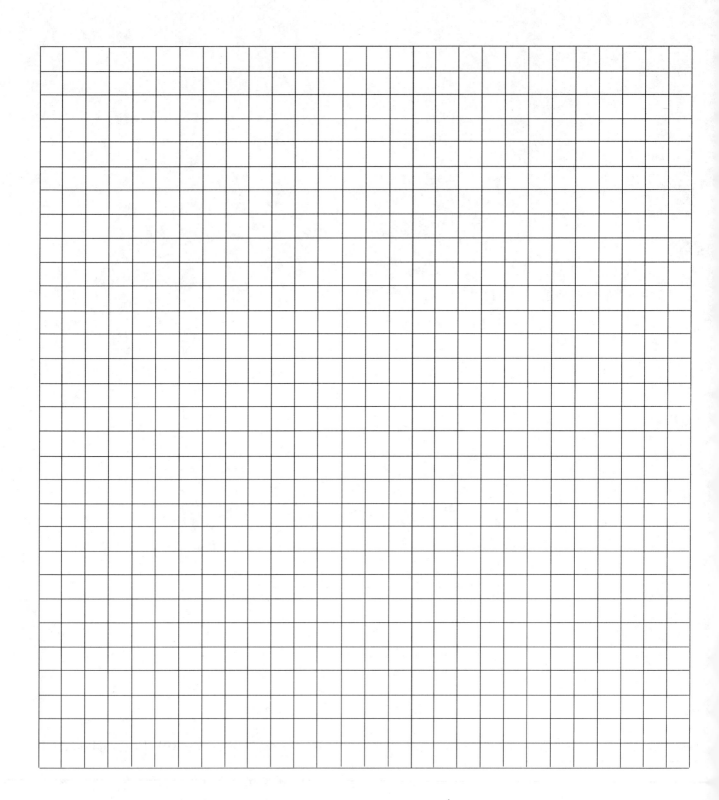

CHAPTER THIRTEEN

UNCERTAINTY

This chapter discusses probability or predicting outcomes based on data. Where is probability used?

- In sports
- In weather forecasting
- In scientific experimentation
- In card playing
- In political projections
- In games

The coach has eight outfielders who were posing in a straight line for a picture. Because he cannot make up his mind, he asked the photographer to take one picture of every possible arrangement. Luckily, the photographer brought 20 rolls of 36-exposure film. Was that enough?

The batter who bats 4th has gotten 120 hits in his previous 300 times at bat. He is now up for the fifth time this game and has already gotten 2 hits. Would you expect him to get a hit this time a bat?

Let us learn how to apply probability.

13.1 Outcomes

Methods of Counting Possible Outcomes

Terms	Definition
Factorial !	successive multiplications of consecutive decreasing integers beginning with a given value and ending with 1 $6! = 6 \cdot 5 \cdot 4 \cdot 3 \cdot 2 \cdot 1 = 720$
Counting Principle	If a 1st event can be done in m ways and a 2nd event can be done in n ways, then in that order both activities can be done $m \cdot n$ ways.
Sample Space or Tree Diagram	shows all possible outcomes of an experiment

Permutations	Arranging items when order matters	AB is different from BA
$_nP_r$	the number of ways n things can be arranged in groups of size r (Order matters.)	$_6P_4 = 6 \cdot 5 \cdot 4 \cdot 3$ $_nP_r = \underbrace{n(n-1)(n-2)\ldots}_{r \text{ times}}$

Combinations	Selecting items, order does not matter	AB is the same as BA
$_nC_r$	the number of ways n things can be arranged/chosen in groups of size r (Order does not matter.)	$_6C_2 = \dfrac{_6P_2}{2!} = \dfrac{6 \cdot 5}{2 \cdot 1} = \dfrac{30}{2} = 15$ $_nC_r = \dfrac{_nP_r}{r!}$

❽ Combination: order does not matter - ABC, BAC, CBA are not considered different because it is the same three letters.

❽ Permutation: order matters - ABC, BAC, CBA are all considered different because the letters, while the same, are in a different order.

Our Turn

Q:

1 Find the value of $\dfrac{5!}{2!}$

Beverages
• Milk
• Soda
• Coffee
• Iced Tea

Desserts
• Pudding
• Cake
• Ice Cream

Given the menu board at left:

2 How many different selections are there of one beverage and one dessert? Use the counting principle.

3 Show the sample space for one beverage and 1 desert.

4 Draw a tree diagram of all possible outcomes of 1 beverage and 1 desert.

5 How many permutations are there of the letters ABCD taken in groups of 2? List them.

6 How many combinations are there of the letters ABCD taken in groups of 2? List them.

A:

1 60

$$\frac{5!}{2!} = \frac{5 \cdot 4 \cdot 3 \cdot 2 \cdot 1}{2 \cdot 1} = \frac{120}{2} = 60$$

2 12

Using the counting principle:

A beverage can be chosen in 4 ways.

A dessert can be chosen in 3 ways.

4 · 3 = 12

3 The sample space lists all the possible outcomes:

Milk, Pudding	Soda, Pudding	Coffee Pudding	Iced Tea, Pudding
Milk, Cake	Soda, Cake	Coffee, Cake	Iced Tea, Cake
Milk, Ice Cream	Soda, Ice Cream	Coffee, Ice Cream	Iced Tea, Ice Cream

4 A tree diagram depicts the space in tree form:

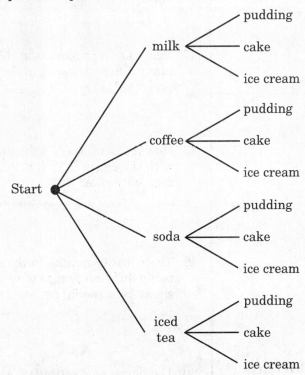

5 12

Four letters used in groups of two. Order matters.

$_4P_2 = 4 \cdot 3 = 12$

AB BA
AC CA
AD DA
BC CB
BD DB
CD DC

6 6

Four letters used in groups of two. Order does not matter.

$$_4C_2 = \frac{_4P_2}{2!} = \frac{4 \cdot 3}{2 \cdot 1} = 6$$

AB
AC
AD
BC
BD
CD

Your Turn

Evaluate:

1   $5!$

2   $\dfrac{8!}{6!}$

3   $_5P_2$

4   $_4P_4$

5   $_5C_2$

6   $_4C_4$

7   $4!$

8   $\dfrac{15!}{14!}$

9   $_3P_1$

10   $\dfrac{(4!) \times (3!)}{2!}$

11   $(9 - 6)!$

12   If job A can be done in 5 ways and job B can be done in 6 ways, in how many different ways can the two jobs be completed?

13   Kirk has 6 pairs of pants and 3 shirts. How many possible outfits consisting of one shirt and one pair of pants can be selected?

14   In how many different ways can the subjects, math, English, social studies, and science be scheduled during the first four periods of the school day?

15   Julia has 6 dresses, 2 coats, and 3 hats. How many different outfits can she wear consisting of a dress, a coat, and a hat?

16   During the softball season, each of six teams played the other five teams only once. What is the total number of games played?

17   There are nine players in the batting order. How many different ways can the first two batters be assigned?

18   How many different 5 digit numbers can be made with the digits, 5, 6, 7, 8, and 9 and using each digit only once?

19   There are 4 sopranos in the special chorus. How many different groups of two can the director select for a special performance?

20   The museum is setting up a show on Impressionists. There are 6 paintings by Monet and only room for 4 of them. In how many different ways can the 4 be selected?

21   At Kyle's pizzeria, pizza is available with a choice of 3 different crusts, 6 different vegetable toppings, and 5 different meat toppings. How many different kinds of pizza can be ordered consisting of one kind of crust, one vegetable topping and 1 meat topping?

22 The letters in the word "math" can be arranged into how many different four letter groupings?

23 There are nine players on the baseball team. If the pitcher must bat last, how many different ways can the first two batters be assigned?

24 After the game, the 6 players on one team shake the hand of each of the 6 players on the other team. How many handshakes are there?

25 Victor knows a telephone number begins 777 and that the last digits are 1, 2, 3, and 4, but he does not know their order. What is the maximum number of calls he would have to make to get the number right?

26 An eight character license plate is made beginning with three letters and ending with five numbers. Using the 26 letter alphabet, how many different 3 letter groupings are possible if no letter is to be used more than once?

27 An eight character license plate is made beginning with three letters and ending in five numbers. Using the 26 letter alphabet, how many different three letter groupings are possible?

28 The 8 people of the Roslyn High School math team are lining up in a single row for a team photograph. In how many different orders can they appear?

13.2 PROBABILITY

DEFINITION

Probability is the chance of an event happening. It ranges from 0 (never) to 1 (always).

THEORETICAL PROBABILITY

$$\text{Probability (Event)} = \frac{\text{the number of ways the specific event can happen}}{\text{the total number of possible outcomes}}$$

EXPERIMENTAL PROBABILITY

$$\text{Probability (Event)} = \frac{\text{actual number of occurrences of the specific event}}{\text{total number of attempts}}$$

PREDICTING OUTCOMES

(number of expected outcomes of an event) = (Probability of the Event) x (number of attempts)

❽ Probability: the probability of event "A" happening is written as: $P(A)$

❽ Not A: $P(\text{not } A) = 1 - P(A)$

RANGE OF VALUES

All probabilities are from 0 to 1 inclusive
0 ——————————————————————————————————— 1
Probability of zero means: The event **never** happens · Probability of one means: The event **always** happens

COUNTING PRINCIPLE

Counting Principle	If event A can be done in m ways and event B can be done in n ways, then the number of possible ways to do event A followed by event B is $m \times n$.

PROBABILITY OF MORE THAN ONE EVENT

Item	Description	Formula	Example
Independent Events	The outcome of the 1st event **does not** affect the outcome of the 2nd event.	$P(A \text{ and } B) = P(A) \times P(B)$	rolling a die ———— The outcome on the 2nd roll is not affected by the outcome of the 1st.
Dependent Events	The outcome of the 1st event **does** affect the outcome of the 2nd event.	$P(A, \text{ then } B) =$ $P(A) \times P(B \text{ after adjust for event } A)$	selecting marbles ———— selecting a 2nd marble from a bag, without replacing the 1st selection
$P(A \text{ or } B)$	the probability of event A, or event B	$P(A \text{ or } B) = P(A) + P(B) - P(A \text{ and } B)$	———

OUR TURN

Q:

1   What is the probability of throwing a 5 on one roll of a die?

2   A class conducts an experiment by flipping a quarter 83 times. 37 times it comes up heads. What is the probability of a tail, based on this experiment?

3   Avery scores 2 goals on every 15 attempts. At this rate, how many goals would he score during a season with 105 attempts?

4   A bag has 4 red marbles and 3 blue marbles. A marble is selected without replacement, then a second marble is selected. What is the probability of a red marble followed by a blue marble?

A:

1 $\frac{1}{6}$

$$P(5) = \frac{\text{number of ways to roll a 5 on a die}}{\text{number of possible values that could be gotten}} = \frac{1}{6}$$

2 $\frac{46}{83}$

$$P(\text{Event}) = \frac{\text{actual number of occurrence of the event}}{\text{total number of attempts}} = \frac{46}{83}$$

3 14

$$\text{Expected} = (\text{Probability of the event}) \times (\text{number of attempts}) = \frac{2}{15} \times (105) = 14$$

4 $\frac{2}{7}$

To begin, there are 4 red and 3 blue; a total of 7.

$$P(\text{red}) = \frac{4}{7}$$

After a red is selected, there are 3 red and 3 blue; a total of 6.

$$P(\text{blue adjusted for the missing red}) = \frac{3}{6}$$

$$P(\text{red, then blue}) = \frac{4}{7} \cdot \frac{3}{6} = \frac{2}{7}$$

YOUR TURN

1 If a letter is chosen at random from the ten letters in the word SUCCESSFUL, find the probability that the letter is a "*C*."

2 The sections of a spinner are shaded in blue and yellow. The probability that the spinner will land on a blue section is $\frac{4}{9}$. What is the probability that the spinner will land on a yellow section?

3 From a jar of red jellybeans and white jellybeans, the probability of picking a white jellybean is $\frac{2}{3}$. If the jar contains 24 jellybeans, how many red jellybeans are in the jar?

4 A bag has only red and blue marbles. All but 4 are red and all but 5 are blue. What is the probability of selecting a red marble?

5 A bag contains five green, six red, and seven black jellybeans. If one jellybean is drawn at random, what is the probability that the jellybean is green or red?

6 If the replacement set of x is {2, 3, 4, 5, 6}, what is the probability that a number chosen at random from the replacement set will make the expression $3x - 1$ an odd number?

Use this data for questions 7–8:
A jar contains 2 red, 6 white, and 5 blue marbles. One marble is selected at random, its color noted, and then it is replaced in the jar. A second marble is selected at random.

7 Find the probability that both selected marbles are red.

8 Find the probability that the first is white and the second is red.

9 The probability of drawing a red marble from a sack is $\frac{2}{5}$, which set of marbles could the sack contain?

A 2 red and 5 green

B 4 red and 6 green

C 6 red and 15 green

D 2 red, 1 blue, and 4 white

10 Giuseppe has 7 blue pens, 6 black pens, and 5 red pens in his desk drawer. If he selects a pen at random, what is the probability that it will be either a blue or black pen?

Use this data for questions 11–15 :
Erin bought a package of marbles and sorted them by color as shown in the accompanying graph.

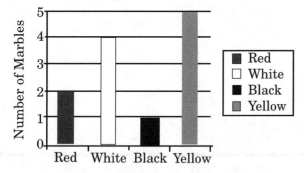

11 What was the total number of marbles in the package?

12 If one marble is selected at random, find the probability that it is red.

13 If two marbles were selected at random, with replacement, find the probability that the first was red and the second was yellow.

14 If two marbles were selected at random, with replacement, find the probability that one of the two marbles was blue.

15 If two marbles were selected at random, without replacement, find the probability that two red marbles were selected.

16 Given the following geometric figures:

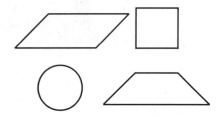

If one of the figures is selected at random, what is the probability it does not have line symmetry?

17 At the end of the season, a baseball player has a batting average of .300. If he was at bat 450 times, how many hits did he have?

18 In the accompanying graph, the color of the pants worn by the students in a class is shown. What is the probability that a student selected at random from the class is wearing black pants?

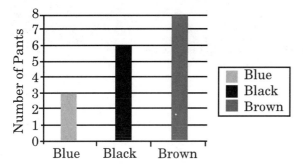

19 If two dice are tossed once, the probability of getting 12 is $\frac{1}{36}$. What is the probability of not getting 12?

20 From a standard deck of 52 cards, one card is drawn. What is the probability that it will be either a club or a diamond?

21 The probability of Team A beating Team B is $\frac{3}{5}$. What is the probability that Team A will win two consecutive games from Team B?

22 A purse contains 3 quarters, 4 dimes, 2 nickels, and 2 pennies. If one coin is pulled out of the purse at random, what is the probability that the coin will be worth less than 11¢?

23 If a number is picked at random from the set {1, 2, 3, 4}, find the probability that the number is a solution for $2x + 5 > 7$.

24 Given the letters: H, T, P, and L, if one is picked at random, what is the probability that the letter chosen has vertical line symmetry?

25 A single card is drawn from a standard deck of 52 cards, what is the probability the card is a five or a diamond?

26 The probability of a particular manufactured widget being defective is $\frac{1}{100}$. How many defective products would be expected in a random sample of 1500 widgets?

27 If a number is randomly selected from the set {1, 2, 3, 4, 5}, what is the probability it is a prime number?

28 If a figure is randomly selected from the set {square, rectangle, trapezoid, rhombus}, what is the probability it is a parallelogram?

29 A set of geometric figures consists of a square, a trapezoid, an obtuse triangle, an equilateral triangle, and a rhombus. If one of the figures is selected at random, what is the probability that all its sides are congruent?

13.3 LONG ANSWER QUESTION: FOR CHAPTER 13

1 When one is headed south, a particular traffic light on the corner of East Broadway and Roslyn Road has the red light on for 30 seconds, the yellow for 10 seconds, and the green for 40 seconds.

PART A

What is the probability of encountering a red light when you arrive headed south at the corner where the light is located? Show all of your work.

Answer _____

PART B

During the year, if I am headed south at this intersection 400 times, how many times should I expect to have a green light? Explain how you arrived at your answer and/or show all of your work.

Answer _____

2 Three friends are going to share a display table at a flea market. The amount of space given to each person is based on the amount of money he pays. Adam is paying $10; Barney is paying $20, and Carl is paying $30.

PART A

What fraction of the table do they each get? Show all of your work.

Answer: Adam: _____

   Barney: _____

   Carl: _____

PART B

Divide the rectangular table shown below to reflect how much space each friend should get. Label each section with A for Adam, B for Barney, or C for Carl. Use the grid on the table to divide the table.

Answer:

PART C

If 240 people at the flea market stop at the boys' table, how many would you expect to examine Adam's merchandise first? Show all of your work.

Answer _____ people

3 There are 3 different roads directly connecting Town A to Town B. There are 4 different roads connecting Town B to Town C, and there are 2 different roads connecting Town C to Town D.

PART A

How many different paths are possible going from Town A to Town D passing through Towns B and C only once?

Answer _____ different paths

Explain how you arrived at your answer and/or show your calculations.

_____

_____

_____

_____

_____

_____

PART B

If one of the roads from Town B to Town C has delays due to construction, what is the probability of being on this road when you go from A to D through Towns B and C as described in Part A?

Answer _____

Explain how you arrived at your answer and/or show all of your calculations.

_____

_____

_____

_____

_____

_____

Example 1: If it rains, I will get wet. Does that also mean that if I get wet, then it rains? The study of logic will help to analyze this.

Example 2: Venn diagrams help to show the overlap between groups. The results of a vote about pizza toppings showed that 8 people liked mushrooms, 7 liked peppers, 7 liked pepperoni, and 4 liked onions. Believe it or not, only 9 people took part in the survey!

Example 3: If it is solid green, it is not striped.
   If it is not solid green, it is striped.
   If it is not striped, it is solid green.
   If it is striped, it is not solid green.

Which statement is logically equivalent to the first statement?

Example 4: Adam told his mom that he had invited 6 people from his math class, 4 people from his science class, and 6 people from his English class to come over and watch the Super Bowl. His mom bought lots of snacks and drinks. Six people showed up on the day of the party. His mom asked Adam when the other people were coming. Adam responded that all the people had come! How is this possible?

Venn diagrams are pictures which show the overlap between and among groups. This chapter will explain logical reasoning and Venn diagrams.

14.1   Logic

If..., Then...

Name	Description	Example
Conditional Statement	the original "if _____, then _____" sentence	If it rains, then I get wet.
Converse	the opposite of the original statement (the sentence reversed)	If I get wet, then it rains.
Inverse	the negation of each part of the original statement	If it does not rain, then I do not get wet.
Contrapositive	the inverse of the converse or the converse of the inverse	If I do not get wet, then it did not rain.

❽   A statement and its Contrapositive always have the same Truth Value as each other.

❽   The Converse and Inverse of a statement always have the same truth value as each other.

Our Turn

Q: Given the statement: "If I study, then I will pass math."

A:

1   Write the converse of the statement.

1   If I pass math, then I studied.

2   Write the inverse of the statement.

2   If I do not study, then I will not pass math.

3   Write the Contrapositive of the statement.

3   If I do not pass math, then I did not study.

Your Turn

Given the following statement: "If the water temperature reaches 100°C, then the water boils."

1   Write the converse of the given statement.

_____

_____

_____

2   Write the inverse of the given statement.

_____

_____

_____

3   Write the converse of the inverse of the given statement.

_____

_____

_____

_____

4   Write the contrapositive of the given statement.

_____

_____

_____

5 What is the converse of the statement: "If you use too much milk, then your cereal gets soggy."

A Soggy cereal is caused by using too much milk.

B If you do not use too much milk, then your cereal did not get soggy.

C If your cereal gets soggy, then you did not use too much milk.

D If your cereal gets soggy, then you used too much milk.

Given the statement: "If company comes, then I will bake a cake."

6 Write the contrapositive of the given statement.

_____

_____

_____

7 Write the inverse of the contrapositive of the given statement.

_____

_____

_____

8 Write the converse of the given statement.

_____

_____

_____

9 Which statement is the inverse of "If I pass this test, then I am happy."

F If I am not happy, then I pass the test.

G If I am happy, then I pass this test.

H If I do not pass this test, then I am happy.

J If I do not pass this test, then I am not happy.

Use the given statement: "If I do not study, then I will not pass math."

10 Write the inverse of the given statement.

_____

_____

_____

11 Write the converse of the given statement.

_____

_____

_____

12 Write the inverse of the converse of the given statement.

_____

_____

_____

13 Write the converse of the inverse of the given statement.

_____

_____

_____

14 Write the contrapositive of the given statement.

_____

_____

_____

14.2 Venn Diagrams

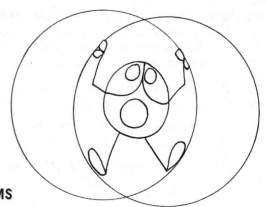

Introduction to Venn Diagrams

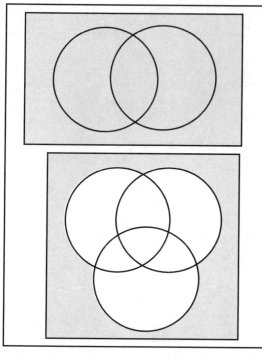

A typical Venn diagram is a rectangular box with two or three overlapping circles inside.

• The rectangle represents the entire universe for the problem.

_____

• The circles represent sets.

Shading Venn Diagrams

Symbol	Shaded Area Represents	People Example
A *B* (shaded circle A)	The shaded area represents event *A*.	The number of people doing event *A*.
A *B* (shaded circle B)	The shaded area represents event *B*.	The number of people doing event *B*.
A *B* (shaded overlap)	The shaded area represents the overlap of event *A* and *B*.	The number of people doing both events *A* and *B*.

Symbol	Shaded Area Represents	People Example
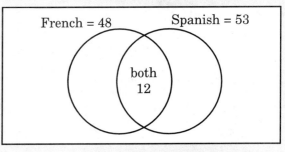	The shaded area represents *A* without *B*.	The number of people doing only event *A* and not event *B*.
	The shaded area represents *B* without *A*.	The number of people doing only event *B* and not event *A*.
	The shaded area represents *A* or *B*.	The number of people doing event *A* or event *B* or both.
	The shaded area represents neither *A* nor *B*.	The number of people doing neither *A* nor *B*.
	The shaded area represents the sum of *A* only and *B* only.	The number of people doing event *A* but not *B* and the number of people doing event *B* but not *A*.

OUR TURN

Q: At HANC Middle School, there are 140 eighth grade students. Forty-eight are taking French, fifty-three are taking Spanish, and twelve are taking both.

1 How many are taking only French?

2 How many taking only Spanish?

3 How many are taking at least one of the two languages?

4 How many are taking neither French nor Spanish?

A:
Draw a Venn Diagram
   Inside the rectangle represents the total of eighth grade students at the school = 140.

- Let circle *F* represent the 48 students taking French.
- Let circle *S* represent 53 students taking Spanish.
- Let the overlap of the circles represent the 12 students taking both languages.

1 36

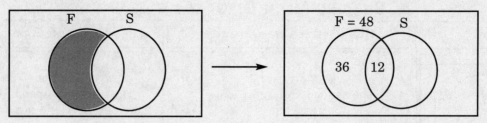

The 48 taking French less the 12 taking both, leaves those only taking French
48 – 12 = 36

2 41

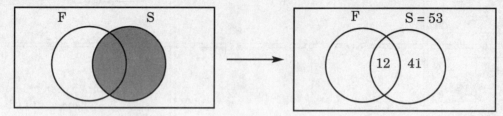

The 53 taking Spanish less the 12 taking both yields those taking only Spanish
53 – 12 = 41

3 89

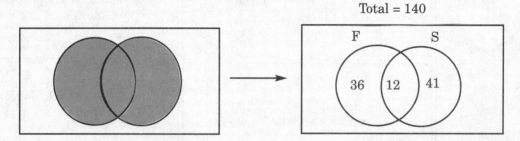

The number of different students taking at least one of the languages is the sum of:

36 taking only French
12 taking both
<u>41 taking only Spanish</u>
89

4 51

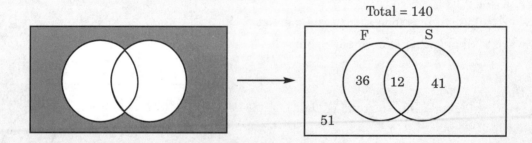

89 of the 140 students are taking at least one of the two languages.
The balance are taking neither: 140 – 89 = 51

YOUR TURN

At a party, 10 people had only ice cream, 4 people had only cake, and 8 had both. If two people had neither, answer the following questions.

1 How many had ice cream?

2 How many had cake?

3 How many had at least one of the two deserts?

4 What is the total amount of people at the party?

Seventy-two of the 140 students in the 8th grade are in the school orchestra, 42 are in the chorus, and 12 are in both. For this 8th grade:

5 How many are in the orchestra only?

6 How many are in the chorus only?

7 How many are in neither?

8 How many different students are there in the combined orchestra-chorus group?

Use the Venn Diagram below to answer questions 9–15.

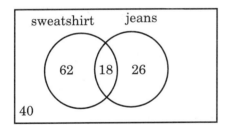

If the diagram represents the entire 8th grade class:

9 How many are wearing a sweatshirt but not jeans?

10 How many are wearing a sweatshirt?

11 How many are wearing jeans but not a sweatshirt?

12 How many are wearing both?

13 How many are wearing at least one of these two items?

14 How many are wearing neither item?

15 How many different students are represented by the diagram?

16 Complete the Venn Diagram below to show the positive integer factors of 30 and 18.

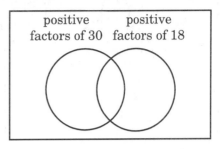

17 Using the Venn Diagram below, how many elements are in the overlap of the two sets?

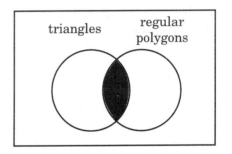

Use the Venn Diagram below to answer questions 18 – 21.

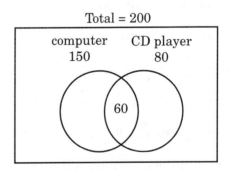

18 How many students have a *CD* player but not a computer?

19 How many have a computer but not a *CD* player?

20 How many have at least one of the two items?

21 How many have neither?

Use the Venn Diagram below to answer questions 22–29.

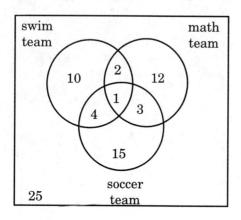

22 How many are on all three teams?

23 How many belong to the swimming and soccer teams, but not the math team?

24 How many belong to only the math team?

25 How many belong to none of the three teams?

26 How many students are represented by the entire Venn Diagram?

27 How many are on exactly two teams?

28 How many are on the soccer team?

29 How many are only on one team?

14.4 LONG ANSWER QUESTIONS FOR CHAPTER 14

1 A marketing company surveyed 400 people in a shopping mall to determine if they owned a *VCR*, a computer and/or a *DVD* player. They compiled the following results:

- 80 owned all three items.

- 110 owned both a computer and a *VCR*.

- 130 owned both a computer and a *DVD*.

- 40 owned both a *VCR* and a *DVD* but not a computer.

- a total of 200 owned a computer.

- a total of 200 owned a *DVD*.

- 20 owned none of the three items

PART A

Label and complete the accompanying Venn diagram based on the survey data.

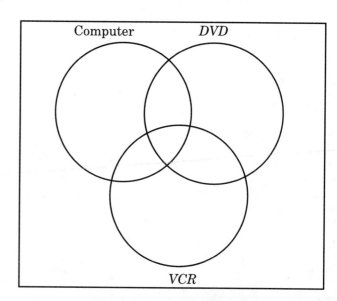

PART B

Based on the data above, how many people surveyed had only a *VCR* (no computer or *DVD* player)?

Answer _____ people

Show your work or explain in words how you arrived at the number of people with only a *VCR*.

_____

_____

_____

2 At a school awards night, 300 guests attended and they all enjoyed pizza. In addition to cheese (which is not considered a topping), some were ordered with meat (pepperoni or meatball), some were ordered with mushrooms, and some were plain cheese.

Label and complete the accompanying Venn diagram in Part *A* based on the following data which reflects the number of people in each category.

- 10 had only mushrooms.
- 20 had both kinds of meat but no mushrooms.
- 30 had pepperoni and mushrooms but no meatballs.
- 40 had none of the 3 toppings (just cheese).
- 50 had only pepperoni.
- 150 had pepperoni.
- 90 had exactly 2 toppings.

PART A

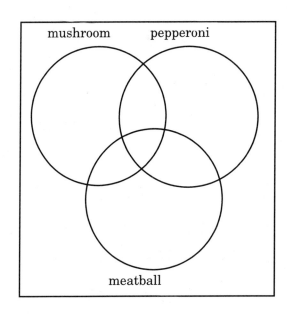

PART B

How many had all 3 toppings?

Answer _____

Explain how you arrived at your answer and/or show all of your calculations.

_____

_____

_____

PART C

How many had only meatballs?

Answer _____

Explain how you arrived at your answer and/or show all of your calculations.

_____

_____

_____

3 Given the accompanying Venn diagram which reflects an 8th grade study about 3 of students' favorite hot foods. Each of the 180 students surveyed liked at least one of the 3 foods.

```
          hot dogs              pizza

             8        x        10

                 40   60   30

                      12

                  hamburgers
```

PART A

How many students like only one of these foods?

Answer _____ students

Show all of your work and/or explain how you arrived at your answer.

_____

_____

_____

PART B

How many students liked hot dogs?

Answer _____ students

Explain how you arrived at your answer and/or show all of your calculations.

_____

_____

_____

Now let us apply all of our learning to a real-world example. The Pizza π Pizzeria will help us see what we have learned and how these skills are used in everyday life. It is guaranteed to make you hungry!

At the Pizza π Pizzeria, cheese is standard on all pizzas and is not considered a topping; however, extra cheese is. Two types of crust are available, thick or thin. It is your choice, and there are no extra charges for either crust. Each pie is cut into 8 equal slices regardless of the size of the pie.

Use the information on page 240 and in the accompanying drawings to help answer the following questions.

1 How many ways can 2 different toppings be selected?

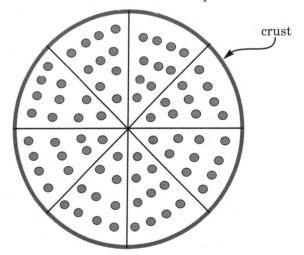

medium pie slice

pepperoni pieces

large pie slice

2 If only 1 extra topping is ordered, how many different pies can be ordered? (Remember to consider types of topping, types of crust, and different sizes.)

5 On the medium and large pies, the pepperoni is arranged as shown in the illustration above. If 120 pies were made during the day, how many more pieces of pepperoni would be used if the 120 were all large pies compared with the 120 being all medium pies? (All pies are cut into 8 slices.)

Use the illustration below to answer questions 6–8.

crust

3 How many ways can 3 different toppings be selected?

4 James spent $71 before tax buying exactly 7 pizzas, each with no extra toppings. How many of each of the 3 sizes did he buy?

6 The pizza has rotational symmetry of how many degrees?

7 What is the length of the crust around a medium pizza to the nearest tenth of an inch. (Use $\pi = 3.14$)

8 Using the illustration, what is the area, to the nearest square inch, of each slice of a large pie? (Use π = 3.14)

11 How many small pizzas are required to equal the same area as 2 large pizzas? (Use π = 3.14)

9 If you are buying a whole pie at the Pizza π Pizzaria, which size pizza, with no extra topping, is the better buy? (The most pizza for the least money.) Show all work.

12 If the delivery service is free and, at 40 mph, a pie can be delivered in 12 minutes, how long should it take to make the same trip at 30 mph?

10 The area of the large pie is what percent bigger than the area of a small pie? (Use π = 3.14) Show all work.

13
PART A

If the local tax rate is 8% and you order 1 large pie with 1 topping and one small pie with "the works," what is the cost including tax? Show all of your work.

Answer: $ _____

PART B

If you pay with 2 twenty dollar bills and a quarter, how much change should you get? Show all of your work.

Answer: $ _____

14 A survey was done of veggie toppings used. The results are shown in the table at the right.

Peppers	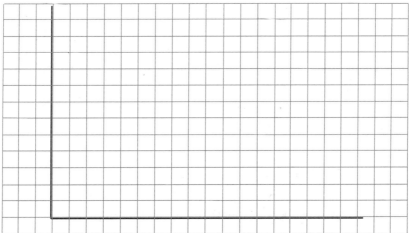
Mushrooms	
Onion	

Part A

Draw a bar graph below showing the survey results. Be sure to label your axes, choose a proper scale, and title your graph.

Part B

If the results from the above table were shown in a Venn Diagram, they appears as shown below. However, the diagram is only partially completed. Complete the Venn Diagram, and explain how you arrived at the missing values called x, y, and z.

pepper = 10   mushroom = 8

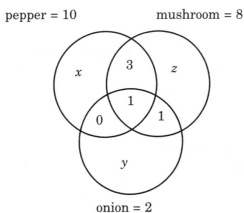

onion = 2

Explain your answer on the lines below:

_____

_____

_____

_____

Answers: $x =$ _____

$y =$ _____

$z =$ _____

15 Answer the following questions assuming a topping was chosen at random.

Part A

What is the probability of choosing meatballs as the topping?

Part B

What is the probability of choosing sausage as the topping?

Part C

What is the probability of choosing peppers or meatballs as the topping?

16 During the day, the owner of the Pizza π Pizzaria sold 12 more small pies than large ones, and 2 more large pies than medium ones, for a total of 130 pies. Let x be the number of large pies sold.

Part A

Write an equation that can be used to solve for x.

Part B

Solve the equation for x and determine how many pies of each size were sold. Show all of your work.

Answers: _____ small pies
_____ medium pies
_____ large pies

ASSESSMENTS: SAMPLE TEST ONE

SESSION 1 PART 1

1 $-15 \times -2.3 =$

  A – 34.5

  B – 3.45

  C 3.45

  D 34.5

2 Which of the following represents the prime factorization of 24?

  F $6 \times 2 \times 2$

  G $4 \times 3 \times 2$

  H $3 \times 2 \times 2 \times 2$

  J $12 + 12$

3 To solve the following expression, which operation should be performed first?

$$14 - (6 + 4) \times 6 \div 2$$

  A +

  B –

  C ×

  D ÷

4 The daily low temperatures during a given week in Buffalo, New York were recorded as follows:

$$7°, -3°, -8°, 0°, 1°, 4°, -2°$$

Which of the following is a list of these temperatures from least to greatest?

  F $0°, 1°, -2°, -3°, 4°, 7°, -8°$

  G $-8°, 7°, 4°, -3°, -2°, 1°, 0°$

  H $-8°, -3°, -2°, 0°, 1°, 4°, 7°$

  J $-2°, -3°, -8°, 0°, 1°, 4°, 7°$

5 Between which two integers does the $\sqrt{38}$ lie?

  A 6 and 7

  B 7 and 8

  C 19 and 20

  D 37 and 39

6 Two coins are tossed. Which tree diagram can be used to find all possible outcomes?

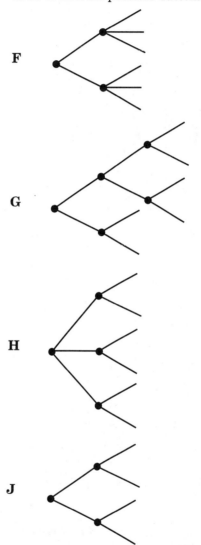

7 Yuri bought CDs from a catalog. Music CDs cost $9.99 each, and game CDs cost $12.99 each. If Yuri paid $55.95 for his CD purchase, (not including tax or shipping) and bought 2 game CDs, how many music CDs did he buy?

  A 1

  B 2

  C 3

  D 4

8 If the following pattern continues, which number will come next?

$$3, 10, 17, 24, \_\_$$

F 31

G 32

H 33

J 34

Questions numbered 9 through 11 are based on the accompanying bar graph which shows the student population at HANC High School in Nassau County.

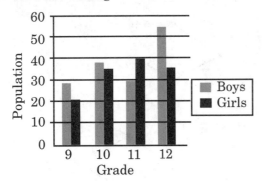

9 How many students are in the school?

A 245

B 265

C 285

D 305

10 Which of the following statements is a reasonable conclusion based on the bar graph?

F There are twice as many boys as girls in the school.

G There is the same number of boys as girls in the school.

H The largest difference between the number of boys and girls occurs in grade 12.

J More students are in grade 10 than in any other grade.

11 Based on the graph, which one of the following statements is true?

A There are the same amount of girls in grade 9 and grade 11.

B There are the same amount of boys in grade 10 and grade 12.

C There are more boys in the school than girls.

D The eleventh grade has the greatest population by grade.

12 Gino paid $8.25 to call California from a coin phone. Using the accompanying prices, how many minutes did the phone call last?

Coin phone rates to California
1st minute: $1.50
Each additional minute: $0.75

F 7

G 8

H 9

J 10

13 If the area of a rectangular garden is 126 square feet and the length is 9 feet, what is the width?

A 117 feet

B 54 feet

C 36 feet

D 14 feet

14 Which inequality is represented by the number line graph below?

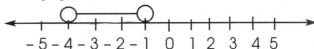

F $-4 < x < -1$

G $-1 < x < -4$

H $-4 \leq x \leq -1$

J $-1 \leq x \leq -4$

15 $T, M, J, E,$ and N are waiting in line to see the newest release at the movies. J stands 2 places in front of T. T stands 3 places behind E, and N is 2 places in front of J. In what order are they standing together in line from front to back? (Note: the front is on the left.)

A T, J, M, E, N

B N, E, J, M, T

C T, M, J, E, N

D T, M, J, N, E

16 Which of the following represents an irrational number?

F π

G 64

H 25%

J $\frac{1}{3}$

17 If $4^{n+1} = 64$, what is the value of n?

A 0

B 1

C 2

D 3

18 Shane practiced the piano every day last week. The accompanying table shows the day of the week and the amount of time he practiced. Based on the table, how many total hours did he practice last week?

Day	Time Spent Practicing
Sunday	$1\frac{1}{2}$
Monday	1
Tuesday	$\frac{3}{4}$
Wednesday	$1\frac{1}{2}$
Thursday	$1\frac{1}{4}$
Friday	$\frac{1}{2}$
Saturday	$1\frac{3}{4}$

F $7\frac{3}{4}$

G 8

H $8\frac{1}{4}$

J $9\frac{1}{2}$

19 Which of the following equations is true?

A $(3 \cdot 4)^2 = 3^2 \cdot 4^2$

B $(3 + 4)^2 = 3^2 + 4^2$

C $(3 - 4)^2 = 3^2 - 4^2$

D $(3 \cdot 4)^2 = 3^2 \cdot 4$

20 Which of the following is an example of the associative law?

F $2 \cdot (3x + 4) = 2 \cdot 3x + 2 \cdot 4$

G $(2 + x) + 3 = 2 + (x + 3)$

H $(2 + x) \cdot 3 = 3 \cdot (2 + x)$

J $(3 + x) + 2 = 2 + (3 + x)$

21 The length of an actual train car is 60 feet. If the model company used a scale of 1 inch represents 12 feet, how many inches long is the model?

A 5

B 8

C 12

D 60

22 Rhett rented 2 video tapes at the same time and returned them at the same time. If his total bill was $12.00, how many days late did he return the tapes. Use the accompanying chart for fees.

Fees per video tape	
Rental	$3.00
Late fee per day	$0.75
Purchase (new)	$20.00
Purchase (used)	$8.00

F 5

G 4

H 3

I 2

23 Using the picture of the cube below, which edge is parallel to $\overline{EF}$?

A $\overline{AD}$

B $\overline{CG}$

C $\overline{DC}$

D $\overline{EH}$

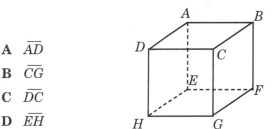

24 Line segment $\overline{AB}$ is shown on the grid below. Point C for a second line $\overline{CD}$ is also shown on the grid.

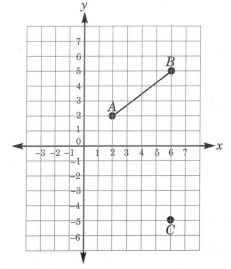

Which set of coordinates for point D will create line segment $\overline{CD}$ as the reflection of $\overline{AB}$ in the x-axis?

F $(2, -6)$

G $(6, -2)$

H $(2, -2)$

J $(2, 2)$

25 Lisa wants to make at least $15 per hour cutting hair. Her earnings include an hourly wage of "w" dollars and "t" dollars per hour in tips. Which inequality best describes the situation?

A $t + 15 \leq w$

B $w + t \leq 15$

C $w + t \geq 15$

D $t > w + 15$

26 A theater is selling tickets to a concert. It charges a service fee of $4.00 per order in addition to $32.00 per ticket. If "$n$" represents the number of tickets sold, which equation shows "C," the total cost in dollars for this order?

F $C = 36n$

G $C = 32(n + 4)$

H $C = 4n + 32$

J $C = 32n + 4$

27 Ariana surveyed a class about favorite colors. The results are shown by the tally below.

Color	Votes
Red	╫╫
Purple	╫╫ ‖
Blue	╫╫ ╫╫ │
Green	‖│
Black	│
Other	‖

Which of the following measurements can best be found using this data?

A the mean

B the mode

C the median

D the range

TEST ONE
SESSION 1 PART 2

28 Bob and Ray are describing the same number. Bob says, "The number is a positive even integer less than or equal to 20." Ray says, "The number is divisible by 4." If Bob's statement is true and Ray's statement is false, what are all the possible numbers?

Answer : _____

Explain your answer on the lines below:

_____

_____

_____

_____

29
PART A
Which of the following numbers are irrational? Circle all the numbers that qualify.

$\sqrt{10}$ 17.1 $\sqrt{81}$ π $\sqrt{.04}$

PART B
Explain in words how you can tell if a number is rational or irrational.

_____

_____

_____

_____

_____

30 The variables a, b, c, and d each represent a different non-zero integer. Given the equations (in the box below), find the values of a, b, c, and d.

Answers: $a =$

$\quad\quad\quad b =$

$\quad\quad\quad c =$

$\quad\quad\quad d =$

$$\boxed{\begin{aligned} & \bullet \quad b + c = d \\ & \bullet \quad a \div c = a \\ & \bullet \quad c + c + c = d \\ & \bullet \quad a - 2b = b \end{aligned}}$$

Explain how you arrived at your answers for the values of a, b, c, d.

_____

_____

_____

_____

_____

31 The graph at the right shows Marie's distance from home (A) to work (F) at various times during her drive.

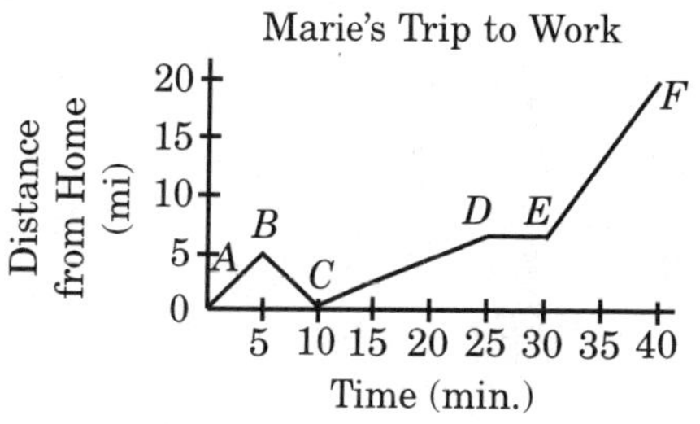

Marie's Trip to Work

PART A

Marie left her briefcase at home and had to return to get it. State which point represents when she turned back around to go home.

Answer: _____

Explain how you arrived at that conclusion.

_____

_____

_____

_____

_____

PART B

Marie also had to wait at the railroad track for a train to pass. How long did she wait?

Answer: _____

Explain how you arrived at your answer.

_____

_____

_____

_____

_____

32 There were seven students running in a race. How many different arrangements of first, second, and third place are possible? Show all of your work.

Answer: _____

33
Part A
Draw all the symmetry lines on the accompanying figure.

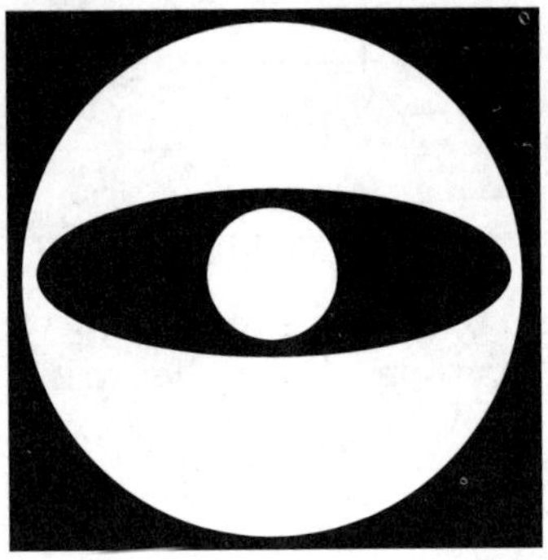

Part B
If the original figure above is rotated about its center, how many degrees of rotational symmetry does it have?

Answer: _____

Explain your answer.

_____

_____

_____

_____

_____

Part C
Does the original figure above have point symmetry?

Answer: _____ (Yes or No)

Explain your answer.

_____

_____

_____

_____

_____

34
PART A

Triangle *SUN* has coordinates *S*(0, 6), *U*(3, 5), and *N*(3, 0). On the accompanying grid, draw and label △ *SUN*.

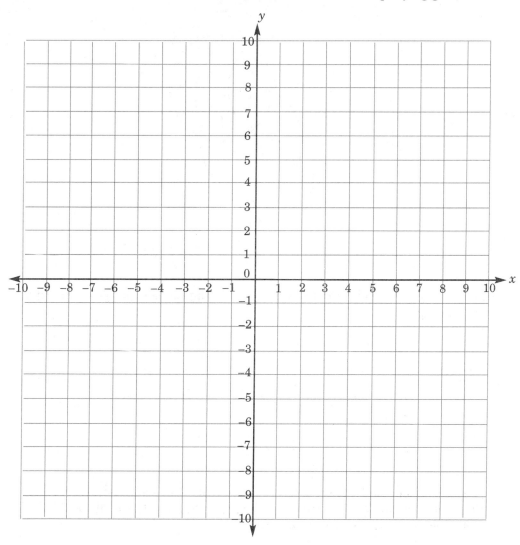

PART B

On the same coordinates graph △ *GHI*, the image of △ *SUN* after a reflection in the *x*-axis.

The coordinates of △ *GHI* are: *G*(,   ) *H*(,   ) *I*(,   )

35 A swimmer plans to swim at least 100 laps during a 6-day period. During this period, the swimmer will increase the number of laps completed each day by one lap. What is the *least* number of laps the swimmer must complete on the first day? Show all of your work.

Answer: _____

36

PART A

The accompanying Venn diagram shows the number of students who take various courses. All students in circle *A* take mathematics. All in circle *B* take science. All in circle *C* take technology. What percentage of the students take mathematics or technology? Show all of your work.

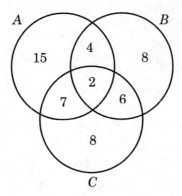

Answer: _____

PART B

Explain how you determined the values to use when calculating the percentage of the students taking mathematics or technology.

_____

_____

_____

_____

_____

37 Keesha wants to tile the floor space shown in the diagram below. If each tile measures 1 foot by 1 foot and costs $3.00, what will be the total cost for tiling the floor? All the lines in the diagram meet at 90° angles and there are no additional costs. Show all your work.

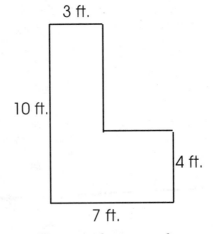

Figure not drawn to scale

Answer: _____

38 The distance from Earth to the imaginary planet Med is 1.7×10^7 miles. If a spaceship is capable of traveling 1,420 miles per hour, how many days will it take the spaceship to reach the planet Med? Round your answer to the nearest day. Show all of your work.

Answer: _____

39 A surveyor needs to determine the distance across the pond shown in the accompanying diagram. He determined that the distance from his position to point P on the south shore of the pond is 175 meters and the angle from his position to point X on the north shore is 35°. Determine the distance, PX, across the pond, rounded to the nearest meter. Show all of your work.

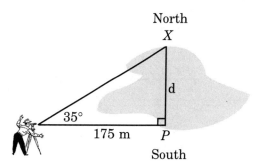

Answer: _____

40

Ashanti is surveying for a new parking lot shaped like a parallelogram. She knows that three of the vertices of parallelogram *ABCD* are *A*(0, 0), *B*(5, 2), and *C*(6, 5). Find the coordinates of point *D* and sketch parallelogram *ABCD* on the accompanying set of axes.

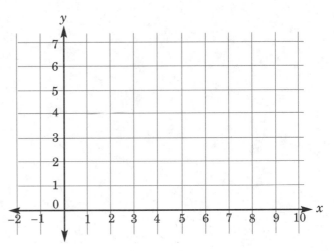

Answer: Coordinates of point *D*(,   )

PART B

Explain how you know that the figure you have drawn is a parallelogram.

_____

_____

_____

_____

_____

41 Jessica is thinking of a number between 20 and 30. The number is prime and not more than 2 away from a perfect square. What is the number?

Answer: _____

Explain how you arrived at your answer.

_____

_____

_____

_____

_____

42 In the accompanying diagram, $\triangle ABC$ and $\triangle ABD$ are isosceles triangles with $m\angle CAB = 50$ and $m\angle BDA = 55$. If $AB = AC$ and $AB = BD$, what is $m\angle CBD$?

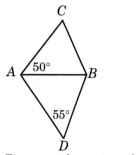

Figure not drawn to scale

Answer: $m\angle CBD$ _____ degrees

Explain how you arrived at your answer for the measure of angle CBD.

_____

_____

_____

_____

_____

43 A newly discovered element, Normonium, has a half-life of 10 days. A half-life is the period of time at which half of what you have disappears.

PART A

If Josh has 2000 grams of Normonium, how much Normonium will there be after 40 days? Show all of your work.

Answer: _____ grams

PART B

If Josh starts with 8000 grams of Normonium, how many days will it take to have 250 grams left? Show all of your work or explain how your arrived at your answer.

Answer: _____ days.

PART C

If Josh has exactly 38 grams of Normonium after 60 days, how many days earlier did he have exactly 76 grams of Normonium? Show all of your work or explain how you arrived at your answer.

Answer: _____ days.

44 The Grimaldis have three children born in different years.

PART A

Draw a tree diagram or list a sample space to show all the possible arrangements of boy and girl children in the Grimaldi family.

PART B

Using information from Part A, what is the probability that the Grimaldis have three boys?

Answer: _____

Explain how you arrived at the probability of the Grimaldi family having three boys.

_____

_____

_____

_____

_____

45 Judy needs a mean (average) score of 86 on four tests to earn a midterm grade of *B*. If the mean of her scores for the first three tests was 83, what is the *lowest* score on a 100-point scale that she can receive on the fourth test to have a midterm grade of *B*?

PART A

Write an equation which can be used to determine Judy's grade on the fourth test. Let "*t*" represent the unknown test grade.

Equation: _____

PART B

Solve the equation you wrote and determine the necessary test grade that Judy needs. Show all of your work.

Judy's fourth test grade: _____

ASSESSMENTS: SAMPLE TEST TWO

TEST 2
SESSION 1 PART 1

1 If $2x + 3y = 18$ and $x = 3$, what is the value of y?

A 3

B 4

C 7

D 10

2 Which of the following is a prime number?

F 37

G 39

H 51

J 57

3 In the figure below, line l is parallel to line m and both are cut by line w. If angle a measures 28°, what is the measure of angle b in degrees?

A 28

B 62

C 118

D 152

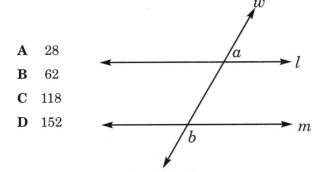

4 The students' recent exam scores in Mr. Urban's class are shown below in the stem and leaf plot. What was the median score on this exam?

F 99

G 88

H 84

J 67

Stem	Leaf
6	7 8
7	4 5 6 7 8 8 9
8	0 4 8 8 9
9	2 6 7 8 8 9 9

5 Which table shows an example of direct variation?

A

x	y
1	4
2	2
3	$\frac{4}{3}$
4	1

C

x	y
2	24
4	12
6	8
8	6

B

x	y
1	$\frac{1}{2}$
2	1
3	$\frac{3}{2}$
4	2

D

x	y
1	1
2	4
3	9
4	16

6 One day in Niagara Falls, NY, it was – 4º F; six months later, it was 87º F. How far apart are these two temperatures?

F 83º

G 84º

H 87º

J 91º

7 Which one of the following is the most appropriate unit to report the speed of a turtle?

A yards per second

B millimeters per second

C kilometers per second

D miles per hour

8 A seagull flying overhead goes in a circular pattern with a diameter of approximately 30 feet. How far, to the nearest foot, does the bird travel in two revolutions? (use $\pi = 3.14$)

F 188 ft.

G 180 ft.

H 94 ft.

J 74 ft.

9 A map of New York State is shown below. Based on the scale, how many miles is it from Albany to Syracuse?

Scale: 1 cm = 30 mi.
Map not drawn to scale.

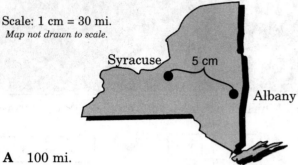

A 100 mi.

B 120 mi.

C 130 mi.

D 150 mi.

10 The planet Saturn is 1,427,000,000 km from the Sun. This distance when expressed in scientific notations is which of the following?

F $1{,}427 \times 10^{6}$

G 14.27×10^{8}

H 1.427×10^{9}

J 1.427×10^{10}

11 Given angle "a" as shown at right, which angle is the complement of this angle?

A

B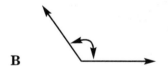

C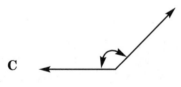

D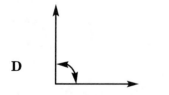

12 Given the following letters, which have vertical or horizontal line symmetry?

Z W S D

F Z and D only

G Z, D, and W only

H Z, D, W, and S

J W and D only

Directions: Use the accompanying spinner and bag of colored marbles to do questions 13–16.

On the spinner the space for letters A, B, and C are equal and the space of D and E are each half of the space for A.

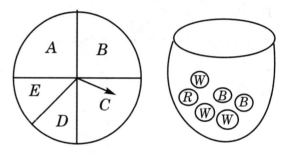

The bag contains 6 marbles of equal size. One is red, two are blue, and three are white labeled, R, B, and W, respectively.

13 If the spinner is used once, what is the probability of it landing in the space marked C?

A $\frac{1}{4}$

B $\frac{1}{5}$

C $\frac{1}{6}$

D $\frac{1}{9}$

14 If a colored marble is selected at random from the bag, what is the probability of selecting a white marble?

F $\frac{1}{6}$

G $\frac{1}{3}$

H $\frac{1}{4}$

J $\frac{1}{2}$

15 The spinner is spun once and then a marble is picked at random. Which of the following can be used to correctly calculate the probability of landing in the E space on the spinner and selecting the red marble?

A $\frac{1}{4} \times \frac{1}{6}$

B $\frac{1}{8} \times \frac{1}{6}$

C $\frac{1}{4} + \frac{1}{6}$

D $\frac{1}{5} \times \frac{1}{6}$

16 If a larger bag of 72 marbles contains the same colors as our bag of 6 marbles and in the same proportion, how many blue marbles will be in the larger bag?

F 12

G 24

H 36

J 48

17 How many faces does a pentagonal pyramid have?

A 5

B 6

C 7

D 8

18 Which of the following diagrams represents a prism?

F

G

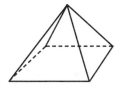

H

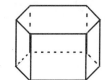

J

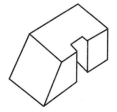

19 On the grid below, triangle NJL is graphed. If points A and B are as shown on the grid, what would be the coordinates of point C to create a similar triangle?

A $(-5, 4)$

B $(1, 4)$

C $(8, 4)$

D $(-1, 4)$

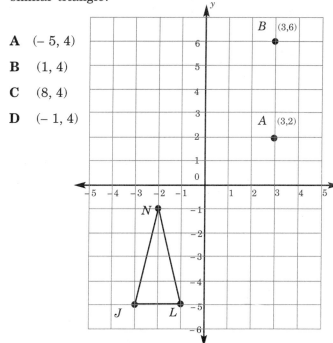

20 Which property is demonstrated in the equation below?

$$a + (2 \times b) = a + (b \times 2)$$

F distributive property

G commutative property of addition

H commutative property of multiplication

J associative property of addition

21 In the accompanying figures: $\triangle ABC \sim \triangle NJL$

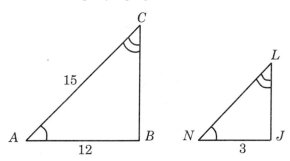

If $AB = 12$ and $AC = 15$, what is the length of NL if $NJ = 3$?

A 6

B 5

C $4\frac{1}{4}$

D $3\frac{3}{4}$

22 Barney is enclosing his rectangular garden with a fence. One side of the garden does not have to be fenced because it is against the entire side of the house as shown in the diagram.

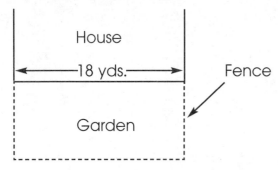

How much fencing is needed to enclose a garden of 108 square yards?

F 6 yards

G 24 yards

H 30 yards

J 48 yards

23 Allison and Jessica each collect stuffed animals. Together they have 30 animals. If Allison has 3 fewer than twice what Jessica has, how many stuffed animals does Jessica have?

A 8

B 9

C 11

D 14

24 Which of the following expressions is a simplification of the expression given below?

$$3(x + 2) - 2(x - 1)$$

F $5x + 8$

G $5x + 4$

H $x + 8$

J $x - 4$

25 Based on the diagrams and dimensions shown below, which two figures have equal area? (Figures not drawn to scale.)

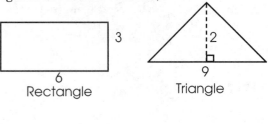

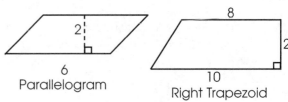

A rectangle and triangle

B rectangle and right trapezoid

C triangle and parallelogram

D parallelogram and right trapezoid

26 Seven friends who had not seen each other in a long time met for lunch. If every person shook everyone's hands only once, how many handshakes took place?

F 7

G 14

H 21

J 28

27 Gary has "d" dimes and "q" quarters. Which expression can be used to represent how many nickels are equivalent?

A $10d + 25q$

B $\dfrac{d}{10} + \dfrac{q}{25}$

C $\dfrac{d}{2} + \dfrac{q}{5}$

D $2d + 5q$

28 Alan, Becky, Janis, and Mariah are four students in the chess club. If two of these students will be selected to represent the school at a national convention, how many combinations of two students are possible? Show all of your work.

Answer: _____

29 Two different surveys were done. In the first survey, 630 people were asked whether they liked Chinese food. In the second survey, 900 people were asked whether they liked Italian food. The results are shown in the graphs at the right.

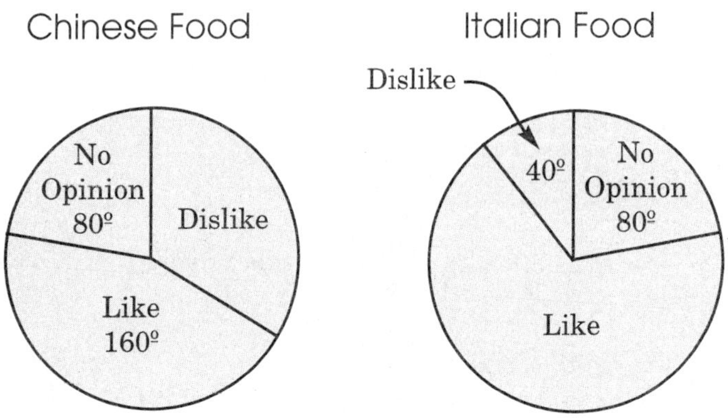

PART A

Based on the Chinese food survey results, to the nearest whole percent, what percent of those surveyed disliked Chinese food? Show all of your work.

Chinese Food

No Opinion 80° Dislike Like 160°

Italian Food

Dislike — 40° No Opinion 80° Like

Answer: _____ %

PART B

Based on the Italian food survey, how many people liked Italian food? Show all of your work.

Answer: _____ people

PART C

How many more people in the Italian food survey had no opinion about Italian food than had no opinion about Chinese food in the Chinese food survey? Show all of your work.

Answer: _____ people

30 Aryeh is building a rectangular dog pen that he wishes to enclose. The width of the pen is 2 yards less than the length. If the perimeter of the dog pen is 16 yards, what is the length of the pen?

PART A

Write an equation, using the letter "*l*" to represent the length, that can be used to find the length, in yards, of the rectangular pen.

Equation:

PART B

Solve the equation to find the dimensions of the pen and the enclosed area. Show all of your work.

Length: _____ yards

Width: _____ yards

Area: _____ square yards

31 The coordinates of endpoints of AB are $A(0, 2)$ and $B(4, 6)$. Graph and state the coordinates of N and L, the images of A and B after AB is reflected in the y axis.

Answer: N (,   ) L (,   )

Explain how you located the coordinates of N and L.

_____

_____

_____

_____

_____

32 A school district offers hockey and basketball. The result of a survey of 300 students showed:

> 120 students play hockey, only
> 90 students play basketball, only
> 30 students do not participate in either sport

Of those surveyed, how many students play both hockey and basketball? Show all of your work or explain in words how you arrived at your answer.

Answer: _____ students

_____

_____

_____

_____

_____

33 Katrina hikes 6 miles north, 5 miles east, and then 6 miles north again (see the accompanying diagram).

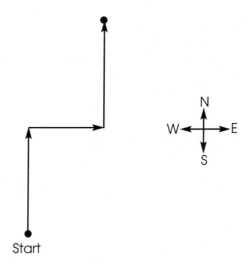

How many miles in a straight line is Katrina from her starting point? Show all of your work.

Answer: _____ miles

34 Howard knows that the length of his rectangular garden is 3 feet more than the width. He also knows that the perimeter of the garden is 26 feet.

PART A

If x represents the width, write an equation that can be used to solve for x.

Equation:

PART B

Using the equation in Part A, solve for the value of x and determine the length and width of the rectangular garden. Show all of your work.

$x =$ _____

length = _____ ft.

width = _____ ft.

PART C

What is the area of the rectangular garden?

Answer: _____ ft^2

35 Tom is holding his kite string 4 feet above the ground, as shown in the accompanying diagram. The distance between his hand and a point on the ground directly under the kite is 80 feet. The angle of elevation to the kite is 55°. (See mathematics reference sheet on page 279)

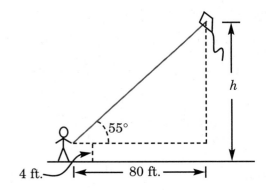

Figure not drawn to scale

PART A

Find the height, h, of his kite, to the nearest foot. Show all of your work.

Answer: _____ feet

PART B

Find the length of the kite string to the nearest foot. Show all of your work.

Answer: _____ feet

36 Sara's telephone service costs $23 per month plus $ .15 for each local call, and long distance calls are extra. Last month, Sara's bill was $36.74, and it included $6.24 in long-distance charges. How many local calls did she make? Show all of your work.

Answer: _____ calls

37 After an ice storm, the following headlines were reported in the *Glacier County Times*:

Monday: Ice Storm Devastates County - 8 out of every 10 lose electrical power

Tuesday: Restoration Begins - Power restored to $\frac{1}{2}$ of affected homes

Wednesday: More Freezing Rain - Power lost by 20% of homes that had power on Tuesday

There are 100 homes in the county, based on these headlines, what fractional portions of homes in Glacier County had electrical power on Wednesday? Show all of your work or explain how you arrived at your answer.

Answer: _____

_____

_____

_____

_____

_____

38 A computer game called "Guess the Pattern" is being played by Dawn. At the right is a table of inputs and outputs which the computer program has supplied so that she can "Guess the Pattern."

Input	Output
1	2
2	5
3	10
4	17
5	26
6	37

PART A
Based on the pattern, what should be the output if 8 is the input? Show all of your work or explain how you arrived at your answer.

PART B
Based on the pattern, what would be the input if 145 is the output?

Answer: _____

39 A target shown in the accompanying diagram consists of three circles with the same center. The radii of the circles have lengths of 3 inches, 7 inches, and 9 inches, respectively.

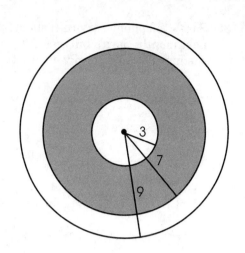

PART A

What is the area of the shaded region to the *nearest tenth of a square inch*? (Use π = 3.14) Show all of your work.

Answer: _____ square inches

PART B

To the *nearest percent*, what percent of the target is shaded? (Use π = 3.14) Show all of your work.

Answer: _____ %

40 The accompanying table shows data collected by two classes about which subject was their favorite.

Subject	Class 8A Votes	Class 8B Votes
Math	3	7
Science	6	3
Social Studies	5	5
Language Arts	7	5
Gym	8	8

PART A

Using the information from the table, construct a double bar graph on the grid below. Be sure to:

- title the graph
- label the axes
- use appropriate and consistent scales
- accurately graph the data
- use an appropriate key

PART B

If a student in class 8B were picked at random, what is the probability that the student voted for math as his/her favorite subject?

Answer: _____

PART C

What subject represents the mode for class A?

Answer: _____

Explain how you chose the mode.

_____

_____

_____

_____

41 Rectangle *RSTV* is intersected by line *LM* as shown below.

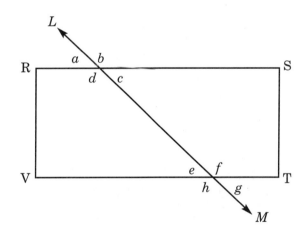

Figure not drawn to scale

PART A

Name two angles that are congruent to angle *f*.

Answer: _____

Answer: _____

PART B

Name three angles that are supplementary to angle *f*.

Answer: _____

Answer: _____

Answer: _____

PART C

What is the best description of the two smaller polygons formed by line *LM* intersecting the rectangle?.

_____

_____

_____

_____

_____

42 A painting that regularly sells for a price of $55 is on sale for 20% off. The sales tax on the painting is 7%.

PART A

What is the final cost of the painting after taxes? Show all of your work or explain your answer in words.

Answer: _____

_____

_____

_____

_____

_____

PART B

Will the final cost of the painting differ depending on whether the sales person deducts the discount before adding the sales tax or takes the discount after adding the sales tax? Show all of your work or explain in words.

Answer: _____

_____

_____

_____

_____

_____

43 The surface area of a cube is 384 cm^2.

PART A

What is the length of an edge of the cube? Show all of your work.

Answer: _____ cm

PART B

What is the volume of the cube? Show all of your work.

Answer: _____ cm^3

44 The Excel Cable Company has a monthly fee of $32.00 and an additional charge of $8.00 for each premium channel. The Best Cable Company has a monthly fee of $26.00 and an additional charge of $10.00 for each premium channel. The Epstein family is deciding to which of these two cable companies to subscribe.

PART A

For what number of premium channels will the total monthly subscription fee for the Excel and Best Cable companies be the same? Show all of your work.

Answer: _____ channels

PART B

The Epstein family decides to subscribe to two premium channels for a period of one year. Which cable company should they subscribe to in order to spend less money? Show all of your work.

Answer: _____ Cable Company

PART C

If the Epstein family decides to subscribe to two premium channels for one year (as in Part *B*), how much money will the Epsteins save in one year by using the less expensive company? Show all of your work.

Answer: _____

---

45 A factory packs CD cases into cartons for a music company. Each carton is designed to hold 1,152 CD cases. The Quality Control Unit in the factory expects an error of less than 5% over or under the desired packing number.

PART A

What is the *least* number and the *most* number of CD cases that could be packed in a carton and still be acceptable to the Quality Control Unit? Show all of your work.

Answer: least _____

Answer: most _____

PART B

Use the number line below to graph your answer to Part A. Be sure to clearly indicate the range of value and label the number line appropriately.

Absolute value (30, 58): The distance a number is from zero on a number line.

Acute (54, 114, 146): Descriptive of angles less than 90°.

Additive identity (60): An operational property in addition whereby adding zero to a number causes the number to maintain its original value.

Additive inverse (32): Characteristic that designates the opposite of a number.

Adjacent angles (118): Exist when two non-overlapping angles share a common side and a common vertex.

Algebra (15, 93-108): A mathematical language that uses variables, numbers, and operational symbols.

Alternate interior angles (118): Congruent angles formed by a transversal intersecting two parallel lines. these are non-adjacent angles, interior to the parallel lines and on alternate sides of the transversal.

Angle (75, 118-113, 114, 116, 118, 121, 130-133, 135-136, 144, 146-147, 145, 152): The figure formed by two rays diverging from a common point.

Arc (134-136, 155-156): A piece of the circumference of a circle.

Area (75, 139, 152, 155-156, 162, 163-164, 170-171): The region enclosed by a flat geometric figure and measured in square units.

Associative Property of Addition (60): An operational rule of addition whereby changing the grouping does not change the sum.

Associative Property of Multiplication (60): An operational rule of multiplication whereby changing the grouping does not change the product

Average (87, 202): The sum of the data items divided by the quantity of data items; also arithmetic mean.

Axes (175-178): Two perpendicular number lines which form the coordinate plane (singular is axis).

Bar graph (207): A graph consisting of parallel bars or rectangles of different lengths used to compare data.

Base (152, 163, 167, 170): The side of a polygon to which an altitude is drawn; the bottom of a three dimensional solid.

Binomial expression (96): A mathematical phrase indicating a polynomial with two terms.

Bisect (116, 132-134): An operation meaning to cut into two equal parts.

Box-and-whisker plot (209-210, 213): Linear display of statistical data by median, extremes, and quartiles.

Capacity (140): See volume.

Celsius (140): A temperature scale that registers the freezing point of water as 0° and the boiling point as 100° under normal atmospheric pressure; after Swedish astronomer Anders Celsius (1701-1744).

Centimeter (cm) (139-140): A unit of length equal to one hundredth (10^{-2}) of a meter.

Chord (155): A line segment that joins two points on a curve.

Circle (155-156, 162, 163, 164): A closed plane figure constructed such that every point is the same distance from a common point called the center.

Circle graph (207): A circular graph having radii dividing the circle into sectors proportional in angle and area to the relative size of the quantities represented; also called a pie chart or pie graph.

Coefficient (94-95, 101, 102, 103, 106, 107): An algebraic term indicating the numerical portion of a monomial.

Circumference (155-156, 162): A term indicating the perimeter of a circle or the distance around the circle.

Combinations (218, 219): One or more elements selected from a set without regard to the order of selection.

Commission (85): A fee or percentage allowed to a sales representative or an agent for services rendered.

Commutative Property of Addition (60): An operational rule of addition whereby changing the order of the terms does not change the sum.

Commutative Property of Multiplication (60): An operational rule of multiplication whereby changing the order of the terms does not change the product.

Compass (126 132-133, 135-136): A V-shaped device used to construct circles and arcs.

Complimentary angles (118): Descriptive of two angles, the sum of whose measures is 90º.

Composite number (35): An integer greater than one with more than two factors.

Conditional statement (230): A sentence containing "if ...then" or cause-and-effect phrases.

Cone (167, 170, 171): A space figure with a vertex and a circular base.

Congruent (75, 116, 121, 135-136, 167): Descriptive of reflecting angles that have the same measure, line segments that have the same length, or geometric figures that have the same shape and size.

Constant term (94): A quantity having a fixed numerical value.

Contrapositive statement (230): The conditional statement formed by taking the inverse of the converse, or the converse of the inverse of an original conditional statement.

Converse statement (230): The conditional statement formed by reversing the "if … then" portions of an original conditional statement.

Conversion factor (137): A quantity by which a measurement can be multiplied or divided to obtain an equivalent measurement in different units.

Corresponding angles (118): Descriptive of angles that are in the same position within two similar or congruent figures or when two parallel lines are cut by a transversal, the corresponding angles are those angles formed by the intersections in the same respective positions or for parallel lines, corresponding angles are congruent.

Cosine (148): In a right triangle, the ratio of the length of the side adjacent to an acute angle to the length of the hypotenuse; Abbr. cos.

Cross multiplication (70): In a proportion, the product of the numerator of the first fraction and the denominator of the second fraction is equal to the product of the denominator of the first fraction and the numerator of the second fraction.

Cube (170): A regular solid having six congruent square faces.

Cubic units (169): A unit, such as a cubic foot, or a system of units used to measure volume or capacity.

Cumulative frequency (205, 206, 212, 213): The progressive summation of frequencies.

Cumulative histogram (208): A bar graph on which the statistical data bars are arranged to include a progressive summation of the current and prior frequencies.

Cumulative relative frequency (204, 205): The sum of the relative frequencies of an occurrence divided by the total statistical data items.

Cylinder (167, 170): A space figure (prism) with circular bases.

Data (204, 205, 207, 208, 209, 201, 212, 213): Factual information, especially information organized for analysis or used to reason or make decisions.

Data interval (204): A set of numbers consisting of all the numbers between a pair of given numbers.

Decagon (144): A polygon with ten angles and ten sides.

Decimal (42, 45, 84): A linear array of integers following a decimal point whose place values are related to the powers of ten.

Denominator (58, 73): The expression written below the line in a common fraction that indicates the number of parts into which one whole is divided.

Dependent events (222): In probability studies, a situation in which the outcome of each preceding event affects all subsequent events.

Diagonal (149, 152, 153): A line joining two nonadjacent vertices of a polygon.

Diameter (155): A chord of a circle passing through the center.

Dilation (195): Mathematical transformation in which an image is enlarged or decreased proportionately from its earlier size.

Direct proportion (70): Two values whose ratio remains constant.

Distance (139): The length or numerical value of a straight line or curve.

Distributive Property of Multiplication over Addition (60-61, 97): An operational rule in equations whereby multiplication can be given out to each part of the addition.

Divisibility (33): Capable of being divided with no remainder.

Edge (167, 170): The line of intersection of two surfaces.

Element (64): A fundamental, essential, or irreducible member of a set.

Equal (75, 116): Having the same of equivalent value.

Equality (180): A statement, usually an equation, that one thing equals another.

Equation (8, 15, 93, 101, 102-104, 106, 107, 182-183, 186): A statement asserting the equality of two expressions, usually written as a linear array of symbols that are separated into left and right sides and joined by an equal sign.

Equilateral (146): A geometric figure having all sides equal.

Exponent (39-40, 56, 62, 94): A number or symbol placed to the right of and above another number, symbol, or expression, as 3 in $(x + y)^3$, denoting the power to which that number, symbol, or expression is to be raised; also called "power."

Exterior angle (144): The outside angle supplementary to one of the inside angles of a polygon.

Factor (35, 36): One of two or more quantities that divides a given quantity without a remainder.

Factorial (218): The successive products of all the positive integers from 1 to a given number.

Fahrenheit (140): A temperature scale that registers the freezing point of water as 32°F and the boiling point as 212°F at one atmosphere of pressure; after German physicist Gabriel Fahrenheit (1686-1736).

Fraction (28, 29, 45-46, 49-50, 84): An expression that indicates the quotient of two quantities.

Frequency (204, 205, 206, 207, 208, 210, 212, 213): The number of times something occurs within a specified condition.

Frequency table (207): Arrangement of data in columns and rows to show the number of times something occurs within a specified condition.

Function (186): A rule of correspondence between two sets such that there is a unique element in the second set assigned to each element in the first set.

Geometry (111-138, Chapters 6-9): The mathematics of the properties, measurement, and relationships of points, lines, angles, surfaces, and solids.

Greatest Common Factor (38-39): The largest factor that a given group of numbers has in common (GCF).

Hexagon (144): A polygon having six sides and six interior angles.

Histogram (208, 213): A type of graph used to display frequency data.

Hypotenuse (148): The side of a right triangle opposite the right angle.

Independent events (222): In probability studies, a situation in which the outcome of each preceding event has no effect on subsequent events.

Inequality (106, 180): An algebraic expression showing that a quantity is greater than or less than another quantity.

Integer (28, 29, 33, 34, 35, 36, 43-44, 64-65, 84): A member of the set of whole numbers or their opposites.

Interest (85): A charge for a loan, usually a percentage of the amount loaned.

Interior angle (144): The angle formed inside the polygon by two intersecting sides.

Inverse proportion (70): Two values whose product remains constant.

Inverse statement (230): The conditional statement formed by negating each portion of an original conditional statement.

Irrational numbers (28-29): Any real number that cannot be expressed as an integer or as a ratio between two integers.

Isosceles triangle (146): A triangle with at least two congruent sides and at least two congruent sides.

Lateral (167): Relating to the side.

Least Common Multiple (38-39): The smallest possible integer into which a given group of numbers can divide without a remainder (LCM).

Like terms (94, 95, 97, 103): Terms in an algebraic expression using the same variables and raised to the same power.

Line (112-113):An endless collection of points extending in either direction along a straight path.

Line ratio (75): The ratio of a polygon side to a corresponding side of a similar polygon.

Line reflection (195): Mathematical transformation in which an image is reflected over a defined line.

Line segment (112-113): Part of a line between two defined end points.

Line symmetry (194): Condition that exists when a figure can be folded over on an imaginary line and the two sides will overlap exactly.

Lower extreme (208, 209, 210, 213): The lowest statistical data value in a presentation.

Mass (139): The physical volume or bulk of a solid body (see weight).

Mean (arithmetic) (202, 205, 212, 213): The value obtained by dividing the sum of a set of quantities by the number of quantities in the set.

Median (202, 208, 209, 210, 212, 213): The middle value in a distribution, above and below which lie an equal number of values.

Mnemonic (56, 148) A formula or rhyme used as an aid in remembering.

Mode (202, 212, 213): The number in a data set that occurs most frequently.

Monomial expression (96): An algebraic expression consisting of only one term.

Multiples (38): A given number multiplied by any or all whole numbers.

Multiplicative Identity (60): An operational rule in multiplication whereby multiplying by one causes the number to maintain its original value.

Multiplicative inverse (32): See reciprocal numbers.

Net (169): In surface areas, a configuration of plane figures that can be folded into a three dimensional figure (e.g., a flattened box).

Non-terminating decimal (28, 29, 47-48): Decimal numbers that go on forever.

Number line (30, 34): A line with equal spacing used to present the integers in sequence.

Numerator (58): The expression written above the line in a common fraction to indicate the number of parts of the whole.

Obtuse (114, 146): An angle greater than 90° and less than 180°.

Octagon (144): A polygon having eight sides and eight interior angles.

Opposites (30-31, 32): Two numbers that are the same distance from zero on a number line but in opposite directions and add up to zero.

Ordered pair (177): In reference to a rectangular coordinate plane, a point defined by coupled (x, y) coordinates.

Origin (176): The intersection of the axes (the zero point on a rectangular coordinate plane).

Parallel (118, 167): Of, relating to, or designating two or more lines or planes that do not intersect.

Parallelogram (163, 164, 167): A four-sided plane figure with opposite sides parallel.

Parentheses (56, 58): The upright curved lines used to enclose a sum, product, or other expression considered or treated as a collective entity in a mathematical operation.

PEMDAS (56): Mnemonic – <u>P</u>lease <u>E</u>xcuse <u>M</u>y <u>D</u>ear <u>A</u>unt <u>S</u>ally – for order of operations (Parentheses, Exponents, Multiplication, Division, Addition, Subtraction).

Pentagon (124): A polygon having five sides and five interior angles.

Percent (45-46, 80, 82, 84, 85): A ratio that compares to 100; indicating the number parts out of 100

Perfect square (43): The square of an integer.

Perimeter (75, 161, 162, 164, 170): The distance around a closed geometric figure.

Periphery: A line that forms the boundary of an area; a perimeter.

Permutations (218-219): An ordered arrangement of the elements of a set.

Perpendicular (115): Intersecting at or forming right angles.

Pi (π) (156, 162, 163, 164, 170-171): A number (not expressible as an integer) – approximately 3.14159 – that expresses the ratio of the circumference to the diameter of a circle and appears as a constant in many mathematical expressions (16th letter of the Greek alphabet).

Pie chart or Pie graph: See circle graph.

Point (112, 177): The mark or dot produced on a rectangular coordinate plane at the intersection of x- and y-coordinate values.

Point symmetry (194):Condition that exists when a figure remains unchanged after rotation about the point of 180 degrees.

Polygon (75, 143, 144, 162): A closed plane figure formed by three or more line segments.

Polynomial (94, 96-97): An expression consisting of one or more terms.

Precision (126, 127): The exactness with which a number is specified; the number of significant digits with which a number is expressed.

Prime factorization (36, 37): Writing a positive integer in terms of its prime factors; found through factor tree method.

Prime number (35): An integer greater than 1 only divisible by itself or one.

Prism (167, 168, 170): A solid figure whose bases or ends have the same size and shape and are parallel to one another, and each of whose sides is a parallelogram.

Probability (87-88, 221-223): A number expressing the likelihood that a specific event will occur, expressed as the ratio of the number of actual occurrences to the number of possible occurrences.

Product (56): Calculation results in multiplication operation.

Proportion (69, 70, 71, 72): An statement which equates two ratios.

Protractor (126, 130-131): A semicircular instrument for measuring and constructing angles.

Pure (never-ending) repeating decimal (47-49): A repeating decimal that has no digits other than those that repeat.

Pyramid (167, 168, 170, 171): A solid figure with a polygonal base and triangular faces that meet at a common point.

Pythagorean theorem (148): The theorem that the sum of the squares of the lengths of the sides of a right triangle is equal to the square of the length of the hypotenuse; after 6th century B.C. Greek philosopher Pythagoras.

Quadrilateral (131, 144, 151-153): A plane figure with four sides and four angles.

Quadrant (176-177): One of the four regions formed by the intersection of the axes on a rectangular coordinate plane; numbered counterclockwise from the upper right.

Quadratic (107, 183): An equation with an x^2 term but no term with a higher power of x.

Quartile (208-210, 212-213): The median in each part when statistical data is divided into a lower half and an upper half.

Quotient (56): Calculation results in division operation.

Radius (155, 156, 163, 164, 170, 171): A line segment that joins the center of a circle with any point on its circumference.

Range (208, 209): The difference between the highest data value and the lowest data value.

Rate (69, 73-74): A ratio of two quantities with different units.

Ratio (13, 71, 80): The relation between two quantities expressed as the quotient of one divided by the other.

Rational numbers (28, 29): A number capable of being expressed as an integer or a quotient of integers, excluding zero as a denominator.

Ray (112-113, 114, 130): A straight line extending from a point.

Real number (28, 29): A number that is rational or irrational, not imaginary.

Reciprocal numbers (32, 39): A number related to another in such a way that when multiplied together their product is one.

Rectangle (149, 151, 152, 153): A four-sided plane figure with four right angles.

Rectangular Coordinate Plane (176): A pattern of regularly spaced horizontal and vertical lines used as a reference for locating points along the x- and y-axes.

Reflex angle (114): An angle greater than 180° and less than 360°.

Relative frequency (204, 205, 190, 191): The number of times for an occurrence in a set divided by the total number of statistical data items involved.

Repeating decimal (47-48, 49): A decimal in which a digit or group of digits recurs endlessly.

Right angle (114, 115, 148): An angle formed by the perpendicular intersection of two straight lines; an angle of 90°.

Rhombus (151, 152, 153): An equilateral parallelogram.

Rotation (194, 195): Mathematical transformation in which an image is turned a defined number of degrees about a point.

Rotational symmetry (194): Property that exists when a figure can be rotated more than 360 degrees about an imaginary center point and still look like the original figure.

Ruler (126, 127, 129): A straightedged strip with precision markings, as of wood or metal, for measuring lengths and drawing straight lines.

Sample space diagram (218-219): Representation of all possible outcomes of an experiment; also tree diagram.

Scale (78): A proportion used in determining the dimensional relationship of a representation to that which it represents.

Scale model (78-79): An object similar to an actual object but of a precisely proportioned, different size (usually smaller).

Scalene (146): A plane figure having three unequal sides; usually referring to triangles.

Scientific notation (41-42): Representation of a number as the product of a number that is at least one but less than ten, multiplied by a power of ten.

Set (64-65): A collection of distinct elements having specific common properties.

Significant digits (127) All of the digits of a measurement known to be accurate plus one estimated digit.

Similar (75, 116, 121): Having the same shape, not necessarily the same size.

Simplest form (94, 95, 101): An expression wherein all like terms are combined.

Sphere (167): A three-dimensional surface wherein all points are equidistant from a fixed point.

Square (151, 152, 163): A plane figure with four equal sides and four 90 degree angles.

Square root (43, 107-108): One of two equal factors of a number.

Stem and leaf plot (208, 209, 212): A system used to display data wherein each number is split into two parts. with the data displayed in two columns – the stem on the left represents the greater place values while the leaves on the right represent the lessor place values.

Straightedge (126): A rigid flat rectangular bar, as of wood or metal, with an unbroken edge for testing or drawing straight lines.

Supplementary angles (118): Two angles, the sum of whose measure is 180 degrees.

Surface area (162, 163, 169, 170): The sum of all the exterior surfaces of a space figure.

Symmetry (193, 194, 195): Exact correspondence of form and configuration on opposite sides of a dividing line or plane or about a center point.

Tangent (148): In a right triangle, the ratio of the length of the side opposite the angle to the length of the side adjacent to the angle; Abbr. tan.

Tax (85): A contribution for the support of a government required of persons, groups, or businesses within the domain of that government; often linked to a rate or percentage of a value (e.g., property tax, sales tax, income tax).

Term (94-95, 96-97): One of the quantities connected by addition or subtraction signs in a mathematical expression.

Terminating decimal (28, 29, 47-48): Decimal numbers that end.

Transformation (193, 194, 195): Mathematical processes in which images are rotated, reflected, dilated, or moved a defined distance.

Translation (195): Mathematical transformation in which an image slides a defined distance.

Transversal (115, 119): A line that intersects a system of other lines.

Trapezoid (151, 152, 153, 163): A quadrilateral figure with one set of parallel sides.

Tree diagram: See sample space diagram.

Triangle (76, 88, 121, 144, 146-147, 148, 163, 164, 167): A polygon having three sides.

Trigonometric ratios (87, 148-149): Precise calculations of relationships between the sides and the angles of triangles (sine, cosine, tangent).

Trigonometry (87, 148-149): The branch of mathematics that deals with the relationships between the sides and the angles of triangles and the calculations based on them.

Trinomial expression (96): A polynomial with three terms.

Unit rate (73): A rate where the denominator is reduced to 1 (e.g., x miles _per_ hour).

Upper extreme (208, 209, 210, 212, 213): The highest statistical data value in a presentation.

Variable (94, 101, 102, 103): A quantity capable of assuming any of a set of values; a symbol representing such a quantity.

Venn diagram (64, 232-238): A diagram using circles to represent an operation in set theory, with the position and overlap of the circles indicating the relationships between the sets.

Vertical angles (118-119): Angles formed by two intersecting lines.

Vertex (118, 130, 167): The point at which the sides of an angle intersect; the point on a triangle or pyramid opposite to and farthest away from its base; plural = vertices.

Volume (139, 161, 169, 170): The amount of space occupied by a three-dimensional object or region of space or its capacity, expressed in cubic units.

Weight (139): A measure of the heaviness of an object (see mass).

X-axis (176, 177): A horizontal number line (perpendicular to the Y-axis at the zero point on a rectangular coordinate plane).
X-coordinate (177): The directed number of horizontal units from zero on a rectangular coordinate plane.

Y-axis (176, 177): A vertical number line (perpendicular to the X-axis at the zero point on a rectangular coordinate plane).
Y-coordinate (177): The directed number of vertical units from zero on a rectangular coordinate plane.

Zero product (60): An operational property whereby multiplying by zero yields a zero product.

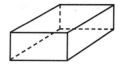

Rectangular Solid　　Total Surface Area $= 2(lw) + 2(hw) + 2(lh)$

Right Circular Cylinder　　Volume $= \pi r^2 h$
Total Surface Area $= 2\pi rh + 2\pi r^2$

Pythagorean Theorem　　$c^2 = a^2 + b^2$

Trigonometric

$$\sin A = \frac{\text{opposite}}{\text{hypotenuse}}$$

$$\cos A = \frac{\text{adjacent}}{\text{hypotenuse}}$$

$$\tan A = \frac{\text{opposite}}{\text{adjacent}}$$

Degrees	Sine	Cosine	Tangent
0	.0000	1.0000	.0000
5	.0872	.9962	.0875
10	.1736	.9848	.1763
15	.2588	.9659	.2679
20	.3420	.9397	.3640
25	.4226	.9063	.4663
30	.5000	.8660	.5774
35	.5736	.8192	.7002
40	.6428	.7660	.8391
45	.7071	.7071	1.0000
50	.7660	.6428	1.1918
55	.8192	.5736	1.4281
60	.8660	.5000	1.7321
65	.9063	.4226	2.1445
70	.9397	.3420	2.7475
75	.9659	.2588	3.7321
80	.9848	.1736	5.6713
85	.9962	.0872	11.4301
90	1.0000	.0000	....

Basic Math Operations & Number Symbols

a = b	a *is equal to* b
a ≠ b	a *is not equal to* b
a > b	a *is greater than* b
a ≥ b	a *is greater than or equal to* b
a < b	a *is less than* b
a ≤ b	a *is less than or equal to* b
+a	a *is positive*
a + b	a *plus* b, b *is added to* a
−a	a *is negative*
a − b	a *minus* b, b *is subtracted from* a
±a	*plus or minus* a
a(b) a **x** b	} a *is multiplied by* b
a · b ab	} a *times* b
a ÷ b $\frac{a}{b}$	} a *is divided by* b

a : b $\frac{a}{b}$	} a *is to* b (*the ratio of* a *to* b)
a%	a *percent*
|a|	*the absolute value of* a
$\sqrt{a}$	the *positive square root* or *principal square root*
$-\sqrt{a}$	the *negative square root*
≈a	*is approximately equal to* a
a ⇒ b	a *becomes* b
.434$3\overline{43}$	43 *repeating*
ax^b	{ a *is the coefficient* x *is the variable* b *is the exponent*

Basic Geometry Symbols

Δabc	*triangle* abc
∠A	*angle* A
m∠A	*the measure of angle* A
a°	a *degrees*
$\overleftrightarrow{AB}$	*line* AB
$\overrightarrow{AB}$	*ray* AB
$\overline{AB}$	*line segment* AB
m(AB)	*the length of* $\overline{AB}$

π	*pi*, ≈3.14, ≈$\frac{22}{7}$
∟	*right angle* (90°)
a ⊥ b	a *is perpendicular to* b
a ‖ b	a *is parallel to* b
ΔABC ~ ΔNJL	triangle ABC *is similar to* triangle NJL
ΔABC ≅ ΔNJL	triangle ABC *is congruent to* triangle NJL

Counting / Uncertainty / Coordinate Symbols

a!	a *factorial*
$_aP_b$	the number of *permutations*[1] of a thing taken in groups of size b
$_aC_b$	the number of *combinations*[2] of a thing taken in groups of size b
P(A)	the *probability*[3] of event A
{a,b}	a *set* with elements a and b
(a,b)	a *coordinate pair* with an x-coordinate of a and a y-coordinate of b

Footnotes:
1 an ordered arrangement or ordered pair of the elements of a set
2 one or more elements selected from a set without regard to the order of selection
3 a number expressing the likelihood that a specific event will occur
4 any of a set of two or more numbers used to determine the position of a point, line, curve, or plane